# FACILIT

# GROWTH

## Experiential Activities
## for Recovery and Wellness

Michelle Cummings M.S.
Marc Pimsler M.A.
Diane Sherman Ph.D.

**Kendall Hunt**
publishing company

www.kendallhunt.com
*Send all inquiries to*:
4050 Westmark Drive
Dubuque, IA 52004-1840

We would like to dedicate this book to those inspirational professionals that illuminated that path before us, our beloved students and participants that teach us more than we could teach them and you, the inspired facilitator seeking to expand and enrich the work that you do. We would each like to also offer a tremendous thanks to our families and friends without whom this book could not have been written.

Sincerely,
Michelle Cummings, Marc Pimsler, and Diane Sherman

80128

# Contents

# About the Authors

## Michelle Cummings

Michelle Cummings MS is the Big Wheel and founder of Training Wheels, a known leader in the Team Development industry. She is also the Co-Founder and Chief Creative Officer for Personify Leadership, a Leadership Development organization. Michelle is an accomplished author and a dynamic, sought-after speaker in the areas of leadership, team building, and experiential learning. Michelle has created a wide variety of facilitation, debriefing, and team-building activities that have collectively changed the way trainers and educators work.

Michelle speaks at more than fifteen local, national, and international conferences each year and authors a weekly team-building newsletter called *The Spokesperson* that has over 15,000 subscribers in sixty-five countries.

Michelle Cummings has authored five books:

1. *A Teachable Moment: A Facilitator's Guide to Activities for Processing, Debriefing, Reviewing, and Reflection*
2. *Bouldering Games for Kids: An Educational Guide for Traverse Walls*
3. *Playing With a Full Deck: 52 Team Activities Using a Deck of Cards*
4. *Setting the Conflict Compass: Activities for Conflict Resolution and Prevention*
5. *Facilitated Growth: Experiential Activities for Recovery and Wellness*

Michelle holds a Bachelor's degree in Psychology from Kansas State University and a Master's degree in Experiential Education from Minnesota State University at Mankato. She grew up on a farm in Norton, Kansas, and currently lives in Littleton, Colorado.

## Marc Pimsler

Since 2004 Marc Pimsler has worked in a variety of counseling and consulting capacities. Marc is as passionate about doing clinical work as he is counselor education and supervision. Marc maintains a private practice where he serves individuals and families in need, specializing in addressing addiction, shame, and trauma. Marc was the 2010 Georgia new counselor of the year for the Georgia Addiction Counselor Association and has been recently inducted into the 2017 National Board for Certified Counselors Minority Fellowship Program—focused in Addictions. Marc is proud to serve the field as the ethics committee chair for the Georgia Addiction Counselor Association. He is certified as a national addictions counselor, certified clinical supervisor, certified yoga and meditation teacher, and is also a certified practitioner with the Institute for Rapid Resolution Therapy. Marc has been intensely trained in experiential therapy as well as psychodrama. Marc is currently working on his Doctoral degree focused on counselor education and supervision. Marc is passionate about recovery, both his own as well as his clients', believing that sometimes all we need is a helping hand and a fresh perspective. Grounded in the belief system that everyone has the capacity to recover, Marc brings humor, spirituality, and creativity to everything he is involved in. For more information or to contact Marc, please visit www.marcpimsler.com and www.mvp-consulting.net

## Diane Sherman, PhD

Dr. Diane Sherman, PhD, a substance abuse professional since 1975, began her career while serving in the U.S. Army in the capacity of Behavioral Science Specialist. She holds the national advanced credential of Master Addiction Counselor, Certified Clinical Supervisor, and Certified Addiction Counselor-II. Dr. Sherman earned her Doctorate in Industrial/ Organizational Psychology from Capella University in 2007. Since 2008 she has taught and supervised students who are in pursuit of the certified addiction counselor credential. She is a national, regional, and state presenter offering topics relevant to addiction professional, clinical, and ethical practices and clinical supervision. Dr. Sherman is the past President of the Georgia Addiction Counselors Association and recipient of the GACA President's Award, and Bernard Carter Humanitarian Award. She also served on the board of the Georgia School of Addiction Studies, and in 2015 was honored to receive the Bruce Hoopes Pioneer Award in Addiction Treatment, a personally meaningful award, for excellence in the addiction profession.

# Introduction

"The tiny seed knew that in order to grow, it needed to be dropped in dirt, covered with darkness, and struggle to reach the light." This quote by author, Sandra Kring truly drives home the process of facilitated growth. The seed could grow even faster and stronger with the proper ingredients like food and water. The goal of Facilitated Growth is to provide the proper ingredients to help participants thrive. According to Webster, to grow is to undergo a natural development by increasing in size and changing physically, also known as a process of maturity. To facilitate means to make an action or process easier. Thus, Facilitated Growth helps the process of change become slightly easier.

Each step along the way has purpose for the seed. At first connected to its source the seed feels safe and secure in its community with other seeds. At some point along the way the little seed becomes separated from its source. All sorts of new experiences transpire for our little seed. Sometimes it flies through the air in the case of a dandelion and sometimes it rolls away like an acorn.

The rain comes and the little seed gets cold and wet, pining for days long ago when it was connected, safe, and protected. The ground, softened by the rain, swallows the little seed up and it is now overcome by darkness deep inside the ground. The seed didn't know what was happening and certainly didn't know why things had to change. The seed began to question himself, had he done something wrong to cause this isolation and darkness? Was this his fault?

At the point in which the seed thought life as he knew it was over, a drop of water came along to soften his hard exterior. The drop of water allowed the seed to begin to change in a way he never knew was possible. Another drop of water came and with it brought some food. The little seed was starving for this type of attention and absorbed what the water and food was offering him. Slowly but surely the little seed grew roots and a stem that began to reach for new heights.

The seed had no idea what was happening to him or where he was headed but he felt a deep connection to the nourishment he was receiving. This nourishment was exactly what he needed to reach into the unknown and grow. Growing can bring up all sorts of feelings. Things like unworthiness, fear, shame, and inadequacy can be common experiences. A facilitator armed with the proper tools can be the nourishment that the participant needs in order to grow.

Finally, the seed rises above the muck and darkness and breaks ground. Connected once again in the land of the living he is reunited with the other seeds that took a similar journey. The seed now transformed sees the light. The seed has learned that there can be no light without darkness, there can be no softening without hardness, and there can be no connection without isolation. Most importantly the seed learned that growing is so much easier with the proper nourishment!

Going back to the definition of the word, facilitate—to make an action or process easier—we find embedded the way we approach facilitation. We believe and have found that if you, as a helping professional are bored with your groups, guess who else is bored? Your participants! However, if you are excited, energized, and inspired then your participants will be as well and their growth will be fueled with fire.

We are very intentional about the language we use. We call those that are helpers "facilitators" and those they serve "participants." This language attempts to depart from many of the stigmatizing or shame-based language that can traditionally be found in centers around the country. We choose participants because we want them to participate in the process of change, participate in the intervention, and certainly participate in their life.

Like the water and food is to the little seed, so too is the experience to the participant. The kindness, compassion, and encouragement from a well-trained facilitator can be the very thing that instills hope in someone who was formerly hopeless. The cohesion created by the group experience can be the very thing that unlocks a closed heart. The celebration of success at the accomplishment of a task can be the very thing that empowers the dispirited.

How participants show up in the experience (treatment, group, individual) is very often similar to how they show up in life. The experience indeed becomes the microcosm of the macrocosm. The group process becomes a place to notice patterns emerging and debriefing becomes paramount to highlight those patterns. As participants see their own patterns emerge they are able to play with new strategies for approaching old problems.

Participants are not only allowed to show up as they are; they are encouraged to do so. If someone refuses to participate, that is more an indication about where they are in the moment than who they are as a person. We often confuse how a person behaves for who they are inside. Remember, just because we have bad actions does not mean we have bad actors. We approach this work from the fundamental belief that wellness and recovery is not about "bad people getting good" but rather it's about "sick people getting well" or "hurt people getting help." Often giving someone permission to just be how they are, can be the fastest way to create a shift, when they are ready to do so. Being a safe, compassionate, and understanding professional allows the participant to turn to you for guidance when and if they need the support.

Marc was once setting up one of his favorite groups and a participant walked into the room and said, "I came here to get clean not play romper room games." Marc looked at him, smiled, remembered what Michelle once said to him when he wasn't feeling well before an activity and said "participate at the level in which you feel you are able." He looked at Marc in a questioning way and decided to take a risk and join his peers. About ten minutes in, this same guy was playing the game with as much enthusiasm as anyone else in the room. It was powerful reinforcement and a testament to the process.

So many of the participants we work with are starved for play. We can go on and on about the stories clients tell us about growing up in homes, gender roles, or communities where play is an afterthought, if thought about at all. Many had to grow up way too soon and often become "the man of the house" or became "caretakers" for those that were supposed to be taking care of them. Certainly, as adults we don't have enough play in our lives and then throw addiction and mental illness into the mix, forget it. Giving participants permission to play opens up the doorway to their own sense of adventure, curiosity, and a world of possibility.

Encouragement can be another powerful tool in the process of change. This is especially true for our population. So often our participants are being picked up, kicked out, thrown away, or otherwise asked to leave. "A word of encouragement during a failure is worth more than an hour of praise after success" author unknown (Morris 2012). When asked what he thought the single most important factor in getting along with other people was, Adlerian psychologist Dreikurs (1971) emphatically stated it was encouragement.

Encouragement differs from praise as it communicates interdependence and worth where praise communicates dependence. When we praise others, it creates an emphasis on perfectionism and is outcome driven. When we lead with encouragement it highlights the principle of progress and focuses on each step of the journey. In this way, we model recovery principles such as progress rather than perfection, living life on life's terms, as well as learning to take things one day/moment at a time.

When facilitators realize that we live in a fishbowl we can recognize the power of our presence, words, and deeds. Participants are always watching to see how we handle circumstances that arise in the group. When a participant is late, doesn't want to show up, breaks a rule, or gets frustrated with the process, other participants are watching to see how we respond. Be mindful of your reactions. Especially when it comes to things like confrontation, it is useful to scan and see what is the motive and where is it coming from. For example, is the motive a reaction or a response and is it coming from my head or my heart? Let's begin to unpack these a bit.

When scanning for motive we look at two things; is it a reaction or response? For the purpose of this discussion we will define a reaction as an automatic action triggered by the facilitator's stuff becoming activated. This can be when we feel a need to control outcomes, become angry, feel the desire to assert authority, be the expert, or otherwise show the participant who's boss. It can also manifest as what Miller and Rollnick call the "Righting Reflex."

The righting reflex as defined by Miller and Rollnick is, "the desire to fix what seems wrong with people and to set them promptly on a better course, relying in particular on directing" (2013). When we "fix what seems wrong in another" we place ourselves in a position that exacerbates the power differential. As a facilitator, we assume the position of guide rather than director. If you imagine the metaphor of white water rafting, the water is the director and the guide is in the boat with the group. The relationship those in the boat have with the water can sometimes be supportive yet can also be adversarial; however, the guide in the boat is always on the same team even when guiding.

Our goal as facilitators is to support the process and allow it to unfold so long as safety is not compromised. Remember the old adage, "If you give a man a fish, he eats for a day; but if you teach him how to fish, he eats for a lifetime." The same is true for the process of change. If you

solve a problem for a participant, that problem is solved for that day; however, if you teach them to solve their own problems they have tools for a lifetime. We find the righting reflex is more about us and our own egos rather than about actually helping others. We strongly encourage facilitators to resist the righting reflex.

So, a reaction is very much like a reflex. It is automatic, often unconscious, and usually about us and our needs. On the other hand, a response is about the participant and what they need. A response requires us to call upon our skills and training as facilitators and the outcome of a response usually helps aid the process of growth. We suggest taking a breath before responding to ensure the frontal lobe is fully engaged thus allowing full access to all your resources. Jim Seckman often says "A good counselor knows what's going on in the group, a great counselor knows what's going on in themselves." Paying attention to what is going on within ourselves sets us up to be the best facilitator we can be for our clients.

When scanning to see if a response is coming from the head or the heart we look to see what it is about. Is what I am about to say what I think (head) is in the best interest of the client? Or is it coming from a place of the heart and unconditional love? Once again the question is, "Is this about me or is it about the participant?" Even in the midst of a confrontation we can bring in the space of the heart so that it feels less like a 2×4 to the head and more like the guide on a raft. We like to refer to this type of confrontation as carefrontation. We will know we have hit our target if the participant walks away feeling cared for rather than beat up.

One of the biggest benefits that we see in using the Facilitated Growth activities is that they foster group cohesion. When we get a group of people working together toward a common goal that requires them to lean on each other physically as well as emotionally, it fosters the type of relationships that support and enhance change. Marc has had the opportunity to bring experiential activities behind the walls of a local city jail. It was so powerful to watch this group as cohesion began to take root. The correctional officers talked about how the entire environment of the pod began to change.

During graduate school in a research and statistics class, Marc once heard from a professor that the largest adult population that commits suicide are Caucasian men. The researchers believed that in part the correlation was around group cohesion. Caucasian men seem to be socialized in a way that doesn't promote cohesion especially in the United States. At the same time, Marc was taking a class on cultural diversity where the subject of White privilege came up. It occurred to him that this privilege and power was literally killing us and if group cohesion was one of the correlations associated with the data it was paramount to create opportunities to give everyone, but especially men the opportunity to experience cohesion.

One of the benefits of using the Facilitated Growth activities are the inherent socio-metric monitoring components built into them. This allows the facilitator to keep their finger on the pulse of the overall health of the group. Sociometry is the study or measure of social relationships. The facilitator properly attuned to the group can pick up on themes and nuances that surface as a result of play. For example, subtle, seemingly benign comments or jabs between participants, noticing how group members react to different leaders emerging, and paying attention to any collusions or toxic pairing between group members can actually unmask problematic relational themes. During the debrief it is encouraged for the facilitator to bring up these themes and allow for group process.

Another benefit we have seen as a result of these activities is in the realm of emotional regulation. We can teach skills, role-play, and talk about strategies or we can create an experience in which participants receive in the moment real-time feedback in a safe space. This safe space allows for new experiences with new strategies. When the reluctant leader takes a step forward and helps solve the puzzle, the group cheers as the problem is solved. The reluctant leader walks away with a new sense of confidence. When the aggressive competitor realizes he simply cannot solve the problem and takes a step back he gets to experience the art of team play. The fearful participant summons new courage in a way that s/he never expected. These experiences or lessons while active in the activity have a way of becoming generalized to other settings.

Interoceptive exposure is a technique used where the individual experiences a wide range of emotions and through the implementation of different strategies finds new ways of being with old emotions and story lines. These new ways of being with old emotions unlock stuck points and creates new possibilities. With this technique it is critical to watch for any abreactions occurring within group members. An abreaction is typically defined as the expression and consequent release of a previously repressed emotion or the reliving of an experience in order to purge it of its emotional excesses—a type of catharsis. The experiential activity experience can trigger participants in ways they might not be expecting. It is the role of facilitator to keep a watchful eye on all group members in order to maintain safety. Having a co-facilitator is encouraged for larger groups.

Karen Carnabucci says, "Action therapy has the potential to help people quickly address hidden issues, feelings and patterns that would take months or even years to address in conventional talk therapy." The recent research on treating trauma points toward the less effective nature of talk therapy and is really highlighting the efficacy of experiential therapy. Since the trauma was an experience that happened to the individual it only makes sense that the transformation really needs to be an experience as well. Facilitated Growth provides a launching pad of experiences that create transformation for the participant.

We get to "re-story" the old stories realizing that the ending can be coauthored by us and the moment. By trying new things, pushing beyond our comfort zones, and stepping into the unknown, the experience begins to change us. Life takes on new meaning for us, our participants, and the group as a whole. Communities come together as never before. Relationships rooted in the experience become powerful agents of change. With the tools and skills, refined by the Facilitated Growth experience, it is our hope that you find a new spirit, new energy, and new approaches to doing this work. Our intention has been to create a book that might be a resource to support you in doing this powerful work. We thank you from the bottom of our hearts for doing your part to make this world a better place. We hope to hear from you and see you on this wild journey.

# How Do Experiential Activities Support Facilitated Growth?

**How do experiential activities support facilitated growth?[1]**

This book provides new and innovative strategies for success in working within arenas of recovery and wellness. Experiential activities are designed to facilitate participant growth, and to support different objectives for participants, including the support of skill development, problem-solving and risk-taking skills, improving insight and critical thinking. It is anticipated that the use of experiential activities helps the participant develop a new outlook of one's future, and to promote and support recovery and wellness. We have designed many of the activities during the provision of educational classes and workshops for students enrolled in a learning process. Students come from various backgrounds—clinical, educational, community-based, summer retreats, professional team building. Most seek new activities or new ways to freshen up their traditional approach to working with participants in a group setting.

Most activities have been drawn from a variety of sources, which may be referenced in the activity description. When adapted from another source, reference is made at the end of each activity.

We encourage you to remain open to the experiential group process, modify activities as needed for your participant population, and use creativity. If you find an activity works better a different way, play with it, experiment with a variation, and see how it turns out.

## Where to Use This Resource

This book is designed for use in any type of setting, recovery and wellness focused environments, and as part of any intervention, regardless of presenting problem or continuum of care. Common settings or environments in the continuum of care include out-patient, intensive out-patient, partial hospitalization, in-patient, residential settings, recovery residences, sober living/independent living homes and aftercare. As well, these activities can be used in any setting that supports recovery, wholeness, and wellness—settings such as retreats, professional development, team-building, conferences and workshops or seminars.

Experiential activities are designed to be used in a group intervention, but can be adapted for individual, couples, and family sessions. Activities can be completed in one session, or used over several sessions. While these activities are designed to promote recovery and wellness, they may be adapted and beneficial in other specialty groups (i.e., trauma group, anger

---

1. Adapted from Jurkovic and Sherman, 2009.

management, anger resolution groups, stress management groups, or community or house meetings in a recovery residence or residential setting).

## How to Use This Resource

One aspect of experiential education is flexibility. We anticipate that activities can be used to meet the various needs of the participants. They can be used to support a psychoeducational lesson plan or a cognitive, emotional, or behavioral skill or objective. The intent of each activity is to create opportunities for one to learn more about oneself within the context of wellness and recovery.

Facilitators will gain the most by first reviewing the contents of this book. We suggest that you first try the activity you have selected to gain an appreciation of the tasks, the process, and your observation of your emotional/cognitive experiences from the activity. The confidence you gain in preparing first before using a selected activity will convey modeling and increase the likelihood of participant's engagement earlier in the experiential process.

## A Standard Approach

When using experiential activities, it is recommended the facilitator use a standard approach to each session. We suggest the following:

► *Check-in.* Rather than asking participants to check-in using a feeling word, which may be difficult for one to identify, we choose to ask participants to check in by offering one or two things they are grateful for, or one or two things they did to support their recovery and wellness. We find that this recovery-based approach supports recovery capital. Also feel free to use any of the check-in or ice breaker ideas in order to inject creativity into your programming.

► *Review homework.* Be sure to review any homework or assignments given from the previous group to support the learning process.

► *Experiential activity.* Select your activity in advance, and understand the purpose for the activity. Consider reviewing the prior activities in a preceding group, connecting it to the present activity, to support the learning or change process. Observe rather than label behavior. Encourage discussion about the purpose of the activity. Do not underestimate the ability of participants to interact and participate in activities—empowering them by inviting them into the process. Perhaps they have an alternate way to attempt completing the task or activity or perhaps a participant evolves into a peer support or peer leader role.

▶ *Debrief activity.* Allow sufficient time to debrief, as this is a critical part of the process, and one where participants can gain a lot through sharing their experience with one another. Use your debriefing questions as a springboard in each activity to the debriefing process.

▶ *Homework assignment.* Homework assignments can be powerful opportunities to reinforce what is learned in group. Only give homework if the facilitator intends to review it—giving homework or assignments without follow-up will not support a change or learning process and in fact often undermines it. Help participants to be accountable by being consistent with reviewing homework assigned at the prior group at the beginning of the next.

▶ *Check-out.* We have found it useful to ask participants one thing that they learned about themselves or one takeaway they are leaving with in the check-out process. It may provide useful information for the facilitator to determine if the purpose or anticipated outcome of the activity was accomplished, as well as provide the participant with a self-reflection process.

## Group Management

Facilitating activities may be met with resistance from participants (Jurkovic and Sherman 2009). If this happens, consider the following options:

▶ Explore behavior and possible solutions rather than labeling it.
▶ Explore with participants their experience of or their resistance to the activity.
▶ Critically evaluate the possibilities for the reaction.
  ☐ What may be connected with the resistance in terms of administration (too boring or tedious) or one's ability (too challenging for participants)?
  ☐ Is the reaction connected to a situation (i.e., a stressful situation that preceded the activity, conflict between participants, or little group cohesion)?
  ☐ Is there emotional disturbance related to one's mental health diagnosis?
  ☐ Do you have the right participants gathered together? Sometime poor selection of group participants may lead to participant disruption.
  ☐ Is the facilitator prepared or lacking in confidence or training?
  ☐ Is the facilitator experiencing countertransference?
  ☐ Is the environment adequate to limit outside distractions and promote confidential exchanges?

General guidelines to manage resistance constructively:

- ▶ Acknowledge that resistance is normal or usual and encourage participants to sit with their feelings, thoughts, or experiences to learn more about themselves.
- ▶ Use redirection skills; encourage the group to observe their experience, sit still with their response, and to consider a different solution or new coping skills.
- ▶ Encourage participants to discuss the resistance, or for some participants to help others with finding a solution to their resistance.
- ▶ Modify the tasks—sometimes activities may be selected that do not fit well with the cohesion of the group. If a group of participants is new, conducting activities that are associated with higher risk are not the best choice until the group has developed better cohesion.
- ▶ Process the issue differently—more succinctly, enthusiastically.
- ▶ Perhaps consider self-disclosure, when it is beneficial for participants.
- ▶ Invite participants' input on how to improve the task.
- ▶ Allow participants the opportunity to opt out or participate to the best of their own ability.

Facilitators can best support the experiential group process by being prepared. Consider these general guidelines:

- ▶ Clarify group guidelines at the beginning of the group. Modify as needed.
- ▶ Include activities that support team building.
- ▶ Determine if your group is best suited as an open or closed enrollment. Closed enrollment is a predetermined number and/or preselected participants, and no others enroll for a selected time frame. Open enrollment is open to any participant for any group session.
- ▶ Consider if any participant(s) can be assigned a role of responsibility, perhaps co-facilitation.
- ▶ Offer three positive affirmations for every critical one.
- ▶ Consider expressive tasks such as psychodrama, physical activity challenges, acting, art, music, humor.
- ▶ Process transference and countertransference with a supervisor or trusted colleague.

# Comfort Zone, Stretch Zone, Panic Zone

When facilitating experiential activities, you will routinely ask people to step outside their comfort zones. Having an understanding of the behaviors associated with this concept is important as you step into the role of a facilitator. Associating these three zones with the colors of a stoplight helps facilitators as well as participants visualize this concept. Green: Comfort Zone. Yellow: Stretch Zone. Red: Panic Zone. When facilitating this concept with a group, draw a bull's-eye and label each ring: Comfort Zone, Stretch Zone, and Panic Zone. Then ask participants to tell you what each zone looks and feels like.

## The Three Zones

### *Comfort Zone*

This is where you are comfortable and feel "safe." Routines are easy, people possess skills that enable them to perform tasks well. Our comfort zone is usually where we spend most of our day. Usually it's with people you know and interact with on a regular basis. Your work routine is familiar and you are used to your environment.

### Comfort Zone Questions

- ▶ What does your comfort zone look like for you?
- ▶ What do you think will be easy for you today?
- ▶ What are some emotions associated with being in your comfort zone?

### Stretch Zone

This is where you are doing something new, allowing yourself to learn, and where you feel energized and engaged. In this zone you are more willing to take risks.

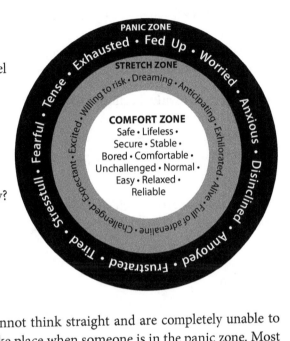

### Stretch Zone Questions

- ▶ What would it look like if you stretched beyond comfortable today?
- ▶ What would we see?
- ▶ What would you like to change?
- ▶ Where will you start?

### Panic Zone

This is where you are paralyzed by fear, cannot think straight and are completely unable to use your resources. No new learning can take place when someone is in the panic zone. Most people go to flight, fright, or freeze mode and are not able to take in new information.

### Panic Zone Questions

- ▶ What would push you into the panic zone today?
- ▶ What are you not ready for?
- ▶ What are your roadblocks?

It may be helpful to review this concept before a meeting or as a new group is forming. After a discussion about the three zones, encourage participants to step outside of their Comfort Zone and into their Stretch Zone with you for the day. New learning takes place in the Stretch Zone. We stop learning once we get into the Panic Zone, and we often go into Fight or Flight mode. That is generally not a place you want to take people. If you introduce this concept early in the program, you can use these terms repeatedly when challenging the group with a new task.

# Sequencing

Sequencing your activities is a very important piece of Experiential Education. If you introduce activities that are above the functioning capability of your participants, it can cause more damage than good. In order to create effective reflection, it is important to start with introductory level activities and proceed to more difficult challenges. Groups need to share simple experiences together before introducing them to activities that have a higher emotional risk to them. As facilitators, it is important to start with activities that are appropriate for the needs of the group, background, or stage in group development.

Sequencing of activities begins with assessing client readiness for each activity. It ends with the activities being placed in an order that makes sense to participants. You wouldn't want to start with a "Trust" activity and then move into a "Get to Know You" activity. The natural order of this would not make sense to the participant if you ask them to trust other participants before they even knew their names.

We recommend starting with an Icebreaker or Check-in activity, then moving to more content related material such as a Symbolic Learning Activity or a Play with Purpose Activity.

# Processing and Debriefing

## Debriefing

Debriefing is a term used in experiential education to describe a question and answer session with participants. These talking sessions are generally thought to be a "sit down" circle where the facilitator asks questions and the participants answer. Although this is an effective debriefing technique, if it is the only technique used, participants can become bored with it and can become easily distracted. Pairing group discussions with partner discussions offers a nice variety to the debriefing process. Incorporating different mediums and learning styles into your activities will also inject energy and creativity into the learning process.

Debriefing an experience helps participants connect lessons and activities they learned in your program to the outside world. It is a very important piece of programming and learning as a whole. If participants are not allowed to reflect on their experiences and relate them to the outside world, then a lot of the learning may be lost. It is important to debrief a group experience, especially after something powerful has surfaced. Mixing up your debriefing activities will keep participants engaged in what they are learning and allow you to create more teachable moments.

Please refer to *A Teachable Moment*, Cain, Cummings, and Stanchfield, for more theory on Processing and Debriefing.

## The Value of Reflection

An excerpt from *A Teachable Moment*, by Cain, Cummings and Stanchfield.

An important concept to consider when implementing experiential education activities is providing opportunities to process or reflect on their educational experiences. The educational philosopher John Dewey (1933), who is known as one of the forefathers of experiential education, believed that in order to truly learn from experience there must be time for reflection.

There is no one set way to debrief or one perfect time to debrief. Using a variety of techniques and using activities that give participants the power to take the lead in the debriefing is the most engaging and effective way of viewing debriefing.

# Symbolic Learning and Play with Purpose

In the pages of this book, you will find two sections, Symbolic Learning and Play with Purpose. We divided the activities into these two sections as the modalities used for the two types are very different. Symbolic Learning uses the effectiveness of imagery, which helps develop a mental blueprint or teachable moment in story format. The Play with Purpose section contains activities that are more active in nature that will surface behaviors through play. The Greek philosopher Plato was once quoted as saying, "I can learn more about a person in an hour of play than a lifetime of conversation." We would whole-heartedly agree with this statement. The Play with Purpose activities will intentionally surface behaviors that participants encounter every day. By following the suggested debriefing questions after each activity, facilitators can successfully walk participants through what happened in the activity and relate it back to the real world. This process will aid participants in their wellness and recovery by letting them "catch" themselves in their own behaviors naturally in the game. They then learn strategies in the debriefing process for how to manage those behaviors back in the real world.

# Disclaimer

All activities contain some inherent risk of injury whether it be physical or emotional. Michelle Cummings, Marc Pimsler, and Diane Sherman have devoted reasonable attention to the safety of the activities in this book. The reader assumes all risk and liability for any loss or damage that may result from the use of the materials contained in this book. It is your responsibility to obtain the expertise and experience necessary to avoid an injury during one of these activities. Liability for any claim, whether based upon errors or omissions in this guide, are the sole responsibility of the reader.

Michelle Cummings, Marc Pimsler, and Diane Sherman and their affiliates are not responsible for the misuse of the information or activities in this book.

# A Note of Thanks

No doubt you will notice, as you read through the pages of this book, that we have been the fortunate recipients of great ideas shared by our friends and fellow facilitators. One of the most outstanding features of the experiential education world is the unique and generous sharing that goes on between members of this field. We are grateful to every person who has allowed us to share their unique insights and their wonderful ideas for exploring conflict resolution and prevention.

In every way we could imagine, we have attempted to thoroughly research the origins and creators of the activities in this book. To the best of our ability, we have tried to credit those who deserve recognition for their contributions.

If, after reading this book, you are aware of any activity for which we have not yet given an appropriate reference or credit, it would be our pleasure to correct this situation in the next printing of this book. Please direct any information you have related to appropriate crediting to Michelle Cummings at michelle@training-wheels.com. We also enjoy hearing from you about your usage of the activities in this book. Please tell us your stories, tales, and experiences with the audiences you serve, both within the United States and abroad. And, if you happen to create a new Facilitated Growth Activity that you would like to share with the world, send us a photo and activity description. If we use it in a future publication, we will send you a copy of that book.

We would also like to thank our teachers and mentors that have guided us along the way and given us the space to grow into the professionals we are. We offer up sincere gratitude for all of our former and current participants, students, and supervisees that teach us more than we could ever teach them. You challenge us with your engagement, curiosity, and hunger for growth. Finally, we want to thank you, the professional reading this book. Your dedication to your participants and professional development is truly inspiring. We know this work is not easy and yet we know just how powerful it can be. We offer this book to you as a resource and a catalyst to your growth, the growth of your participants, and the advancement of our field.

Sincerely,

Michelle Cummings, Marc Pimsler, and Diane Sherman

# Play with Purpose

# 7 Up

**Group Size:** 9–50

**Purpose:** Increase frustration tolerance, problem solving, communication skills, group cohesion, and increase mindfulness skills. This task sounds easy, but in reality it is difficult to achieve. Participants will most likely reach a level of frustration with the task and one another.

**Props Needed:** Seven tossable items for every ten people. These could be koosh balls, rubber chickens, bean bags, hackey sacks, etc.

## Activity Preparation:
1. Prep time needed: 5 minutes.
2. Prior to class make sure you have all your props.
3. Place 7 tossable items into small stuff sacks for every 10 people.

## Time Needed:
- ▶ Directions: 2 minutes
- ▶ Activity: 10 minutes
- ▶ Debrief: 15 minutes

## Safety:
- ▶ Physical—For participants with physical issues like back pain this activity might be one they want to sit in a chair rather than stand.

## Activity Directions:
- ▶ Have group gather around to discuss.
- ▶ Divide groups into 9–10 people and have them stand in a circle.
- ▶ This activity is somewhat involved but quite worth the effort to learn. Circle up the players and let them know that you will be introducing Tossable Objects into the group 1 at a time. The activity must follow a certain set of rules. If a rule is broken, the activity starts over from the first object.
- ▶ **Rule 1:** Players must start each toss from a circle position. One person will be the designated Tosser, and will be adding an Object each round. Tell the group that the Tosser will toss the Object up into the air with the aim of the Object landing in the center of the circle.
- ▶ **Rule 2:** All tosses must be at least as high as the tallest player in the group and players may not move positions.

- ▶ **Rule 3:** Objects cannot touch the ground. If the first item is tossed and caught, the group can move onto Object #2. Both items will then be tossed in to the center of the circle. Both items must be caught for the activity to continue. If one of the objects is dropped, the group must start over with one item.
- ▶ **Rule 4:** All tosses must happen on the word "Toss."
- ▶ **Rule 5:** Any player in possession of an Object must toss their object into the center of the circle.
- ▶ The activity is over when all 7 items are tossed and caught.

**Facilitator Script:** "Hey everyone gather around. I need you to divide yourself into small groups, with 9–10 people per group. Please stand in a circle with your small group. *(Wait for this to happen.)* I'm going to demonstrate what to do with this group. *(Include yourself in one circle.)* I'm going to give one person in each group a small bag that has seven tossable items in it. Whoever the tosser is, will pull one item out of the bag. This person will say 'One, two, three toss,' and toss this item into the center of the circle. This item must be caught by someone else in the group in order for the activity to continue. *(Demonstrate this.)* OK, since Patty caught this first item, the game may continue. Next, I am going to select another item out of the bag. Again, I will say, 'One, two, three toss.' Both Patty and I will both toss the items at the same time into the center of the circle. If both items are tossed and caught, the game can continue. This process continues until all seven items have been successfully tossed and caught. If an item is dropped at any time, the group must start over with one item and work their way back up. All tosses must be at least as high as the tallest player in the group, and players may not move positions. You must also stay in a circle formation. All items must be tossed into the center of the circle. Please be careful to avoid any head-on collisions while attempting to catch an item. Nothing is worth getting hurt over today. Are there any questions? *(Pause for questions.)* You may begin!"

## Debrief:

- ▶ What were some of the strategies you and your group came up with to be successful at this activity?
- ▶ How many of you thought this sounded like an easy task?
- ▶ How many of you got frustrated during the process? Describe something that frustrated you.
- ▶ What did it feel like when you had to start over?
- ▶ How does this relate back to the real world?
- ▶ What could some of the tossable items represent in your life?

▶ Who are the people in your life that are helping you successfully toss and catch the important parts of your recovery?

**Recovery/Wellness Metaphor:** Recovery sounds like an easy process. There are many times we have multiple things in the air and trying to manage it all can be overwhelming. There are also times when we have to rely on others and simply can't complete the task ourselves. The first word in the first step is "we." Learning to work in a "we" sets up for success in recovery.

**Role of Facilitator:** Safety monitor. Reinforce that items must be tossed into the center of the circle.

**Source:** *Possibles Bag Manual,* Chris Cavert

# As If

**Group Size:** 8–50

**Purpose:** To serve as an icebreaker activity for mini-role-plays. Allows participants to practice skills learned in class before experiencing them in the real world.

**Props Needed:** none

**Activity Preparation:** none

**Time Needed:**

- ▶ Directions: 2 minutes
- ▶ Activity: 10 minutes
- ▶ Debrief: 15 minutes

**Activity Directions:**

- ▶ Have group gather around to discuss.
- ▶ Divide your group into pairs. Have the pairs stand about 6 feet apart from one another and face each other.
- ▶ Instruct them to walk forward toward one another and greet one another AS IF they were . . . and give them a role to play out.
- ▶ Each interaction is approximately 60 seconds in duration.
- ▶ After the interaction is over, ask them to get back into their original stance, about 6 feet away from one another.
- ▶ Debrief that round.
- ▶ Proceed with a different role-play.
- ▶ Debrief the second round.
- ▶ Proceed with a third role-play.
- ▶ Debrief the third round.

**Facilitator Script:** "Please find a partner and stand about 6 feet away from them and face one another. *(Pause until they are ready.)* This activity is called 'As If'. In a moment I'm going to give you a role I'd like you to play out with your partner. Once I say 'Go', I want you to walk toward your partner and greet your partner *AS IF* you were in the role I'm about to give you. I want you to stay in this role for about 60 seconds. Once you hear me say 'STOP!' that round is over and I want you to get back into this starting position, where you are standing 6 feet away from your partner. Are there any questions? OK, for this first interaction, I want you to greet your partner **AS IF** you were long-lost college roommates. Ready? Go!"

Let this interaction go on for about 60 seconds. It will be loud and energetic. When 60 seconds is up, yell out STOP (or use a noisemaker to get their attention). Ask them to get back into their original 6-feet-away position. Then ask these debriefing questions:

► What was that interaction like?
► It appeared to be pretty high-energy. Was there anyone **not** excited to see their college roommate?
► What were some of the things you talked about?

Then move onto your second role-play.

**Facilitator Script:** "OK, the beauty of this activity is that we can change the roles to be whatever we want them to be. Let's have this next round be a little harder. This time I want you to pretend that you and your partner are coworkers, and the two of you got into an argument yesterday. It's now the next day and you walk in and see one another for the first time. Go ahead and greet your partner **AS IF** you are seeing one another for the first time since your argument yesterday. Ready? Go!"

Let this interaction go on for about 60 seconds. This interaction will have multiple different responses. Some of the pairs will take accountability and resolve their conflict. Other pairs will ignore each other altogether. Some will start out with a "pretend" angry tone, then start to work toward a resolution. When 60 seconds is up, yell out STOP (or use a noisemaker to get their attention). Ask them to get back into their original 6-feet-away position. Then ask these debriefing questions:

► What was that interaction like?
► Did you resolve your conflict in that 60-second time period? Wouldn't it be great if that's the way it happened out in the real world?
► What made this interaction awkward?
► How do you respond to conflict in the real world?

Then move onto a third role play.

**Facilitator Script:** "OK, let's do one more. This time, I need one person to be someone who has had multiple years of sobriety, and the other person to be a newcomer to group meetings. Decide who is going to be in each role. *(Pause a few moments.)* This time, I want the person who has had multiple years of sobriety to welcome the newcomer to their first group meeting. Go ahead and greet your partner **AS IF** you are seeing one another for the first time at a group meeting. Ready? Go!"

Let this interaction go on for about 60 seconds. This interaction will have multiple different responses. Some of the pairs will be talkative, some pairs will be more quiet. When 60 seconds is up, yell out STOP *(or use a noisemaker to get their attention)*. Ask them to get back into their original 6-feet-away position. Then ask these debriefing questions:

- ▶ What was that interaction like?
- ▶ Let's hear from the newcomers first, what was that experience like for you?
- ▶ Now let's hear from those that portrayed having multiple years of sobriety. What was that experience like for you?
- ▶ How does this relate to our groups? What kind of environment do we want to foster for our newcomers?

**Additional Ideas for Role-Plays:**

- ▶ Going out on a job interview
- ▶ Attending a party where there is your drug of choice being passed around
- ▶ You saw an old drug dealer at a gas station
- ▶ You are making amends to someone you hurt in addiction
- ▶ You are welcoming someone back from a relapse
- ▶ You are celebrating 1 year clean and sober
- ▶ You see someone in a meeting you used to use with

**Recovery/Wellness Metaphor:** These role-plays help to creatively practice a variety of different situations. This is also a great activity to increase group cohesion.

# Body Part Check-In

**Group size:** 5–50

**Purpose:** Gather information about where participants are at today and what they need, increase group cohesion, and stimulate metaphoric thinking. This is a great way to start a full day program.

**Props Needed:**
1. Pictures or stress balls in the shape of feet, spine, heart, hand, brain, lips, and ears.
2. 50-foot rope (optional)

**Activity Preparation:**
1. Prep time needed: 5 minutes
2. Prior to class create an open space for body parts. If you are indoors, put chairs around the perimeter of the room. If you are outside, find an open space to play that is free of debris or obstacles.
3. Obtain stress balls in the shape of body parts (heart, hand, brain, lips, and ears) or print pictures from the Internet. (Remember to use images that are representative of your population.)

**Time Needed:**
- ▶ Directions: 5 minutes
- ▶ Activity: 10 minutes (depending on size of group)
- ▶ Debrief: 5 minutes

**Set-Up:**
1. Create a circle with large rope.
2. Scatter body parts around the circle so participants can gather around and see all 7 body parts from any angle.

**Activity Directions:**
- ▶ Have the participants stand in a circle. Include yourself in the circle.
- ▶ Ask participants to select a body part that represents what they need for today.
  - ☐ Foot—a stronger foundation to stand on or maybe needing to feel more grounded
  - ☐ Spine—more courage and the ability to stand up for yourself
  - ☐ Heart—more in touch with feelings

- ☐ Hand—ask for help when needed
- ☐ Brain—open mind to learn new things
- ☐ Lips—to speak and give voice to what is going on with me
- ☐ Ears—to listen more
  ► Go around the group and have everyone check in with the body part they selected and why.
  ► Short debrief of what participants noticed.

**Facilitator Script:** "Let's form a circle to hear the directions for today's check-in. You may have noticed all the body parts scattered around the circle. Today we are going to do our check-in a little differently. I would like to use the body as a metaphor for what we need, so when you check in you are going to choose one of the body parts to metaphorically represent where you're at today.  For example, if you choose the Foot, it could represent needing a stronger foundation to stand on, or the Spine might represent the need to gain more courage or to stand up for myself.  If you choose the heart it might represent needing to be more in touch with your feelings, or maybe a Hand in order to ask for help when I need it. The Brain could represent having an open mind to learn new things or Lips in order to speak and give voice to what is going on with me. And finally, the Ears could represent the need to be a better listener.

So you are going to choose a body part and then tell us how it represents either a need or where you are at today.

Any questions? *(answer questions)* OK great, who would like to start?" *(then go around the circle until everyone checks in)*

**Debrief:**
  ► What did you notice about check-in today?
  ► What were your thoughts as you entered the room and saw all the body parts?
  ► How is this check-in different from others we have done?

**Recovery/Wellness Metaphor:** This check-in is helpful as it is a way to gather information about your participants in a slightly different way. This is a safe, easy way to engage the subconscious and access information that clients might not automatically share by just having a verbal check-in.

**Role of Facilitator:** Make sure to spread out body parts so each participant can see each body part. We recommend having at least 4–6 sets of each body part.

**Variations:** Feel free to add in additional body parts as needed.

**Where to Find It/How to Make It:** You can purchase spare body parts from training-wheels. com or feel free to print off pictures in a public domain from the Internet. We have found that if you are going to use pictures it might be helpful to have them laminated so that they can be reused and do not get crumpled.

# Bull Ring Cup Stack

**Group size:** 8–50

**Purpose:** To provide an opportunity for team work, and a discussion on the important foundations of wellness and recovery.

**Props Needed:** Small cups, rubber bands, string, and writing utensils

**Activity Preparation:**
1. Prep time needed: 15 minutes. Purchase materials, cut strings into desired lengths. (18″–36″ recommended.)

**Time Needed:**
- ▶ Directions: 2 minutes
- ▶ Activity: 10 minutes
- ▶ Debrief: 15 minutes

**Activity Directions:**
- ▶ Have group gather around to discuss.
- ▶ This activity can be done sitting at a table or sitting on the floor.
- ▶ Give each group a minimum of 10 cups, 1 rubber band, and 1 string per person.
- ▶ Have groups tie the strings onto the rubber band using an overhand knot. You can also pre-tie these if you desire.
- ▶ Have the group scatter the cups on the surface in front of them. Make sure several cups are tipped over on their side. After the cups are scattered, they may not touch the cups with their hands.
- ▶ Have participants write words associated with recovery and wellness on their cups. For example: trust, sobriety, sponsor, patience, forgiveness, etc. Before participants begin stacking, ask them to put the worded cups in order of importance, starting with a strong foundation and building up from there. This allows for great dialogue in the group during the activity.
- ▶ The pair must then work together to stack cups in a pyramid using the rubber band device to pick up and move the cups. If multiple cups are lying down on their sides it increases the difficulty level of the activity.

**Facilitator Script:** "I need everyone to get into groups of six and take a seat at one of the tables. In the center of the table you will find a rubber band, some strings, and some Dixie Cups. Please tie one string onto the rubber band for each person you have at your table. *(Pause while the group performs this task.)* Next, I need everyone to think about what some of the most important parts of recovery and wellness are. Please write some of the words you come up with on the Dixie Cups provided. *(Pause while the group does this task.)* Now I'd like each group to scatter the cups in the center of the table, making sure that some of them are on their sides. *(Pause while group does this task.)* Now, from this moment on, you may not touch the cups with your hands. Take your dominant hand and put it behind your back. You are not allowed to use your dominant hand. Together as a team, you must stack the cups into a pyramid. You may use the rubber band/string device to move your cups around. I'd like for you to discuss at your tables which words for recovery and wellness are the most important to you, and place these cups on the lower level of your pyramid. These will be your strong foundation on the base of your pyramid. Build up from there. Are there any questions? *(Pause for questions.)* You may begin!"

**Debrief:**

- ▶ Describe how you and your partners worked together.
- ▶ How much planning did you do before you began?
- ▶ Did your strategy change throughout the process?
- ▶ How did you communicate with your teammates?
- ▶ What were some of the words you put on your cups?
- ▶ How did you choose which cups were on the foundation level?
- ▶ What can you apply from this exercise to your daily life?

**Recovery/Wellness Metaphor:** Sometimes the solution is right before our eyes, yet we might need a team of creative thinkers working together in order to reach the solution. This solution requires a team approach much as does our recovery. We simply do not have to do it alone.

**Variation:** Have participants write words on their cups that reflect important traits of working together. For example: trust, teamwork, laughter, positive work environment, leadership, etc. Before participants begin stacking, ask them to put the worded cups in order of importance, starting with a strong foundation and building up from there. This allows for great dialogue in the group during the activity.

**Variation:** Create a series of obstacles the group has to transport the cups around before they can place them on the pyramid. If they drop a cup along the way they must start over.

**Variation:** Fill the cups with water! See if they can stack cups filled with water into a pyramid.

**Where to Find It/How to Make It:** Dixie Cups are inexpensive and readily available in stores. You can also use the cups designed for Speed Stacking. Use masking tape to write words on the cups. You can find these at www.speedstacks.com.

Surveyor string found at hardware stores makes for inexpensive, colorful string. Using different colors of string allows for flexibility of facilitators to add in more complex rules such as, if you are touching the yellow string you may not talk. If you are touching the blue string you must assume a leadership role in the activity, etc.

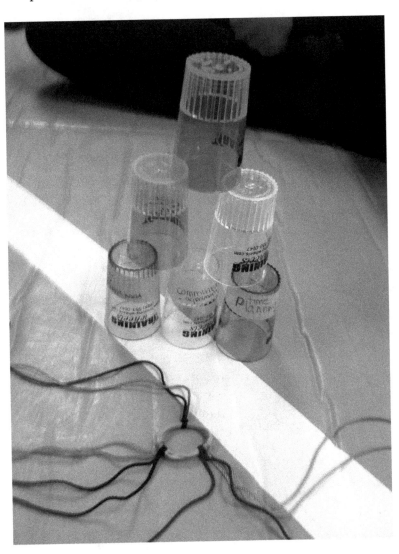

# Clean and Messy

**Group Size:** 8–20

**Purpose:** To show that other people can undo the work we've done. Have a strategy to keep on track, even if other people try to sabotage your success.

**Props Needed:** 10–20 soccer cones

**Activity Preparation:**
1. Prep time needed: 5 minutes
2. Prior to class make sure you have all your props.
3. Clear a large space in the room or go to a large space.
4. Spread the cones out in the space, with half of them standing and the other half lying down.

**Time Needed:**
- ▶ Directions: 2 minutes
- ▶ Activity: 10 minutes
- ▶ Debrief: 15 minutes

**Safety:**
- ▶ Physical—Remove any tripping hazards from the activity area. Control pace of participants. Encourage a walking pace.

**Activity Directions:**
- ▶ Have group get into a circle.
- ▶ Randomly identify half of the participants as the mess makers and the other half as the cleaners.
- ▶ Tell the participants that if they are mess makers, they are trying to tip all the cones over. If they are cleaners, they are trying to stand the cones back up. This is all to be done in a walking pace. For safety reasons, no one is to run.
- ▶ Tell the participants that you will give them one minute either to make messes or to clean them up.
- ▶ Remind the participants to use a walking pace.
- ▶ Yell "go" and begin the time. (If they are having fun, you may extend the time.)
- ▶ After one round, have everyone switch roles and try it again.

**Facilitator Script:** "Hey everyone gather around. Let's count off by two's. *(Pause while the group counts off.)* You'll see that I have a variety of soccer cones scattered about here in the middle of the room. One's are going to be designated as 'Mess Makers.' Your goal in the activity is to tip all of the cones over that are standing upright. Two's are going to be the 'Cleaners.' Your goal is to stand all of the cones back up. We will play for one minute, and we'll see who is the closest to achieving their goal. For safety purposes, this is a walking game. Please do not run. Are there any questions? *(Pause for questions.)* Ready? Go!"

### Debrief:

- ▶ What was difficult about your job?
- ▶ Did you have any strategy to your mess making or clean-up process?
- ▶ How did you react when someone undid what you had just done?
- ▶ Did anyone work together in teams?
- ▶ Where do you see this kind of process outside of this activity?
- ▶ How does this activity relate back to the real world?
- ▶ Do you ever feel like you make progress in one area, then someone undoes your progress?
- ▶ How does this relate back to recovery and wellness?

### Recovery/Wellness Metaphor:

**Role of Facilitator:** Timekeeper and walking pace monitor.

**Where to Find It/How to Make It:** Soccer cones can be purchased at any store carrying sports accessories.

**Source:** *Journey Towards the Caring Classroom,* by Laurie Frank

# Conflict Animals

**Source:** The idea for this activity came from *Resolving Interpersonal Conflicts*, Chapter 8, pp. 254–257. The initial concept of these "conflict styles" (animals metaphor) came from Johnson & Johnson (1981) and was adapted from *Group Dynamics in the Outdoors: A Model for Teaching Outdoor Leaders* by Maurice L. Phipps of Western State College of Colorado and *Wilderness Educator in The Wilderness Education Association Curriculum Guide*, which was edited by David Cockrell. It was further developed by Michelle Cummings and Mike Anderson.

**Group Size:** 5–50

**Purpose:** Gather information about how participants approach conflict, increase group cohesion, and stimulate metaphoric thinking. This is a great way to start a discussion around community conflict such as bullying and collusion.

**Props Needed for Conflict Animal Check-In:** Pictures of or physical models of a variety of different animals.

**Props Needed for Variation #1:** Pictures of or physical models of the following animals: turtle, shark, bear, fox, and owl.

**Props Needed for Variation #2:** Pictures of or physical models of the following animals: turtle, shark, bear, fox, owl, camel, bull, lion, mouse, panther, parrot, rabbit, cobra, chicken, elephant, horse, and mule. You will also need blank index cards and writing utensils for each participant.

**Activity Preparation:**
1. Prep time needed: 5 minutes
2. Prior to class create an open space for Animals. If you are indoors, put chairs around the perimeter of the room. If you are outside, find an open space to play that is free of debris or obstacles.
3. Obtain stress balls or pictures in the shape of the animals being used.

**Time Needed:**
- ▶ Directions: 5 minutes
- ▶ Activity: 10 minutes (depending on size of group)
- ▶ Debrief: 5 minutes

**Set-Up:**

1.  Place animals around so participants can gather around and see.

**Activity Directions:**

▶   Place animals in the center of group so all participants can see them.
▶   Have participants check in with their conflict management style.

Here are some examples of different animals and their conflict management styles:

▶   Turtle (withdraw)—Withdraws from the conflict; hides until it is safe to emerge.
▶   Shark (force)—Forces and tries to make opponents accept his/her decisions; often threatening and intimidating.
▶   Bear (smooth)—Avoids the conflict when possible; ignores their own goals and resolves conflict by giving into others.
▶   Fox (compromise)—Sly, sneaky, tricky, and able to persuade others to give up part of their most important and valued positions.
▶   Owl (problem-solver)—Known throughout children's books as the wise old owl . . . the owl views conflicts as problems to be solved, confronting the situation and seeking solutions that will satisfy both parties.
▶   Camel—Carries others' burdens without taking care of their own needs first.
▶   Bull—Hits the issue head-on when provoked. Certain triggers ignite anger.
▶   Lion—Very proud, works within a group; King of the jungle. Another metaphor to work with is the "cowardly lion"; those that tuck their tail and run when faced with conflict.
▶   Mouse—Very timid, runs from conflict, easy target.
▶   Panther—Slinks around in the background, stalks his prey, and pounces for the kill.
▶   Parrot—Repeats everything that is heard. Often annoying and loud.
▶   Rabbit—Runs and hides from any kind of conflict.
▶   Cobra—Deadly and dangerous when provoked. Can be charmed by some and submit to those in authoritative positions.
▶   Chicken—Everyone has heard the phrase, "You're just being a chicken!" when referring to someone who is shying away from a situation or opting out because they are scared. Chickens tend to flee from conflict and frighten easily.
▶   Elephant—The strongest animal on earth, has an amazing memory, yet when faced with small restrictions, such as a rope around their foot, it paralyzes them from moving forward.

► Horse—Can be tamed to do whatever their manager wants them to do. Very loyal when treated properly. When faced with conflict it rears back and attempts to protect itself. Able to handle a great deal of weight and workload.

► Mule—Very stubborn. Will not move forward unless given something positive in return.

**Facilitator Script for conflict animal check-in:** "Let's form a circle to hear the directions for today's check-in. You may have noticed all the animals scattered around the circle. Today we are going to use these animals to take a look at different conflict management styles. I would like for our check-in to be around how we have handled conflict in the past, and how we would like to handle conflict in the future. So when you check in you might say 'In the past I was a shark, forceful and aggressive. I would do whatever I had to in order to meet my needs not caring much about the needs of others. In the future, I would like to be more like lion; King of the jungle. He knows how to be a loving part of a family and is also strong and protective.'

So you are going to choose an animal that represents how you handled conflict in the past and then choose an animal that represents how you would like to handle conflict in the future.

Any questions? *(answer questions)* OK great, who would like to start?" *(then go around the circle until everyone checks in)*

**Debrief:**

► What did you notice about check-in today?
► What were your thoughts as you entered the room and saw all the animals?
► How is this check-in different from others we have done?

**Recovery/Wellness Metaphor:** This check-in is helpful as it is a way to gather information about your participants in a slightly different way. This is a safe, easy way to engage the subconscious and access information that clients might not automatically share by just having a verbal check-in.

**Role of Facilitator:** Make sure to spread out animals so each participant can see each animal. We recommend having at least four to six sets of each animal for larger groups.

**VARIATION #1:**

**Directions:** Place the five animals in the center of the group (turtle, shark, bear, fox, and owl). Begin the conversation about conflict styles by asking your participants to share with you what they know (stereotyping) about the animal in question. It is important that you also know some basic biological information about each animal.

Once the group shares enough information, you can ask the participants to place themselves into those roles according to how they typically deal with conflict. Some questions to ask might include: Would you like to work for a "shark"? Do you know a "turtle" in your peer group or family? Who do you know that is an "owl"?

After a short discussion, place the animals around the room. Ask everyone to move to the location in the room with the animal that best represents their own conflict style. You could also put chart paper and markers in these same areas and have participants write down the similarities and differences in interpretation of each animal's qualities. The rule of feet applies at all times, meaning, participants can walk away or remove themselves if they so desire. When each group is finished, encourage them to partner up with someone that was not in their conflict style group and discuss the information the small groups developed.

**The Competing Shark (force)**—Forces and tries to make opponents accept his/her decisions; often threatening and intimidating.

- ► Sharks use a forcing or competing conflict management style
- ► Sharks are highly goal-oriented
- ► Relationships take on a lower priority
- ► Sharks do not hesitate to use aggressive behavior to resolve conflicts
- ► Sharks can be autocratic, authoritative, uncooperative, threatening, and intimidating
- ► Sharks have a need to win; therefore, others must lose, creating win-lose situations

**Advantage:** If the shark's decision is correct, a better decision without compromise can result.

**Disadvantage:** May breed hostility and resentment toward the person using it.

Appropriate times to use a shark style:

- ► When conflict involves personal differences that are difficult to change
- ► When fostering intimate or supportive relationships is not critical
- ► When others are likely to take advantage of noncompetitive behavior
- ► When conflict resolution is urgent; when decision is vital in crisis
- ► When unpopular decisions need to be implemented

**The Avoiding Turtle (withdraw)**—Withdraws from the conflict; hides until it is safe to emerge.

▶ Turtles adopt an avoiding or withdrawing conflict management style
▶ Turtles would rather hide and ignore conflict than resolve it; this can lead them to being uncooperative and unassertive
▶ Turtles tend to give up personal goals and display passive behavior, which creates lose-lose situations

**Advantage:** May help to maintain relationships that would be hurt by conflict resolution. Turtles carry their safe place with them at all times.

**Disadvantage:** Conflicts remain unresolved; overuse of the style leads to others walking over them.

Appropriate times to use a turtle style:

▶ When the stakes are not high or issue is trivial
▶ When confrontation will hurt a relationship
▶ When there is little chance of satisfying your wants
▶ When disruption outweighs benefit of conflict resolution
▶ When gathering information is more important than an immediate decision
▶ When others can more effectively resolve the conflict
▶ When time constraints demand a delay

**The Accommodating Teddy Bear (smooth)**—Avoids the conflict when possible; ignores his/her own goals and resolves conflict by giving in to others.

▶ Teddy bears use a smoothing or accommodating conflict management style with an emphasis on human relationships
▶ Teddy bears ignore their own goals and resolve conflict by giving into others; unassertive and cooperative, which creates a win-lose (bear is loser) situation

**Advantage:** Accommodating maintains relationships.

**Disadvantage:** Giving in may not be productive; bear may be taken advantage of.

Appropriate times to use a teddy bear style:

▶ When maintaining the relationship outweighs other considerations
▶ When suggestions/changes are not important to the accommodator
▶ When minimizing losses in situations where outmatched or losing
▶ When time is limited or when harmony and stability are valued

**The Compromising Fox (compromise)**—Sly, sneaky, tricky, and able to persuade others to give up part of their most important and valued positions.

▶ Foxes use a compromising conflict management style; concern is for goals and relationships

▶ Foxes are willing to sacrifice some of their goals while persuading others to give up part of theirs

▶ Compromise is assertive and cooperative; result is either win-lose or lose-lose

**Advantage:** Relationships are maintained and conflicts are removed.

**Disadvantage:** Compromise may create less-than-ideal outcome and game playing can result.

Appropriate times to use a fox style:

▶ When important/complex issues leave no clear or simple solutions

▶ When all conflicting people are equal in power and have strong interests in different solutions

▶ When there are no time restraints

**The Collaborating Owl (problem solver)**—Known throughout children's books as the wise old owl . . . the owl views conflicts as problems to be solved; confronting the situations and seeking solutions that will satisfy both parties.

▶ Owls use a collaborating or problem-confronting conflict management style that values their goals and relationships

▶ Owls view conflicts as problems to be solved; works to find solutions agreeable to all sides (win-win)

**Advantage:** Both sides get what they want and negative feelings are eliminated.

**Disadvantage:** Takes a great deal of time and effort.

Appropriate times to use an owl style:

▶ When maintaining relationships is important

▶ When time is not a concern

▶ When peer conflict is involved

▶ When trying to gain commitment through consensus building

▶ When learning and trying to merge differing perspectives

The chart below illustrates, depending on the importance of the result, which conflict style we might utilize in any given situation . . . the value of the goal versus the relationship is often the determining factor.

**Owl (Problem Solver)**
—Initiate negotiation
—Seeking agreement that maximizes joint benefit

**Shark (Force)**
—At all costs

**Fox (Compromise)**
—Give up part of the goal
—Sacrifice part of the relationship

**Bear (Smooth)**
—Give up goals
—Maintain relationship

**Turtle (Withdraw)**
—Give up goals
—Give up relationship

**Goal**

**Relationship**

## VARIATION #2

**Directions:** Place a large collection of animals in the center of the group. Begin the conversation by asking your participants to share with you how each animal deals with conflict. Go through each of the animals you have in the center of the group. During the discussion ask the participants to be thinking about which animal conflict styles match their own conflict styles. Encourage them to think of other animals not represented by the props you have in the center and add them to the discussion.

After this discussion, pass out one index card and a few writing utensils to each participant. Ask them to pick three or four of the animals whose conflict styles match their own. Invite them to morph these three or four animals into one and draw it on their index card. Then ask them to re-name their new animal with a combination of the three animals. For example: If a participant chooses a tiger, a horse, and a dog for their three animals, they might draw the body of a horse with the arms of a tiger and the tail of a dog. They might name this new animal a "Hors-ger-og."

Give plenty of time for each participant to complete their index card. Offer assistance to those that appear to struggle with the concept. After everyone has completed their card, invite them to share their card and their conflict style with the group.

Here are some examples of different animals and their conflict styles:

- ▶ Turtle (withdraw)—Withdraws from the conflict; hides until it is safe to emerge.
- ▶ Shark (force)—Forces and tries to make opponents accept his/her decisions; often threatening and intimidating.
- ▶ Bear (smooth)—Avoids the conflict when possible; ignores their own goals and resolves conflict by giving into others.
- ▶ Fox (compromise)—Sly, sneaky, tricky, and able to persuade others to give up part of their most important and valued positions.
- ▶ Owl (problem solver)—Known throughout children's books as the wise old owl . . . the owl views conflicts as problems to be solved, confronting the situation and seeking solutions that will satisfy both parties.
- ▶ Camel—Carries others' burdens without taking care of their own needs first.
- ▶ Bull—Hits the issue head-on when provoked. Certain triggers ignite anger.
- ▶ Lion—Very proud, works within a group; King of the jungle. Another metaphor to work with is the "cowardly lion"; those that tuck their tail and run when faced with conflict.
- ▶ Mouse—Very timid, runs from conflict, easy target.
- ▶ Panther—Slinks around in the background, stalks his prey, and pounces for the kill.

- ► Parrot—Repeats everything that is heard. Often annoying and loud.
- ► Rabbit—Runs and hides from any kind of conflict.
- ► Cobra—Deadly and dangerous when provoked. Can be charmed by some and submit to those in authoritative positions.
- ► Chicken—Everyone has heard the phrase, "You're just being a chicken!" when referring to someone who is shying away from a situation or opting out because they are scared. Chickens tend to flee from conflict and frighten easily.
- ► Elephant—The strongest animal on earth, has an amazing memory, yet when faced with small restrictions, such as a rope around their foot, it paralyzes them from moving forward.
- ► Horse—Can be tamed to do whatever their manager wants them to do. Very loyal when treated properly. When faced with conflict it rears back and attempts to protect itself. Able to handle a great deal of weight and workload.
- ► Mule—Very stubborn. Will not move forward unless given something positive in return.

**Where to Find It/How to Make It:** You can purchase *Conflict Animals* from training-wheels. com or feel free to print off pictures in a public domain from the Internet. We have found that if you are going to use pictures it might be helpful to have them laminated so that they can be reused and do not get crumpled.

# Coping with the Stuck Points

**Group size:** 5–50

**Purpose:** Increase frustration tolerance, problem solving, communication skills, trust, group cohesion, and learning how to fail brilliantly.

**Props Needed:**
1. Maze
2. Facilitator Map
3. Noise Maker (bell, buzzer, or facilitator voice)

**Activity Preparation:**
1. Prep time needed: 5 minutes
2. Prior to class, create an open space for play. If you are indoors, put chairs around the perimeter of the room. If you are outside, find an open space to play that is free of debris or obstacles.

**Time Needed:** Total time 45 minutes
▶ Directions: 5 minutes
▶ Activity: 25 minutes
▶ Debrief: 15 minutes

**Set-Up:** In order to do this group you must first make a maze. This is a grid of boxes. We recommend going to a hardware store and getting a blue plastic tarp that is 8' x 10' and some duct tape. We recommend using a fun and contrasting color to help members clearly see the grid. It is important to print out the facilitator grid so that you can keep track of the pathway through the maze.

**Safety:** When a person is in the maze and has lost the resource of their sight ensure safety by removing all obstacles that might be harmful. Pay attention to the emotional tone of both the individuals as well as the collective whole. This activity might increase frustration; however, it will also give participants an opportunity to work through their frustration.

## Activity Directions:

▶ Group members are instructed that their task is to get five members through this maze.

▶ Once a member enters the maze if they hear the bell that is their clue that they have reached a stuck point and must exit the maze.

▶ In order to enter into the maze again all members of the group must have a turn. Much like the lineup at a baseball game participants must cycle through the lineup.

▶ Remember there is only one way in and one way out.

▶ You may not use the resource of your pens, papers, or electronics.

**Facilitator Note:** Don't tell the participants this but there are five rounds. A round is completed once they have successfully moved a participant through the maze.

▶ Round 1—Participants may not use the resource of their pens, papers, or electronics

▶ Round 2—Participant in the maze may not use the resource of their eyes

▶ Round 3—Participants out of the maze may not use the resource of their voice

▶ Round 4 and 5—1 participant in the maze may not use the resource of their eyes and the participants outside of the maze may not use the resource of their voice.

**Facilitator Hint**—When the next member walks into the maze for round 4 tell them they don't have the resource of their eyes and say those of you outside of the maze have lost the resource of your voice. The solution here is that two group members must be in the maze; one with their eyes closed and the other guiding them through either by the resource of voice or touch.

**Facilitator Script:** "OK everyone gather around the tarp in order to hear your mission." *(Stand at the side of the maze that is the exit. This will help you visualize the maze as each member goes through. Wait until everyone is standing around the tarp.)* Great! Here is your mission. You are standing around a maze. There is one way in *(point at entrance)* one way through, and one way out *(point at exit)*. You can step on any square you want when you hear this sound *(make the noise)* it will signify you have misstepped. The good news is that you can always start over. Whenever you hear this sound *(make noise again)* the person's turn in the maze is now over and you cannot have another try until everyone else has gone. Therefore, everyone needs to participate and get a turn at the maze. Oh and you may not use the resource of pens, papers, or electronics. You have completed your mission once you have successfully moved five participants through the maze without hearing *(make the sound)*. Any questions?

OK, who wants to go first? (*Make sure you have the facilitator grid that will allow you to track if they are on the right path. Pay close attention, as it is important to remain consistent and on track. Each time someone has a misstep make the noise; when someone makes a correct step nod your head yes.*)

(*When someone has made it through the maze successfully the group advances to round two.*) Great job everyone, now you are ready for round 2. For round 2 the person in the maze has lost the resource of their eyes.

(*When someone has made it through the maze successfully the group advances to round three.*) Great job that's two, now you are ready for round 3. In round 3 everyone out of the maze has lost the resource of his or her voice.

(*When someone has made it through the maze successfully the group advances to round 4 and secretly 5.*) Great job that's 3, now you are ready for round 4. In round 4 everyone out of the maze has lost the resource of his or her voice and one person in the maze has lost the resource of sight.

(*Usually the members will pick up on the fact that you said 1 person in the maze thus indicating that 2 people can be in the maze. Each person in the maze has to go through the correct path so it might mean that they have to get close and work together. Sometimes the guide will focus too much on the person without sight that they themselves misstep; make sure to make the noise and let them know that there was a misstep.*)

(*When both people make it through the maze successfully the group has completed its mission.*) Awesome and that's 4 and 5!" (*This may be news to the group as they forget to count the guide.*)

## Debrief:

- ▶ What was this activity like for you?
- ▶ What strategy did you use to solve the problem?
- ▶ What strategies did you use to cope with the stuck points?
- ▶ How did you feel every time you heard the buzzer?
- ▶ What did it feel like the first time someone completed the maze?
- ▶ How did it feel to become stuck again after completing it the first time?
- ▶ What was it like once you lost the resource of your sight and voice?
- ▶ How does this relate to coping with stuck points in recovery?
- ▶ What is a relapse oriented approach to coping with stuck points?
- ▶ What is some recovery oriented approaches to coping with stuck points?

## RECOVERY/WELLNESS METAPHOR:

### Role of Facilitator:

**Variations:** Play with the rules or limitations of the different rounds as well as the complexity of the maze. We find that the below example takes participants about 30 minutes to complete the mission as outlined above. Clients will want to know if they will use a square more than once or if they will be going diagonal. Typically, I answer these types of questions with the recovery slogan, "More will be revealed."

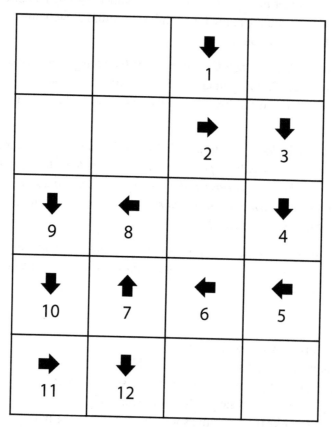

### Where to Find It/How to Make It:

## CREATING THE MAZE

**Materials:** 8 × 10 plastic tarp, duct tape, measuring tape, sharpie, helpful friend

Get a friend to help, this is much harder than it needs to be with one person doing it. Lay out the 8′ × 10′ blue tarp. First let's start with making the columns of the grid. Measure out 2′ across the 8′ side of the tarp until you have four marks 2′ apart from each other. Then go to the opposite side of the tarp and do the same thing. Now take the duct tape and tape down the long columns. This should give you four columns. Now let's create the rows. Use the measuring tape to measure out rows 2′ apart from each other along the 10′ side of the tarp. Once completed this should give you five marks. Then go to the opposite side of the tarp and do the same thing. Now take the duct tape and tape down the rows. This should give you five rows and a sense of accomplishment as you have created your maze tarp that you can use for a long time to come.

NOTE: It is important that the boxes are 2′, as they need to be big enough to accommodate 2 group members within each box. One of the problem-solving components might include having two people in one box at a time.

### Facilitator Grid:

Print off the facilitator grid in this book as you will need to be able to keep track of the solution while participants are attempting to move through it. It is important to remain consistent, otherwise trust can be broken between participants and facilitator. Also draw out your maze on the grid in a yellow highlighter so it doesn't show through to participants.

## Facilitator Grid

| | | | |
|---|---|---|---|
| | | | |
| | | | |
| | | | |
| | | | |
| | | | |

# Digital Contract

**Source:** The idea for this activity came from *Digital Contract, The Empty Bag* (2003), Cavert and Hammond and was adapted from *Training Wheels Challenge Kit Field Guide*, 2nd ed. (2012), Michelle Cummings.

**Group Size:** Any number of people.

**Purpose:** Introduction of guidelines/safety

**Props Needed:**

1. Your hand.

**Activity Preparation:**

1. Prep time needed: 5 minutes

**Time Needed:**

- ▶ Directions: 5 minutes
- ▶ Activity: 10–20 minutes
- ▶ Debrief: 10 minutes

**Set-Up:**

1. Locate participants in a physical space free from debris or objects that may create a safety hazard.

**Activity Directions:**

- ▶ Have the participants seated, where the facilitator is in the front of the room, or participants can be standing in a circle facing toward the facilitator.

---

**Facilitator Script:** "Let's form a circle. Before we begin any activities today, we want to go over a few guidelines about safety and your participation. As we think about experiential activities and your participation, we want to start with a few reminders. We intend to create an experience that helps you to grow. In so doing we need to establish and observe safe practices. By creating a safe physical and emotional place today, we allow ourselves the opportunity to experience each activity to its fullest for our own growth.

This activity is called Digital Contract. When we think of a contract we often think of commitment. A contract is a vehicle for which each party agrees to the terms.

You may notice that I do not have any props. But I do—my hand! *(Hold hand above your head for all to see)* And on my hand are my fingers, also called digits. I am going to review five guidelines using my hand to help you to remember some important guidelines about experiential activities as we go through the day. As we go through the five digits I want you to hold up your hand along with me.

**The Little Finger**—*Hold up your hand to visibly show your pinky finger*

The first digit we have is the little finger, often called the pinky finger, and it is our smallest. It is the one that can be easily hurt. Today we want to avoid anyone getting hurt, either emotionally or physically. I want you to consider what will be helpful for you to be safe.

**The Ring Finger**—*Hold up your hand to visibly show your ring finger*

The next digit, the ring finger, is the one that represents commitment. If you think of this finger, it often wears a ring or ornament that may symbolize commitment. Today we are asking you to make a commitment to the group, to your authentic self, and to your journey toward wellness and recovery.

**The Middle Finger**—*Point to this finger, not at others. You may hold up your hand in a way that all fingers are up to avoid flinging this finger toward someone.*

The third digit, the middle finger, is the one that can represent strong, often derogatory, words intended to put down others. Today we want to remember to be respectful of all in the group, avoiding putdowns, derogatory words and statements.

**The Index Finger**—*Hold up your hand to visibly show your index finger*

The pointer finger represents pointing things out in others. This is often used in a defensive way, pointing *(gesture)* toward others as we are strongly getting our own point across. I want you to notice that when you have your pointer finger poking at others, you also have three fingers pointing to yourself. So for every one thing you point out about others, I ask that you point out three things about yourself.

**The Thumb**—*Hold up your thumb, gesturing Thumbs Up!*

The final digit, the thumb, is the one finger we would use for encouragement. Thumbs Up. I want you to use a Thumbs Up to give encouraging feedback to your fellow participants.

To review—*(Here go over the digit with the word associated, asking participants to echo the guideline.)*

- ▶ Pinky Finger—safety
- ▶ Ring Finger—commitment

- ▶ Middle—avoid strong derogatory works
- ▶ Pointer Finger—one finger points outward, three fingers point inward
- ▶ Thumb Finger—encouragement; thumbs up

Now, who would like to take a turn to recite The Digital Contract?

(**Facilitator Note**—Encourage participants to practice reciting it, and help them with filling in details as they recite it to the group.)

Now as in any contract, there is a final expression of personal commitment. Usually a contract is signed by each party. Another way to affirm commitment is the handshake. So now, take time to shake hands with your fellow participants to seal the deal of your Digital Contract."

## Debrief:

- ▶ What are your thoughts about introducing guidelines in this way?
- ▶ What skills did it take?
- ▶ What challenges might you experience in sharing the Digital Contract with a group?
- ▶ What is one thing you can do to address your challenge?

**Recovery/Wellness Metaphor:** In every journey of recovery and wellness there can be challenges. Growth requires expanding beyond one's comfort zone with guidelines for trust and safety. Using the Digital Contract is one way to explore the need for safety, commitment, avoidance of putdowns of self or others, pointing out things in self and others, and exploring encouragement of self to grow, get outside of one's comfort zone, and expand one's horizons and support network.

**Variations:** Conduct activity without speaking, using your hand as the prop, and with participants communicating the details of each digit. Participants can pair up and rehearse the Digital Contract.

**Where to Find It/How to Make It:** N/A.

# Emotional Jenga

**Group Size:** 5–25

**Purpose:** Increase emotional intelligence, group cohesion, and insight

**Props Needed:**
1. Jenga blocks with emotions written on them

**Activity Preparation:**
1. Prep time needed: 30 minutes
2. Make the emotional Jenga set by writing an emotion on each block

**Time Needed:**
- ▶ Directions: 5 minutes
- ▶ Activity: 25 minutes
- ▶ Debrief: 15 minutes

**Set-Up:** Prior to class, set up the Jenga set as a tall tower following the instruction on the box. Set up block on a table if using a small set; if using a jumbo set of blocks, you can set them up on the floor. This is completely up to you as a facilitator and the population you are working with.

**Activity Directions:**
- ▶ Have the participants stand in a circle around the Jenga set.
- ▶ Remind participants of the rules of Jenga.
- ▶ Have clients pull a block and use the word on the block (see variations below).

---

**Facilitator Script:**

"Let's form a circle around this table to hear the directions for our game today. We are going to play a version of Jenga today. Now here's how the game is played. You are going to take a block from the tower. You can pick any block as long as it is not from the top. Your block will have a feeling word written on it. During round one when you have your block please tell us a short story of the last time you felt that way. Then put the block back on top of the tower. We will continue until everyone has had a chance. *(Give everyone a chance to pull their block and share their story of the last time they felt that way.)*

*(For round two)* Great job everyone. OK, are you ready for round two? This time you will pull three blocks. Use one of your blocks to define the feeling using your own words and then select another feeling and share how this feeling could be a potential trigger to use negative coping skills such as alcohol or drugs."

*(When and if the tower falls down start clapping in excitement as if the participant did something great. This is an intentional way of replacing the feeling that the participant has lost. There are no losers in emotional Jenga.)*

## Debrief:

- ▶ What did you notice about this version of playing the game?
- ▶ What was it like recalling the last time you felt a certain way?
- ▶ What was challenging about this version of Jenga?
- ▶ What was something you learned about yourself/your peers/the group?

## Recovery/Wellness Metaphor:

**Role of Facilitator:** Keep the game going and help participants remember what they are supposed to do with the feeling words.

**Variations:** Use the feeling words as a check-in or debrief. Also write an action or coping skill on each block to get more use out of the set of blocks.

Use emotional words to:

- ▶ Describe the last time you felt that way
- ▶ Define the emotion in your own words
- ▶ Describe how that emotion can be a trigger for relapse

**Where to Find It/How to Make It:** Purchase a set of Jenga blocks. They can be bought online or even found in Goodwill from time to time. Using a Sharpie write out a mixture of positive and negative emotions. For your convenience, we have attached a list that we have used in the past.

# List of Positive/Negative Emotions

1. Blessed
2. Brave
3. Clever
4. Confident
5. Excited
6. Fantastic
7. Free
8. Friendly
9. Glad
10. Happy
11. Honest
12. Important
13. Interested
14. Joyful
15. Loved
16. Miracle
17. Optimistic
18. Quiet
19. Relaxed
20. Reliable
21. Safe
22. Satisfied
23. Surprised
24. Thankful
25. Trustworthy
26. Wonderful
27. Worthwhile

28. Abandoned
29. Aggressive
30. Angry
31. Bad
32. Belittled
33. Betrayed
34. Bored
35. Chaotic
36. Competitive
37. Confused
38. Cowardly
39. Devastated
40. Disorganized
41. Flawed
42. Fragile
43. Gloomy
44. Hateful
45. Impulsive
46. Inferior
47. Irritable
48. Jealous
49. Lazy
50. Misunderstood
51. Nervous
52. Offended
53. Pain
54. Resentful

# Fabric Check-In

**Group Size:** 5–20

**Purpose:** Gather information about where participants are at today and what they need, increase group cohesion, and stimulate metaphoric thinking. This is a great way to start a full day program.

**Props Needed:**
1. As many different fabric cuttings as possible. It is useful to gather a collection of fabrics with different textures, colors, and prints.

**Activity Preparation:**
1. Prep time needed: 5 minutes
2. Prior to class create an open space. If you are indoors, put chairs around the perimeter of the room. If you are outside, find an open space to play that is free of debris or obstacles.
3. Put the fabrics in a circle in the middle of the group.

**Time Needed:**
- ▶ Directions: 5 minutes
- ▶ Activity: 10 minutes (depending on size of group)
- ▶ Debrief: 5 minutes

**Set-Up:**
1. Create a circle of fabrics in the middle of the group.

**Activity Directions:**
- ▶ Have the participants gather in a circle. Include yourself in the circle.
- ▶ Ask participants to select a fabric that represents where they are currently.
- ▶ Go around the group and have everyone check in with the fabric they chose and why.
- ▶ Short debrief of what participants noticed within themselves and each other.

---

**Facilitator Script:** "Let's form a circle to hear the directions for today's check-in. You may have noticed all the fabric swatches around the circle. Today we are going to do our check-in a little differently. I would like to use the fabrics as a metaphor for where we're at. So when you check in you might say I chose this piece of fabric because . . . and then tell us why you chose it or what it represents.

Any questions? *(answer questions)* OK great, who would like to start?" *(then go around the circle until everyone checks in)*

---

### Debrief:

- ▶ What did you notice about check-in today?
- ▶ What were your thoughts as you entered the room and saw all the fabric?
- ▶ How is this check-in different from others we have done?

**Recovery/Wellness Metaphor:** This check-in is helpful as it is a way to gather information about your participants in a slightly different way. This is a safe, easy way to engage the subconscious and access information that clients might not automatically share by just having a verbal check-in.

**Role of Facilitator:** Make sure to spread out fabric so each participant can see each swatch. We recommend having more than you need so participants can have plenty of a selection.

**Variations:** Feel free to use fabrics in any way as needed.

**Where to Find It/How to Make It:** You can purchase fabrics from any fabric store.

# Group Juggle

**Group Size:** 5–25

**Purpose:** Increase frustration tolerance, problem solving, communication skills, group cohesion, and increase mindfulness skills.

**Props Needed:** Various sizes and shapes of throwable objects. It would be good to have at least one per person.

**Activity Preparation:** none

**Time Needed:** Total time 50 minutes
- ▶ Directions: 5 minutes
- ▶ Activity: 30 minutes (depending on how long it takes group to complete task)
- ▶ Debrief: 15 minutes

**Safety:**
- ▶ Physical—For participants with physical issues like back pain, provide seating options.

**Activity Directions:**

Instruct them that they need to establish a throwing pattern. The facilitator starts the pattern and tosses the ball to someone across from them in the circle. Then that person throws the ball to someone across the circle from them that has not received the ball yet. Continue this process until everyone has received the ball one time. The last person to receive the ball throws it back to the facilitator. After one ball has circulated through the system, ask the group if they remember who they threw it to and who threw it to them. You may want to practice the pattern one more time to make sure everyone remembers.

Once the pattern is established pick up three balls/items. Tell the group you are going to add a few items to the pattern, but to continue throwing and receiving to/from the same people. When the group is ready start with the first ball, wait a few seconds and throw the second ball into the pattern, wait a few more seconds and throw the third ball into the pattern. After all three items circulate through the pattern, ask the group how they thought they did. After some discussion ask them how many items they think they could successfully keep going at one time (hence the group juggle!). Let the group set a goal around how many items they think they can successfully toss through the sequence, with as few drops as possible. Then give them as many attempts as you see fit for them to accomplish their goal.

**Facilitator Script:** "Hey everyone let's form a circle. We are going to create a pattern by tossing the ball. The rule is you cannot throw it to someone who has already had the ball and you cannot just pass it to the person next to you. It needs to go across the circle to someone new. Does anyone have any questions? *(If no questions toss the ball to the person across from you and let the group figure out a pattern. If they throw to someone that already had the ball have them start over.)*

*(After one ball has circulated through the system, ask the group if they remember who they threw it to and who threw it to them. You may want to practice the pattern one more time to make sure everyone remembers).* OK, let's try the same pattern again. Does everyone remember who they caught it from and threw it to? *(Do the pattern one to two more times.)*

*(Once the pattern is established pick up three balls/items.)* OK, now let's add a few balls to the pattern but continue throwing and receiving to and from the same person.

*(When the group is ready start with the first ball, wait a few seconds and throw the second ball into the pattern, wait a few more seconds and throw the third ball into the pattern. After all three balls circulate through the pattern ask the group how they thought they did.)* Good Job! What was that like? What did you notice? *(allow for some discussion)*

OK, so how many balls do you think you can get through the pattern?" *(Let the group set a goal around how many items they think they can do. Then give them as many attempts as you see fit for them to accomplish their goal.)*

---

**Debrief:**

- ▶ How successful do you think the group was at this activity?
- ▶ What was difficult?
- ▶ What were some helpful tricks you learned?
- ▶ How many different things do you juggle in your life on a daily basis?
- ▶ What are some things that you juggle?
- ▶ What happens at work/school/home when someone "drops the ball"? Who picks up the slack?
- ▶ Who do you lean on for support to help you with the many things you juggle?

**Recovery/Wellness Metaphor:** Show that we can work together to create creative solutions to our problems.

**Variations:** Add possible restrictions to increase the difficultly level of the task. This can be a great name game. Have each person come up with an alliteration that goes with the name they go by.

**Where to Find It / How to Make It:** Purchase a full Group Juggle set from Training Wheels, www.trainingwheelsgear.com. Make your own by gathering several soft, throwable items.

# Gutterball

**Group Size:** 2–30

This activity can be done with two people. Please allow each person to have two gutters each if facilitating a small group. If the group has more than five people, then restrict the number of gutters to one per person.

**Purpose:** Increase communication, problem-solving, frustration tolerance, emotional regulation, and group cohesion.

**Props Needed:**

► 1' long gutters (1–2 per participant)
► Couple of different sized marbles
► One jar or bucket

**Activity Preparation:** Have a clear space so participants can line up with enough gutters for each participant.

**Time Needed:** Total time 1 hour or so.

► Directions: 5 minutes
► Activity: 30 minutes (depending on how long it takes for participants to solve the problem)
► Debrief: 15 minutes

**Activity Directions:**

A team-building activity where each participant gets one short length of half-pipe, and the group must work together to deliver a marble down the pipes from start point to finish. However, when the marble is in contact with your pipe, you may not move your feet. This requires a high level of communication and teamwork.

► This is a group problem-solving and communication exercise.
► This activity involves moving marbles or different sized balls (or even water) down lengths of half-pipe or gutters.
► Each participant has only one short length of pipe each, and the start and finish points can be separated by an obstacle course.

► As facilitator, you can control how hard or easy to make this task. You can take them over obstacles, down stairs, around trees, etc. If, for example, the group is in the forming stage, put only one minor obstacle in the path and create opportunity for fairly instant experiential success of teamwork. If the team is functioning cohesively, make the obstacle course longer and harder and more physically challenging in order to deepen their experience of what they can achieve together.

► Brief the participants on the start line and the finish point (a distinctive container is helpful), and give them any extra rules you may wish to add to the task, such as every person must carry the marble at least once; participants need to take turns in a certain order; or both feet must remain on the floor at all times. Get creative if you want to add challenge.

► Important rule: When the marble is in contact with your pipe, you may not move your feet.

► Give the group the pipes and the marble and 5 minutes planning time.

► Allow the group several attempts if you have the time and they have the motivation, or keep it to one attempt and draw out the key points in the debrief.

**Facilitator Script:** "Gather around everyone. Today your mission is to get these balls (*hold up marbles*) into this container (*hold up jar*). Here is the trick—you can only touch the marbles with these gutters and it has to pass through everyone's gutter at some point in the process of getting it from my hand into the jar. You will have 5 minutes to strategize and then it will be time for your first attempt. When the ball is in your gutter it cannot touch your body and you cannot move your feet. If you drop the ball, move your feet, or allow the ball to touch any part of your body then you must start over.

Any questions? OK, here we go . . ."

## Debrief:

► How do you feel about your performance?

► Were you open to hearing ideas from other participants?

► If you were in a conflict with other participants, how difficult would it be to hear his/her perspective?

► How did you communicate with your peers?

► How did the size of your group affect the outcome? How would the outcome be different if the group was a different size?

**Recovery/Wellness Metaphor:** We often have far more courage and strength than we might initially think we have. Discuss how to work through frustration tolerance and how they respond to leaders emerging in the group.

**Role of Facilitator:** safety, Safety, SAFETY

**Variations:**

► Challenge the group to see how fast they can get the marble through the obstacle course. Time the group, and ask them to "tender" for how fast they think they can really do it. Then give them another go. Requires debriefing.

► For added problem-solving under pressure, do not give the gutters and marble to the group during planning time.

► Create a more intensive obstacle to include going through doorways, stairs, around trees, or whatever else you can imagine.

**Where to Find It/How to Make It:** You can purchase a Gutterball set through the Training Wheels website, www.training-wheels.com. Or, if you are handy with tools, you may purchase O-shaped PVC pipe at your local hardware store. First cut the pipe into 1′ sections. Then cut the tube in half lengthwise to create two U-shaped tubes. Be sure to sand the edges to prevent any splinters. Corner door molding can also be cut into 1′ sections and makes great gutters.

# Have You Ever

**Group Size:** 8–50

**Purpose:** Icebreaker, increase group cohesion and connection.

**Props Needed:** One physical spot marker for each participant. One spot must be red in color. Sample spots could include carpet squares, construction paper, plastic or foam squares. You could even use masking tape X's on the floor and use a red marker to make one spot red.

### Activity Preparation:
1. Prep time needed: 5–15 minutes
2. Prior to class create an open space for play. If you are indoors, put chairs around the perimeter of the room. If you are outside, find an open space to play that is free of debris or obstacles.

### Time Needed:
- ► Directions: 3 minutes
- ► Activity: 10 minutes
- ► Debrief: 5 minutes

**Set-Up:** Place spot markers on the ground in a circle. Make sure you include one red spot.

### Safety:
- ► Physical—Small risk of participants colliding into one another.

### Activity Directions:
- ► Place spot markers on the ground in a circle. Make sure you include one red spot.
- ► Have the participants stand on one of the spots in circle. Include yourself in the circle and stand on the red spot.
- ► The participant occupying the Hot Spot (the red spot) states a true statement about themselves.
- ► Other participants who also share that in common would move off of their spot. The next person occupying the Hot Spot states a new true statement.
- ► Play for 5–8 minutes.

**Facilitator Script:** "Let's form a circle to hear the directions for our first game. I need each person to stand on one of these spots. *(Wait until everyone is occupying a spot. Remove extra spots.)* What we're going to do in this game is find out things that are true for you, and find out things we have in common with one another. Do you see how I am standing on a red spot? This spot is called the Hot Spot. Whoever is occupying the Hot Spot needs to say 'Have you ever . . .' And then state something you have done before, or something that is true about you. For example, since I am standing on the Hot Spot, I will say something that is true about me. *(Come up with your own, but following is an example.)* I will also say this loud enough so that everyone can hear me. 'Have You Ever . . . been to Mount Rushmore?' Now if you also have been to Mount Rushmore, then you will move off of your spot and try to find a new spot. Once I have said my true statement I will also move off of the Hot Spot and try to find a new spot as well. The person that ends up in the Hot Spot after everyone has moved will be the next person who will announce a 'Have You Ever' statement. Let's practice one round to make sure everyone understands the rules. Let's go ahead and use my example, 'Have you ever been to Mount Rushmore?' So if you have also been to Mount Rushmore, then you would move off of your spot and try to find a new spot. *(Start to move off of your spot. Everyone else that has been to Mount Rushmore should also be moving off of their spot.)* Great! Now see how Peter is in the Hot Spot now? Now Peter must come up with the next 'Have You Ever' statement. But before Peter takes his turn, I want everyone to think of one true statement that they can use when they get to the Hot Spot. Think of one now so you are prepared when it is your turn in the Hot Spot. It's amazing how your mind goes blank when you are put on the spot. Think of things you've done or places you've been. Please keep this clean and appropriate. Everyone have one? OK Peter, get us started with our first Have You Ever . . . "

### Debrief:

  ▶   Did you learn something new about others in our group?
  ▶   Why is it important to learn new things about others in our group?

**Role of Facilitator:** Monitor statements. If participants start to make questionable Have You Ever statements, step in and ask participants to rephrase the question or choose an alternate question.

**Recovery Metaphor:** We can often get too caught up on the differences between us and our peers. This activity, as does recovery, offers us an opportunity to focus on the similarities rather than the differences.

**Where to Find It/How to Make It:** Use carpet squares, plastic discs, or pieces of paper for your spot markers. Purchase a full set of Have You Ever spot markers from Training Wheels, www.trainingwheelsgear.com.

# Helium Pole

**Group Size:** 10–20

**Purpose:** Increase frustration tolerance, problem solving, communication skills, trust, group cohesion, and increase mindfulness skills.

**Props Needed:**

▶ One tent pole approximately 16 feet long

**Activity Preparation:** Determine if more than one pole is needed based on group size.

**Time Needed:** Total time 45 min.

▶ Directions: 5 minutes
▶ Activity: 25 minutes (depending on how long it takes group to complete task)
▶ Debrief: 15 minutes

**Safety:**

▶ Physical—For participants with physical issues like back pain, knee or hip injuries, this activity might be one they want to observe.

**Activity Directions:**

▶ Have the team line up in two lines, facing each other, with their index finger extended from the hip.
▶ Instruct the group that the object of the activity is to lower the pole to the ground.
▶ Demonstrate "proper form" for fingers (thumb up and pointer finger straight out, no bending or curling under or around the pole) for the pole lying on the TOP of the pointer finger.

---

**Facilitator Script:** "Gather around everyone. Today we are going to play a game called Helium Pole. For this game we are all one team and I will ask you to line up in two lines facing each other. The goal of this activity is to lower the pole down to the ground. This is the proper positioning for your fingers. Thumb straight up, pointer finger straight out, and the other fingers curled. No bending or curling your fingers around the pole. The pole must lay on top of the pointer finger at all times. Also you must remain in contact with the pole at all times.

In a moment I will lower the pole onto your fingers. Everyone bend your arms so they are at a 90-degree angle at hip level. Everyone decide on a starting height. OK, here comes the Helium Pole. *(Lay the pole down on the group, and watch what happens.)* Remember, you must remain in contact with the pole at all times."

*(During the activity, it is useful to repeat this phrase—)* "Remember, you must remain in contact with the pole."

*(Monitor the frustration levels of group members as this will be important to debrief. When pole is too high above participant's head you can call a time-out and restart. This may occur several times before the group successfully lowers the pole to the ground.)*

### Debrief:

- ▶ How do you feel the group did as a team?
- ▶ What did it take to lower the pole?
- ▶ How did you feel the team communicated?
- ▶ What was this activity like for you?
- ▶ What strategy did you use to solve the problem?
- ▶ What strategies did you use to cope with the experience?
- ▶ Did you find yourself blaming others when the pole would not go down?
- ▶ How does mindfulness play a part in surrender?
- ▶ What were the steps you took to eventually make this a successful activity?
- ▶ What would you do differently if we were to do this again?
- ▶ What do you want to remember about this experience?

**Recovery/Wellness Metaphor:** This can be a powerful activity. Highlight that the task was to surrender to a power greater than ourselves. You can further highlight this by picking up the pole and simply dropping it. Ask the group what is a power greater than themselves they needed to surrender to? Yes, gravity! Powerful to debrief what surrender looked like in this activity.

**Role of Facilitator:** It's called Helium Pole because usually the pole will end up above the participant's heads before it will end up on the ground. The pole is light enough that any amount of pressure will raise the pole, which is the opposite direction of where they want to go. Groups really have to focus and work together to get the pole to do what they want it to.

Facilitate this one carefully as some groups will get so frustrated that they may want to give up. Often, you will see people blaming others for not going down, and while they are blaming, their fingers are not touching the pole. Great example of being worried about what others are doing and not taking care of your own responsibilities.

**Variations:** Using a Hula Hoop will make the activity a little easier as the group can see everyone in the group but the Hula Hoop will act very similar to that of the pole or stick. If you have a large group either split your group in half or if you have a large hoop have each person use only one finger instead of two.

**Where to Find It/How to Make It:** Purchase the Helium Pole from Training Wheels, www. trainingwheelsgear.com, or use a long, straight tent pole from a tent.

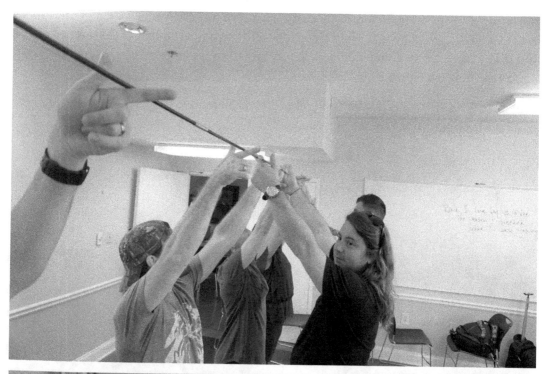

# Human Camera

**Original Game Source:** Karl Rohnke, Silver Bullets

**Group Size:** 6–30

**Purpose:** To learn how to trust others. To experience three specific visual experiences to debrief.

Activity Trust Level = High Risk

**Props Needed:** None

**Activity Preparation:** Group needs wide open space with no tripping hazards. Have the group partner up.

**Time Needed:** Total time 35 minutes
- ► Directions: 5 minutes
- ► Activity: 15 minutes
- ► Debrief: 15 minutes

**Safety:**
- ► Physical—Remove any tripping hazards from the activity area.

**Activity Directions:**
- ► Have the participants stand in a circle. Include yourself in the circle.
- ► Instruct the group to find a partner and stand next to them.
- ► After having made appropriate comments about how a camera is like a human eye, ask the pairs to determine who will be the camera first and who will be the photographer first. The roles will switch after some pictures are taken.
- ► The "photographer" will ask the "camera" to close his/her eyes, and then lead them to a spot where there is an interesting object that you would like to record on retinal film. Using the human camera body as an infinitely mobile tripod, set up your partner's head (the camera) in such a way that his/her closed eyes are directly in front of the chosen object. Say "Click" to activate the shutter. At this encouragement, the "camera" opens and closes the eyelids (shutter) for about 3 seconds in order to record the scene. Take three pictures before switching roles. After each person has had a chance to be in both roles, rejoin the group to discuss the experience and the pictures that were taken.

►   This activity is not only a shared experience of high quality, but also a trust sequence that leads to good feelings and a useful pairs' rapport. Be sure to talk about trust and personal boundaries before beginning. You may also ask for the "cameras" to walk with their "bumpers up" (hands out in front of them) while they are walking with their eyes closed.

**Facilitator Script:** "Let's form a circle to hear the directions for our first game. I need everyone to find a partner and stand next to them. *(Pause until everyone has a partner.)* In this game, one of you is going to be the photographer and the other person is going to be the camera. Don't worry, we will switch roles halfway through so you will get to be both parts. Decide who will be the photographer first. *(Pause so the pairs can decide.)* OK, if you are the camera you are going to close your eyes. The photographer will safely and verbally lead their camera to an interesting area or object. Once there, the photographer will say 'Click!' When the person in the camera role hears this, they will open their eyes for 3 seconds and look at what is in front of them. Then they will close their eyes again. The photographer will then safely lead them to a different object or area and say 'Click!' again. The camera will open their eyes again and mentally record what they see. Then they will close their eyes again. The photographer will then safely lead them to one more object or area and take one more picture. Then we will stop and debrief what happened before we switch roles. Photographers, it is very important that you be trustworthy and keep your cameras safe. Be caring and supportive of your camera. Cameras, please put your hands out in front of you like this *(demonstrate this)*. We will call these your bumpers, so you don't bump into anything. You may hear me say, 'Bumpers up!' during the game. This is just to help make sure that everyone stays safe. Are there any questions?"

## Debriefing Topics:

►   What was it like to be a photographer?
►   What was it like to be the camera?
►   Did your photographer keep you safe?
►   What were some of the pictures that were taken?
►   What were some feelings that came up for you?
►   Why is it important to build trust between partners?
►   How are the three pictures you mentally recorded like a snapshot of your recovery?
►   How does this relate to real life?
►   What is one take-away you will remember from this experience?

**Recovery/Wellness Metaphor:** Show that we can do together what we can never do by ourselves. This activity requires that we rely on our partner.

# Human Knot

**Source:** The idea for this activity came from *Human Knot-So-Fast, The Empty Bag* (2003), Cavert and Hammond and was adapted from *Training Wheels Challenger Kit Field Guide*, 2nd ed. (2012), Michelle Cummings.

**Group Size:** 6–15

**Purpose:** Group problem solving. Building frustration tolerance.

**Props Needed:** None

## Activity Preparation:
1. Prep time needed: 5 minutes
2. Space free from objects.
3. Since this is an activity that involves people being in very close space proximity to one another, be sure to consider safety and trust issues.

## Time Needed:
► Directions: 5 minutes
► Activity: 15–30 minutes
► Debrief: 10 minutes

## Set-Up:
1. Physical space free from debris or objects.
2. If using activity props, one bandana, piece of cloth or piece of rope per participant.

## Activity Directions:
► Locate participants in a physical space free from debris or objects that may create a safety hazard.
► Have the participants stand in a circle facing inward.

**Facilitator Script:** "Let's form a circle. Look around you and be sure there is nothing around you that can create a safety problem. This activity is called Human Knot—and is one that will create an opportunity for problem solving. First I want you to take a good look at your partner to your left and your right. Good. Now that you know who is next to you take a look around the circle.

Next I want you to hold your right hand overhead. Shake it around and let's be sure that you have your **right** hand up. Now extend it into the center of the circle. Now grasp the right hand *(or prop: bandana, rope, piece of cloth)* of another participant different from the one to your immediate left or your right.

Double-check—are you holding the hand of someone other than the one to your immediate left and your right? Good.

Now hold up your **left** hand overhead. Shake it around. Extend it into the circle and grab the left hand *(or prop: bandana, piece of rope, or cloth)* of a different participant, again, not to your immediate left or right.

So now you should be holding the right hand of one participant, and the left hand of a different participant, neither are immediately next to your left or your right.

The object is to untangle the group without breaking hand-to-hand contact and returning to a circle formation.

Any questions? *(Facilitator answers questions)* And Start."

## Debrief:

- ► How did you successfully untangle?
- ► What skills did it take?
- ► What did you notice about group interaction from beginning to end?
- ► What did you notice if you/the group encountered stuck points?
- ► What did you notice about yourself? About others?
- ► Did some lead versus follow?
- ► If you identify yourself as a leader did you choose to interact differently than your leader style? Why or why not?
- ► If you identify yourself more as a follower, did you choose to interact differently? Why or why not?
- ► What would it take to interact in an experience different than the way you naturally identify?
- ► What is the message to yourself about overcoming frustration or communication challenges?
- ► What are two things you will do differently to help you overcome those challenges?

**Recovery/Wellness Metaphor:** This is an energetic way to explore problem solving. This is also a way to explore frustration tolerance, when to hang together with one another, and when to let go. It can help participants consider that their recovery/wellness path may encounter barriers or challenges, and how they view themselves when encountering those barriers or challenges. It may also help those who typically isolate in their recovery/wellness path consider the benefits and challenges of remaining isolated, getting connected, or how a group can accomplish a goal of improved recovery/wellness compared to isolating.

**Role of Facilitator:** Be sure to have space free of debris or other objects that may create a safety hazard.

**Variations:** Conduct activity silently without speaking or giving any form of communication. Connecting participants may include pieces of rope, cloth, or large bandanas.

**Where to Find It/How to Make It:** You can purchase your own bandanas, or make your own with a yard of cloth cut into 36"–strips, enough for two people to hold. Be sure the cloth has a texture that is not too slippery. Purchase rope from home supply store and cut into 36" pieces.

# Icebreaker Thumball

**Group Size:** 5–50

**Purpose:** Fun icebreaker to create group cohesion.

**Props Needed:** Thumball

**Activity Preparation:** Need some space to sit/stand around room.

**Time Needed:** Total time 5–15 minutes (depending on group size)
- ► Directions: 1 minute
- ► Activity: 8 minutes (depending on group size)
- ► Debrief: 5 minutes

**Safety:**
- ► Physical—Encourage participants to toss the ball gently using an underhanded throw.

**Activity Directions:**
- ► Toss Thumball to first player and have them answer what is under their thumb.
- ► Toss ball around group until everyone has had a chance to answer.

**Facilitator Script:** "Hey everyone we are going to get started with a fun icebreaker. Let's make a circle. The ball we are going to use in this next activity is called a Thumball *(hold up thumball)*. It's called a Thumball because when you toss it, catch it, and then look under your thumb, you answer the question that is printed on the panel your thumb landed on *(toss up ball and catch it to show where your thumb landed)*. When you catch it please say your name and answer the question *(model it for the group to see and hear)*. Any questions? Great, here we go." *(toss ball to first participant)*

**Debrief:**
- ► What made this activity fun?
- ► What did you learn about your peers?
- ► What did you notice?

**Recovery/Wellness Metaphor:** This activity is a fun way to create group cohesion.

**Role of Facilitator:** Keep the ball moving.

**Variations:** Find Everyone Who—Facilitator uses the ball to pick category for the group. Example "favorite childhood toy." Participants will have a second to think about what their "favorite childhood toy" was and then mingle with the rest of the group to see if they can find anyone else who has the same toy in mind. Once in a group have them stand together so there is distinction between the groups and then facilitator tosses ball again for a new category. You can also create your own categories if you would like.

**Where to Find It/How to Make It:** Purchase the Icebreaker Thumball from Training Wheels, www.trainingwheelsgear.com, or use a beach ball and a marker to create your own.

# Jacobson's Progressive Relaxation Technique

**Group Size:** Any

**Purpose:** To teach participants a strategy for relaxation for anxiety. Jacobson's relaxation technique is a type of therapy that focuses on tightening and relaxing specific muscle groups in sequence. It's also known as progressive relaxation therapy. By concentrating on specific areas and tensing and then relaxing them, you can become more aware of your body and physical sensations.

**History:** Dr. Edmund Jacobson invented the technique in the 1920s as a way to help his patients deal with anxiety. Dr. Jacobson felt that relaxing the muscles could relax the mind as well. The technique involves tightening one muscle group while keeping the rest of the body relaxed, and then releasing the tension.

**Props Needed:** Copy of relaxation prompts

**Activity Preparation:**

1. Prep time needed: none, or you can use yoga mats or towels for people to lay on.

**Time Needed:**

- ► Directions: 2 minutes
- ► Activity: 20 minutes
- ► Debrief: 15 minutes

**Activity Directions:**

- ► Invite participants to lay down on the floor.
- ► Ask participants to close their eyes.
- ► Read relaxation prompts in a slow and monotone voice.
- ► Debrief the experience.

---

**Facilitator Script:** "I'd like everyone to find a place to lie down on the floor. Be sure to give yourself enough space between you and the person next to you. This activity is called Jacobson's Progressive Relaxation Exercise. The purpose of this is to teach you an exercise you can do on your own back home if you are feeling anxious or having a hard time falling asleep. By focusing on tensing and relaxing different muscle groups at a time, it can help you relax. I'm going to ask everyone to close their eyes for the duration of the activity. I'm going to walk you through a series of relaxation prompts that will take about 20 minutes. I encourage you to go with the process and let your mind freely wander. Are there any questions before we begin? (*Pause for questions.*) Go ahead and close your eyes now."

**Debrief:** Encourage everyone to stand up, stretch, then take a seat in a circle for the debrief.

- ▶ How is everyone feeling?
- ▶ What were some of the thoughts you had as you were going through the exercise?
- ▶ Were you able to relax?
- ▶ How could this process help you back at home?
- ▶ Final thoughts: Progressive relaxation therapy is generally safe and doesn't require a professional's guidance. Sessions typically last no more than 20–30 minutes, making it manageable for people with busy schedules. You can practice the techniques at home by recording the instructions from the handout, or purchase an audio recording that takes you through the exercises.

**Recovery/Wellness Metaphor:**

### Jacobson's Progressive Relaxation Technique Prompts

Read these prompts in a slow, monotone voice.

Take a deep breath, hold it for 3 seconds, then let it out.

Do this again. Take a deep breath, hold it for 3 seconds, then let it out.

Imagine yourself in a relaxed place.

Allow yourself to feel really comfortable.

We're going to start with your right hand. Clench your right hand into a fist . . . tighter . . . tighter . . . study the tension in your fist, hand, and forearm. Be sure the rest of your body is relaxed.

Now relax your right fist . . . loosen fingers . . . observe the contrast in feeling between your right fist tense and relaxed, and the difference in the way your right and left hands feel now.

Relax all over. Attend to your body's feelings. Try to enjoy the sensation of your body as you relax.

Now tighten your left fist and repeat the same procedure as for your right fist. Clench your left fist . . . tighter . . . tighter . . . study the tension in your fist, hand, and forearm. Be sure the rest of your body is relaxed.

Now relax . . . loosen fingers . . . observe the contrast in feeling between your right fist tense and relaxed, and the difference in the way your left and right hands feel now.

Now repeat the procedure for both fists. Tighter . . . Tighter . . . Be sure the rest of your body is relaxed. And relax. Loosen your fingers.

Bend your elbows . . . tense both biceps and try to keep hands and fingers loose . . . relax and let your arms rest at your sides. Notice the difference in feeling between the tension and the relaxation.

Straighten your arms so that you tense your tricep muscles in the back of your upper arms . . . Now relax your arms at your sides. Relax all over.

Notice that your arms feel comfortable and heavy. Feel the relaxation spread up your arms. Notice that your arms feel heavier and heavier as you relax more and more. See if you can go one step further in relaxing.

Take a deep breath in and out.

Now we'll work on relaxing the face, shoulders, neck, and upper back.

Begin by wrinkling your eyebrows up toward your scalp. Be sure the rest of your body is relaxed. Now smooth your brow. Relax.

Now frown hard . . . and relax.

Tighten your eyes. Tighten the muscles deep in your eyes as well as the facial muscles around your eyes. Relax . . . keep eyes closed.

Now bite your teeth together. Study the tension in your jaw. Relax . . . slightly part your lips.

Relax lips . . . eyes . . . forehead . . . scalp. Feel the difference.

Press your tongue hard against the roof of your mouth. Study the tension. Relax . . . slightly part lips.

Feel the relaxation in your cheeks . . . scalp . . . eyes . . . face . . . arms . . . hands.

Relax further.

Now press your head back against the floor and feel the tension in your neck . . . Relax.

Now bring your head forward toward your chest. Feel the tension in your neck. Relax.

Shrug your shoulders to your ears. Be sure the rest of your body is relaxed. Notice the difference between how your shoulders feel in contrast to the rest of your body. Relax.

Let relaxation flow into your back . . . neck . . . throat . . . jaws . . . and face. Let relaxation spread and go deeper. Now relax your entire body. You experience a comfortable, heavy feeling. You experience a good feeling . . . the force of gravity.

Now for the chest, stomach, and lower back. Breathe deeply—hold. Notice the tension. Now exhale and study the feeling. Breathe slowly, normally in and out. Notice how you feel more relaxed exhaling. Let your chest walls grow loose as you breathe out.

Now take in another deep breath. Hold. Breathe out. Feel the release of tension. Let relaxation spread to your shoulders, neck, back, and arms. Let go to the relaxation.

Now tighten your stomach. Make it hard. Now relax. Notice the well-being that accompanies your relaxation.

Now, gently tighten the muscles of your abdomen, but don't strain. Relax.

Do this again. Notice the tension for a few moments. Then release . . . notice the relaxation.

Become aware of the difference between the tensed muscles and the relaxed muscles.

Be aware again of your breathing. Notice how exhaling relaxes your lungs and stomach. Try to let go of all the contractions in the body.

Now for your lower back. Arch up. Feel the tension along your spine. Relax the rest of your body. Locate the tension in your lower back. Relax your lower back, upper back, stomach, chest, shoulders, arms, face . . . Relax further, even further.

Now tighten your buttocks and thighs by pressing down on your heels. Relax the rest of your body. Relax. Feel the contrast.

Press your feet and toes downward to tighten calves and feet. Relax.

Now curl your toes toward you to create tension along your shins. Relax. Relax further. Now, as I mention parts of the body, let go more and more of those parts.

Feet relax . . . ankles relax . . . calves and shins . . . knees and thighs . . . buttocks and hips . . . Feel the heaviness of your lower body. Stomach . . . Waist . . . Lower back . . . Let go more and more. Upper back . . . chest . . . shoulders . . . arms . . . all the way down to your fingertips . . . Let relaxation take over . . . Throat . . . neck . . . jaws and face . . . all relaxed.

To deepen the effects of the relaxation, think about lifting one leg. Think of the muscles you'd need to use. Can you spot any tension that has crept back into that part of your body as you think of lifting it? Relax it . . . Can you notice tension disappearing? Now think about moving the other leg. Relax . . . Lie and relax this way, choosing other body parts and relaxing the tension.

When you are ready, count backward from four to one, stretch and sit up.

# Knee Coup

**Group Size:** 8–20

**Purpose:** To surface the topics of integrity and judging.

**Props Needed:** none/boundary markers

**Activity Preparation:**
1. Prep time needed: 5 minutes
2. Prior to class make sure you have all your props.

**Time Needed:**
- ▶ Directions: 2 minutes
- ▶ Activity: 10 minutes
- ▶ Debrief: 15 minutes

**Safety:**
- ▶ Physical—Participants with knee issues should observe, rather than play.

**Set-Up:** Many moons ago, when Indian tribes warred against one another, honor and bravery often counted for more than ultimate physical victory on the field of battle. An Indian warrior, for example, could prove his bravery in combat by simply touching an opponent and voicing the words "Counting Coup." In the game Knee Coup, we have adapted some of these same philosophies.

**Activity Directions:**
- ▶ Have group gather around to discuss.
- ▶ Establish boundaries with marker cones.
- ▶ **Round 1:** Emphasize that the only way to get other participants out of the game is to tag them on their kneecaps. Now the tricky thing about tagging on the kneecaps is that it is a very small area. Usually only the person who owns the kneecap will know whether or not they have been tagged.
- ▶ Once someone has been tagged on the kneecap they are to take themselves to the outside of the boundaries.
- ▶ Players cannot cover or hide their kneecaps during game play.
- ▶ Play for 3 minutes.

- ▶ **Round 2:** Now tell the participants that they do not have to remove themselves from the game until their kneecaps have been tagged twice.
- ▶ If you catch yourself judging someone else you must remove yourself from the circle. So if you catch yourself telling someone they are out you remove yourself from play. This way, the person who owns the kneecap will be the sole judge on whether or not their exact kneecap was tagged.
- ▶ Players cannot cover or hide their kneecaps during game play.
- ▶ Play for 3 minutes.

**Round 1 Facilitator Script:** "Let's form a circle to hear the directions for our next game. We are going to play a tag game called Knee Coup. Many moons ago, when Indian tribes warred against one another, honor and bravery often counted for more than ultimate physical victory on the field of battle. An Indian warrior, for example, could prove his bravery in combat by simply touching an opponent and voicing the words 'Counting Coup.' In the game Knee Coup, we have adapted some of these same philosophies. In a moment, I'm going to start the game. When I say 'Go' everyone is 'It', and you are going to try and tag another player by tapping their kneecap. Now the tricky thing about tagging on the kneecap is that it is a very small area. Usually only the person who owns the kneecap will know whether or not they have been tagged. If you get tagged on the kneecap, then remove yourself from play and stand on the outside of the boundary markers. Players cannot cover or hide their kneecaps during the game. We will play the game for 3 minutes. Are there any questions? *(Pause for questions.)* Ready? Go!"

**Round 2 Facilitator Script:** "OK, great job! Now we are going to play the game again but I'm going to add in a few new rules. First, we are still tagging people on the kneecap, so that part is the same. This time you do not have to remove yourself from play until you have been tagged twice on the kneecaps. Again, usually the person who owns the kneecap will know whether or not they have been tagged. If you get tagged on the kneecap twice, then remove yourself from play and stand on the outside of the boundary markers. Players cannot cover or hide their kneecaps during the game. One additional rule I am adding to this round is this: If you find yourself judging another player, please remove yourself from play. So if you find yourself saying, 'Hey, you are out!' or 'Hey, I got you!' in your mind or out loud, then you must also take yourself out of the game. We will play the game for 3 minutes. Are there any questions? *(Pause for questions.)* Ready? Go!"

## Debrief:

- ▶ What was difficult about this activity?
- ▶ Did everyone follow the rules?
- ▶ In Round 1, who was the winner of the game? (Many people will say whoever the last few players were at the end.) Could we assume that the last few people could possibly be the biggest liars? Could the winners be anyone who played by the rules?
- ▶ How did honesty and integrity come into play in this game?
- ▶ In Round 2, did anyone remove themselves from the game for judging someone else? Anyone care to admit what the scenario was?
- ▶ Was it difficult not to judge others? Why or why not?
- ▶ How does this relate back to recovery?
- ▶ How do we protect our recovery like we did our knees?
- ▶ When we are confronted with an opportunity to be honest or cheap what did we choose?
- ▶ What does honesty and integrity mean to me?

**Recovery/Wellness Metaphor:** There is a saying in recovery that honesty is the principle behind the first step and the most important person to be honest with is yourself. How does this game represent the challenges we face in recovery?

**Role of Facilitator:** Observer

# Knot Exchange

**Group Size:** 12 or more

**Purpose:** To experience making a mess, then cleaning up someone else's mess. This activity also increases frustration tolerance, problem solving, and group cohesion skills.

**Props Needed:** One 5-foot rope or cord for each pair of people in the room

## Activity Preparation:

1. Prep time needed: 15 minutes
2. Prior to class make sure you have all your props.

## Time Needed:

- ▶ Directions: 2 minutes
- ▶ Activity: 10 minutes
- ▶ Debrief: 15 minutes

**Set-Up:** Lay three to four ropes on the ground in an asterisk formation for each group. Divide participants into groups of six to eight, and have each group form a circle around an asterisk of rope.

## Activity Directions:

- ▶ Figure out the group size that you want beforehand. Ideally, every team will have six or eight people in it. You will need an even number of people for this activity to work.
- ▶ Lay three (or four) ropes on the ground in an asterisk formation for each group. Divide participants into groups of six (or eight), and have each group form a circle around an asterisk of rope.
- ▶ Instruct the group that you would like everyone to reach down and pick up one end of a rope. Have them lift it off the ground and hold on to it. Have them imagine that the rope is now superglued to their hand. In other words, they may not let go of the rope or break contact with the rope.
- ▶ Tell the group that when you say, "Go" you want them to take two minutes to make the biggest tangle of rope or knot that they can. The more they weave over and around one another, the bigger and more tangled it will be. Restate that they may not let go of the rope.
- ▶ After two minutes, ask the group to carefully lay their rope ends back on the ground and let go of the ropes.

- ▶ Instruct participants to step away from their knotted mess and exchange knots with another group. They will now have to untangle another group's knot.
- ▶ Ask them to pick up the ends of the rope and begin untangling. They may not break contact with their end of the rope once they pick it up.
- ▶ Optional: You can have this be a competition to see who can untangle the mess the fastest.

**Facilitator Script:** "Hey everyone, I need you to divide into groups of six people and make a circle around the rope asterisks that are laying on the ground. *(Pause until everyone is in a group.)* In a moment, I'm going to ask everyone to bend over and pick up one end of one of the ropes on the ground. As a group you will then all stand up together. Once you have picked up your end of the rope, you may not break contact with the rope. Pretend that the end is superglued to your hand. I'm going to give each group two minutes to create the biggest knot or mess that you can. You may go over, under, around and through—whatever you would like to create the biggest knot that you can in two minutes. Any questions on what we are doing? *(Pause for questions.)* Ready? Go!"

*(After the two minutes is up, ask the group to carefully lay their rope ends back on the ground. Then ask them to step away from their mess and admire their fine work. Then, have them move to a different group's knot. Time them to see how long it takes to untangle someone else's knot.)*

**Debrief:**

- ▶ Which took longer, making a mess or untangling a mess?
- ▶ What was your reaction when we switched to a new tangle of rope?
- ▶ How did your group work together to untangle the knot?
- ▶ What was it like making a mess compared to undoing someone else's mess?
- ▶ How does this activity relate to the real world?

**Recovery/Wellness Metaphor:** In recovery we are asked to "face life on life's terms," sometimes cleaning up other people's messes is a part of that. At other times we want people to clean up our mess. This activity gives us the ability to increase problem-solving skills while gaining appreciation for what it is like to clean up somebody else's mess.

**Role of Facilitator:** Timekeeper

**Where to Find It/How to Make It:** You can purchase any kind of rope at a hardware store. Wrap ends of cut rope with electrical tape to prevent fraying, or use a heated rope cutting blade that melts the rope as it is being cut.

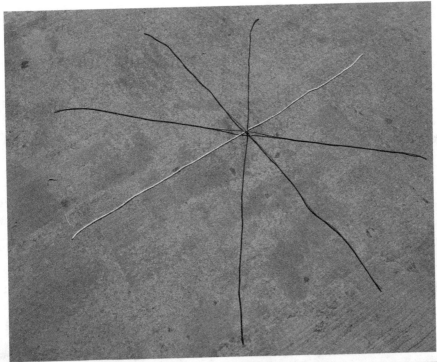

# Labyrinth Walk

**Activity Source:** A Teachable Moment

**Group Size:** 1–25

**Purpose:** Mindfulness, meditation, personal reflection.

**Props Needed:**

1. Labyrinth

**Activity Preparation:** None, with the exception of creating the Labyrinth.

**Time Needed:**

▶ Directions: 2 minutes
▶ Activity: 10–45 min (depending on how many participants walk the Labyrinth)
▶ Debrief: 15 minutes

**Activity Directions:**

▶ Explain the concept and purpose of a Labyrinth.
▶ Have each participant walk the Labyrinth either one at a time or as a group.
▶ Upon completing an activity, or even after journaling, the facilitator encourages participants to reflect on their experience, while traversing the labyrinth.
▶ The typical goal is to reach the center of the labyrinth, and return to the outside, without crossing any lines, and without talking.
▶ Movement with meditation and introspection are the key.

**Facilitator Script:** "Let's gather around to hear the directions for our next activity. Today we are walking the labyrinth. The labyrinth has been around for many centuries and is used by many of the world's religions and spiritual paths as a way of personal reflection, meditation, and connection. The typical goal is to reach the center of the labyrinth, and return to the outside, without crossing any lines, and without talking. Movement with meditation and introspection are the key. The labyrinth becomes a metaphor for our own journey. As we wind through the labyrinth consider your own journey inward and as you return from the core of the labyrinth consider how you will move out from here. Consider all that it took to arrive to this moment and all the amazing tools you take with you as you prepare to go forward."

**Recovery/Wellness Metaphor:** The journey to recovery is rarely a straight line between two points. Life takes us on a windy journey filled with many turns and unexpected movements. The journey of the labyrinth can be very much about finding recovery or it can be about finding ourselves, our higher power, or any type of meditation.

**Debrief:**

- ▶ What did you notice as you were about to walk into the labyrinth?
- ▶ What was the journey like for you?
- ▶ What are you taking with you as a result of the journey?
- ▶ What was this activity like for you?

**Where to Find It/How to Make It:** You can purchase a mobile labyrinth though training-wheels.com or find many examples online with how to make your own.

For more information about the labyrinth, see the book *Exploring the Labyrinth: A Guide for Healing and Spiritual Growth*, by Melissa Gayle West, 2000, Broadway Books, New York, NY ISBN 0-7679-0356-0 or contact the Worldwide Labyrinth Project, 1100 California Street, San Francisco, California 94108. Website: www.gracecathedral.org

# Look Up, Look Down

**Group Size:** 8–50

**Purpose:** A lively energizer.

**Props Needed:** none

**Activity Preparation:**
1. Prep time needed: none

**Time Needed:**
- ▶ Directions: 2 minutes
- ▶ Activity: 10 minutes

**Activity Directions:**
- ▶ Invite participants to get into groups of nine to ten people and stand in a circle.
- ▶ **Phase 1:** Ask the participants to get into a circle and look at an imaginary spot on the floor in the center of the circle. Instruct them that when you announce, "LOOK UP!", each person is to look up and look directly into the face of another participant. If they do not make eye contact with another person they stay still. If they make eye contact with that person, they are to point and scream (with conviction!) at that person. Then you will announce, "Look Down" and the whole group will look down.
- ▶ Play this way six to seven times and then move on to Phase 2.
- ▶ **Phase 2:** Phase 2 has the same rules as Phase 1, but this time if you make eye contact with another participant, you are to point, scream, and then run and join another circle (that is, if you have multiple circles).

**Facilitator Script:** "OK, everyone. I need you to get into small groups of nine to ten people and stand in a circle. This energizer is called Look Up, Look Down. I want each of you to find an imaginary spot on the floor in the center of your circle. When I say Look Down! I want you to stare at this spot. Let's practice this. LOOK DOWN! OK, good! You are with me so far. Next, if you hear me say, Look Up! then I want you to pick ONE person that you are going to immediately look straight at their face. If they did not choose you, then they will be looking at someone else and you do nothing. If they did choose you, the two of you will be looking directly at one another. If this happens I want you to point at them and scream with conviction.

Let's give this a try, Look Down! . . . LOOK UP! (*If they didn't scream with conviction, add in a few comments about how to scream with conviction.*) OK, now that didn't sound like screaming with conviction. Let's try that again. Look Down! . . . LOOK UP! (*Usually it will be better this time.*) Now that's more like it! Let's do this a few more times. Look Down! . . . LOOK UP! (*Do this four to five more times.*) OK, great! Now we are going to add a rule. This time, if you make eye contact with another participant, you are to point, scream, and then run to another group. Any questions on what we are doing? OK, here we go! Look Down! . . . LOOK UP! (*Give them a few moments for anyone who moved to get settled into their new group.*) Look Down! . . . LOOK UP! (*and repeat four to five more times.*)

## Debrief:

▶ There isn't really a debrief for this activity. The purpose is to raise the energy level of the group. This is a good activity to do if you have been sitting for a long time, or if you notice the energy level and attention spans of the participants start to drop.

# Lycra Tube

**Group Size:** 5–10

**Purpose:** Gather groups together, increase group cohesion, and be more comfortable sitting on the ground. This tool can be used for either check-in, activity, debrief, or processing.

**Props Needed:** One Lycra tube per group.

**Activity Preparation:** Have a Lycra tube ready for each group of 8–10 participants depending on size.

**Time Needed:**
- ▶ Directions: 5 minutes
- ▶ Activity: 10 minutes (depending on size of group)
- ▶ Debrief: 5 minutes

**Set-Up:** None needed

**Activity Directions:**
- ▶ Stretch the Lycra tube out and have everyone stand in the center.
- ▶ Have each person back up until the Lycra tube is fully stretched.
- ▶ Next, instruct the group to simultaneously sit down in the Lycra tube.
- ▶ This creates a comfortable setting in which to check in or process. You could do other activities, like Body Part Debrief, while sitting in the Lycra tube.
- ▶ If it happens to be a sunny day, and there are few trees in sight, the Lycra tube can be used to provide shade for the group. Just stretch the Lycra tube into a large circle, and lift the top of the Lycra tube over the heads of all participants by about 24 inches. The stretch within the Lycra tube will create a canopy that blocks the sun. This also creates a visual barrier between your group and other groups or other distractions that are nearby.

**Facilitator Script:** "Let's form a circle to hear the directions for today's check-in. We are going to check in while sitting in this Lycra tube. Here is how you get in it. It is like a large doughnut. Get in the center and then stretch it out. Once everyone is in you can sit down" (*support group in getting in*).

*(Now you can introduce the check-in, activity, or process.)*

**Debrief:**

> ► What did you notice about being in the tube?
> ► What were your thoughts as you first heard the activity?

**Recovery/Wellness Metaphor:** This is a fun way of gathering the group together in a different way. This tool can be very useful for outdoor gathering as it provides a chair for everyone.

**Role of Facilitator:** Make sure everyone is able to get in safely.

**Variations:** Feel free to use fabrics in any way as needed.

**Where to Find It/How to Make It:** You can purchase Lycra material at most fabric stores. Ask for the highest quality of Lycra to ensure longevity of your Lycra Tube. Allow for 5 feet of Lycra per tube. Sew together with a French seam. See the Lycra Tube write-up in *Teamwork and Teamplay*, by Jim Cain, for more information.

Lycra Tube can also be purchased from Training Wheels.

# Mask Making

**Group Size:** 8–20

**Purpose:** To see ourselves as others see us, outwardly, so that we may begin to understand our uniqueness.

**Props Needed:**

1. First aid plaster gauze strips, often used in wrapping broken arms, cut into 2 to 3" strips, with approximately forty pieces per person. Also cut some small ½" triangular pieces to fit around the nose and other contours. Carapace "Original Formula" plaster bandages, extra fast setting, are recommended. Size: 3" wide by 3 yards long. Available at medical supply stores.
2. Scissors.
3. Snack size plastic bags to put plaster pieces in.
4. Several large bowls.
5. Warm water source.
6. Towels/sheets for participants to lay on.
7. Several rolls of paper towels.
8. 1 small jar of Vaseline for every 2 people.
9. Reflective, instrumental music to play in the background.
10. A bathroom sink for participants to wash their face after their mask has been removed.

**Activity Preparation:**

1. Prep time needed: 30–45 minutes
2. Pre-cut the plaster gauze and put these pieces into plastic bags for easy distribution, one per participant.
3. Set several mask stations by laying towels or sheets out on the floor. Leave plenty of space between each station. The towels and sheets are essential for keeping the plaster drippings from staining the floor.
4. Set one bowl of warm water at each station. Switch out the water when the participants switch places.
5. Place one jar of Vaseline and one roll of paper towels at each station.

**Time Needed:**

▶ Directions: 10 minutes
▶ Activity: 45 minutes per participant, 90 minutes total
▶ Debrief: 15–30 minutes

## Activity Directions:

To mentally prepare the group for the seriousness of this activity, talk to them about trust and how to care for others. This activity will require someone to "give up control" of their sight and in doing so, will force them to trust their partner. Talk to them about caring for others and how they would like to be cared for. Tell them to use a soft, calm voice and tell their partner what they are doing when they are doing it (i.e., "I'm going to apply a piece to your left cheek"). Tell them to position themselves to where a part of their knee or arm is in contact with the receiver at all times. This will help alleviate any abandonment feelings during the application and drying process.

- ▶ Talk to the group about personal reflections. How do people see them on the outside and how is that different from what's on the inside? What is unique about you? etc.
- ▶ Tell the group that this is a quiet activity to allow for personal reflection. Play reflective instrumental music in the background.
- ▶ Have the group choose partners (or assign them). Have them decide which person will apply the mask first and which will go second.
- ▶ Have the mask receiver lie down on the towel/sheet and close their eyes. Instruct them to put a VERY generous portion of Vaseline on their partner's face, covering at hairline and around to front of ears and down the neckline. Make sure that the eyelashes and eyebrows are well covered. The Vaseline is what keeps the plaster from permanently adhering to the face and hair, so definitely apply enough to cover the face completely, but still allow the plaster to define the face. If the receiver has a beard, apply an extra generous portion of Vaseline.
- ▶ The person doing the mask (the giver) then proceeds to dip each strip into warm water, smear the plaster together, and place on the face of their partner. Start with the outline of the face and work inward.
- ▶ Apply two to three layers of pieces and cover all of the face, including the eyes. Make sure verbal warnings are given before the pieces go over the eyes (talking allowed).
- ▶ The only place left exposed should be the nostrils for breathing. Even the mouth should be covered. This works best when the giver shapes the gauze on the face of the partner so that the facial features are well-defined.
- ▶ Few people are allergic to these products, but be cautious.

**Very Important:** It is recommended that the giver do not remove their hands/knee from their partner at any time. Especially when waiting for the gauze to dry and the application process is finished. While this is happening, play soft music and allow no talking, other than placement statements. When all gauze has been put on the face, allow five minutes for it to dry. It will get warm as it dries and hardens. You can do a small squeeze test to see if it gives a little or if it has hardened. After the mask has hardened you can help them remove their mask. Facilitators may need to help with this and assure the participants that there is nothing to fear. Ask the mask receiver to scrunch up their face underneath the mask several times so it starts to release from their face. The mask giver and/or facilitator can start to work the edges of the mask to find a spot where the mask is starting to come off of the face. Gently work the mask off of the face. After the mask is off have the mask giver walk their partner to a sink so they can use paper towels and water to remove the Vaseline from their eyes and face. This will require a lot of paper towels. To allow the mask to finish drying, wad up several paper towels and put them in the face of the mask. Place the mask with the other completed masks on a tabletop until everyone has finished.

When this is done, have them switch and the receiver then becomes the giver.

## Debrief:

A great way to start the debrief for this activity is to have each mask maker present the mask they made to their partner and share something unique they see in them.

- ▶ Describe the experience of having a mask made.
- ▶ What were some of the feelings that came up for you as you had your eyes closed while the mask was being applied?
- ▶ How did you trust your partner?
- ▶ What did you learn about yourself throughout this process?
- ▶ What were some feelings you had when you were the mask maker?
- ▶ Describe what it was like to take care of someone else.
- ▶ How do you think others see you when they look at your mask?
- ▶ What do others not know about what is happening on the inside?

An added exercise would be to have them decorate the masks in whatever way they feel is appropriate. They could decorate the outside of the mask how other people see them. The inside of the mask could be how they see themselves.

This exercise should be done early in the program and the masks saved so that they can have them at the end. A lot of reflection and insight can be gained from this exercise, too. You could have them share how they feel about themselves while they are holding their masks, both at the beginning and end of the program.

Be sure to have them tag their mask on the backside with their name so they can find it easily at the end of the program. You could also write their name on a sticky note and place it in front of the mask while it is drying.

**Recovery/Wellness Metaphor:** This powerful activity can stimulate a discussion about the masks we wear, finding our authentic self, and increasing our awareness about how other people see us. Recovery tends to invite us to take off our masks and get real.

**Where to Find It/How to Make It:**

You can get the plaster from:
    Carapace, A LOHMANN Company, Tulsa, OK 74147-0040
    Search online for Plaster Cloth Gauze Bandage.
    Online Retailers:
    Amazon.com, Craft Wrap brand or Activa Rigid Wrap Plaster Cloth.
    www.superiormedical.com 800-268-7944, Gypsona Plaster of Paris

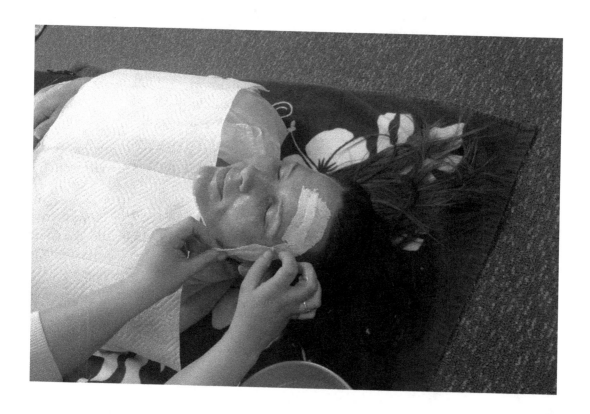

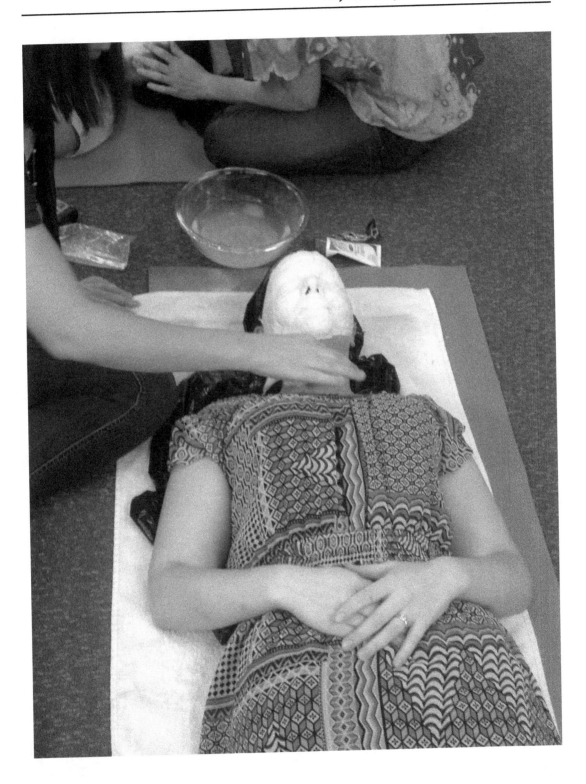

# Mousetrap Trust Sequence

**Original Source:** Sam Sikes, Raptor

**Group Size:** 5–50

**Purpose:** Learn about trust, support, and coaching by setting and unsetting mousetraps.

Activity Trust Level = High Risk (if going all the way through to minefield. Trust level can be modified by stopping before minefield).

**Props Needed:**

1. Mousetraps (we recommend using *Victor Easy Set, Metal Pedal Mouse Traps*)

**Activity Preparation:**

Inspect your mousetrap for wear and tear and set them somewhere out of sight until you want participants to use them. It is a good idea to have more traps than necessary in case any traps break while using them.

**Time Needed:** Total time 45 minutes

- ▶ Directions: 5 minutes
- ▶ Activity: 45 minutes (depending on how many stages the group goes through)
- ▶ Debrief: 15 minutes

**Safety:**

Physical—Make sure group takes this activity seriously as traps can hurt when they are snapped on body parts. This is not a time for horsing around. When a person has lost the resource of their sight ensure safety. Pay attention to the emotional tone of both the individuals as well as the collective whole. This activity might increase anxiety or frustration; however, it will also give participants an opportunity to work through their feelings.

**Activity Directions:** We will be going through a multi-stage process using the mousetrap. (Explain to the group the true and false hazards of mousetraps on bodies. Also demonstrate how to set a mousetrap.)

> Orientation: Orient group to the loading of the Trap (approximately 3 minutes)—Facilitator should orient group to parts of the traps and proper way to hold and set trap.
>
> Stage 1: Setting the Trap (approximately 3 minutes)—Partners should teach and coach each other to set the trap. Everyone should have an opportunity to set a trap.
>
> Stage 2: Setting the Trap with Your Eyes Closed (approximately 3 minutes per partner)—Partners should teach and coach each other to set the trap while the "setter" has his eyes closed and the partner coaches verbally and visually.
>
> Stage 3: Unsetting the Trap (approximately 2 minutes)—One person holds his hand flat with fingers together and places his hand over the top of a loaded trap. Then, when he is ready, he lifts his hand quickly.
>
> Stage 4: Partner Unset the Trap Blindly (approximately 4 minutes)—One person sets the trap, lays it on a table or floor, and coaches verbally while the partner sets a trap as directed above, except that his eyes are closed the whole time.
>
> Stage 5: Mouse Trap Minefield (time depends on how many participants go through)—If you think the group is ready, introduce Mouse Trap Minefield to the group.

**Facilitator Note:** Don't tell the participants this but there are five stages. A stage is completed once they have successfully moved through that stage. Not all groups will be appropriate for all five stages.

---

**Facilitator Script:** "Hey everyone, find a partner and have a seat (*once everyone is seated with their partners*). Today we are going to do some work with a common household tool . . . the mousetrap (*hold up a trap and allow group to respond and settle down*). OK, so before I pass out the mousetraps I want to orient you all to it. Please pay close attention so that we all stay safe. It is important that we all approach this activity with safety at the forefront of our minds."

**Orientation**

(*Hold up a trap and say*) "This is a mousetrap. You want to hold it in your non-dominant hand with your thumb on the Red V. This is the safety zone on the mousetrap. When you are handling the trap, please make sure that your thumbs and fingers are in this area. In order to set the trap, with your dominant hand pull the lever back and hold it down with your non-dominant thumb. *(Demonstrate this.)* Now pay attention so that the lever doesn't snap back. Hold it steady with your thumb. This is the arm of the trap *(hold up arm)*, as you can see at the end of the arm is the neck. The neck is the little ridge at the end of the arm. To set the trap, you want to bring the neck toward the catch. The neck doesn't go inside the catch, it just rests under it. With your thumb, slowly release pressure on the lever to increase the tension. If it is set correctly the catch will engage with the neck. Once the catch is engaged with the neck the trap is set." *(Hold the set trap up in your non-dominant hand to show the group. Then drop the trap on the floor to disengage it.)*

## Stage 1: Setting the Trap

"OK, we are ready for stage 1. *(Pass out the unset traps)* Everybody needs a trap. Take one and inspect it to make sure you are familiar with each part of the trap. We are each going to set a mouse trap. Once you have set the trap, drop it in front of you to set it off. If you get stuck ask for help and someone can help you. *(Pay close attention to the mood of the group to ensure safety. Help participants who seem anxious or afraid. Let peers help those that seem stuck.)* Has everyone set their trap at least once? You need to be very comfortable with this stage before we move on *(if everyone has set a trap at least once the group is ready to move on)*. Does anyone feel they need additional support in setting a trap? If so, partner up with a confident peer near you."

## Stage 2: Setting the Trap with Your Eyes Closed

"Good job everyone. So now we are ready for stage 2. Does everyone have a partner? With your partner determine who will be partner A and partner B *(give a few seconds to do that)*. Partner A is going to coach Partner B in setting the mousetrap. Partner B, however has lost the resource of their sight. They will be setting the trap with their eyes closed. This is known as the Blind Set. Partner A can only give verbal directions, you may not physically assist Partner B. Once Partner B has successfully set a trap with their eyes closed, you may drop it on the floor to disengage it. Then, I want you to switch roles so that you both get a chance to be the coach." *(Keep safety in mind as you observe the pairs working together.)* Once both partners have gone, the group is ready to move on to the next stage.

## Stage 3: Unsetting the Trap

"OK, moving right along to the next stage. In this stage we are going to unset the trap with our hands. Here is how it works. *(Demonstrate this as you give the instructions to the group.)* First, set your trap. Then place the trap carefully in the outstretched palm of your non-dominant hand. Be careful, as you have a live trap in your hand. Take your dominant hand and hover it about 6 inches above the trap with a flat palm, fingers together. Now to unset the trap, press your top hand straight down onto the trap and then release straight up and let the trap fall to the floor. The trap will unset underneath your palm. Keep your bottom hand steady and let your top hand do all the work. *(It might be useful to do this twice for groups that seem to have anxiety around this stage.)* Here watch me do it again . . ." *(Demonstrate this again.)*

## Stage 4: Partner Unset the Trap Blindly

"OK, we are now ready for stage 4. Stage 4 is a combination of Stage 1, 2, and 3. Each person will take a turn setting and unsetting the mousetrap with their eyes closed. Partner A will be the coach and Partner B will have their eyes closed. Partner B will set the trap, then unset it all with their eyes closed. Then switch roles. Once both have gone you will complete this stage."

*(It is perfectly OK to stop at any of the previous stages depending on the security, stage, and cohesion of the group. Not to mention the time you have for this activity. This next stage cannot be rushed and needs ample time for debriefing. This requires time and trust to make sure that you as facilitators and the group as participants are ready for this next stage prior to moving on. If you are unsure it is better not to do it.)*

## Stage 5: Mouse Trap Minefield

"We are moving on to the final stage. I could use your help in setting traps and placing them on the floor randomly. *(Begin to set live traps and place them in a roped off or otherwise designated area to be known as the minefield. The more traps that are set the greater the risk.)* OK, we have a minefield here full of live mousetraps. I need everyone to take off their shoes. With your partner determine who will be a walker and who will be a coach. Walkers you will lose the resource of your sight and will be guided through the minefield by your coach; however, you do not have to close your eyes. Instead, you will place your hands underneath your eyes like this (demonstrate this, see picture for reference), so that you can see your coach, but you cannot see your feet or the traps. Coaches will stand on the other side of the minefield from the walkers. If you have balance issues, someone can walk alongside you on the outside of the minefield and place their hand on your shoulder for balance support. You may practice with your coach outside of the minefield beforehand if you'd like. Talk with one another about how you would like to be communicated with when you are the walker. The goal is to get through the minefield without setting off any traps. In order to do this, it will be useful to pay close attention to your coach. If you have long pants on, please roll them up above your ankles to avoid any clothing accidentally setting off a trap. Are there any questions before we begin?"

## Debrief:

- ▶ What was this activity like for you?
- ▶ What strategies did you use to cope with the stuck points?
- ▶ How does this activity build trust?
- ▶ What changes have you noticed since you finished the stages?

- ▶ How did you overcome any anxieties?
- ▶ How well did you coach your partner?
- ▶ What do you value in a coach?
- ▶ What did it feel like to have your eyes closed while handling a mousetrap?
- ▶ Was it easier to give directions or to lead?
- ▶ What did the observers gather about the guides and walkers?
- ▶ What were the guides doing to instill confidence in the walkers?
- ▶ What were some strategies for getting across the minefield?
- ▶ How did the mousetraps affect your performance?

**Recovery/Wellness Metaphor:** Show how we often have far more courage and strength than we might initially think we have. Bring out for the group the things they value in a coach or guide in their recovery.

**Role of Facilitator:** safety, Safety, SAFETY

## VARIATIONS:

**Variation 1:** One variation we might implement for this activity would be to create three roles in the activity: observer, walker, and guide. The observer should watch for subtle interactions between the walker and the guide with special attention to the walker's reactions to the behaviors of the guide.

Only walkers are allowed within the roped off area with "mines." The walker should focus only on his guide's eyes, without looking down at his own feet or the "mines" on the floor.

All the groups of three will begin simultaneously. The walkers should make their way across the diameter of the roped off area while only looking into the eyes of the guide. The guide may give both verbal and nonverbal commands from outside the circle. When the walker completes the crossing, ask the trio to switch roles.

Notes: What often happens is that the walker will look down at the "mines" when the guide seems unsure or untrustworthy. Usually the walkers are unaware that they have glanced down. Some walkers have more trouble than others.

**Variation 2:** Allow the coach to be inside the minefield with the walker to walk with them. In order to increase the challenge, you could tell the coach that they have lost the resource of their voice.

**Where to Find It/How to Make It:** Mouse traps can be ordered online or purchased at any hardware store. You can also purchase a full set at Training Wheels, www.trainingwheelsgear.com.

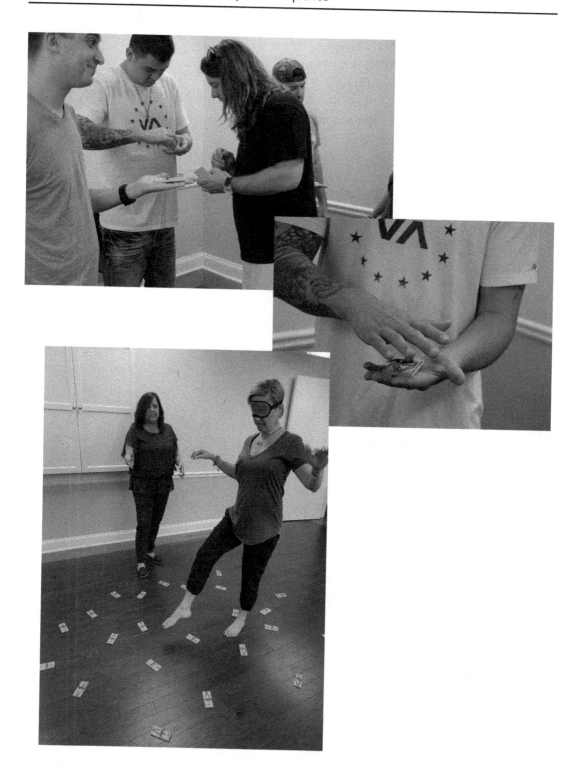

# Pokerface

**Activity Source:** *Playing With a Full Deck,* by Michelle Cummings

*Setting the Conflict Compass,* by Michelle Cummings

**Group Size:** 8–52

**Purpose:** To surface feelings of being left out or treated differently by others.

**Props Needed:** playing cards

**Activity Preparation:**

1. Prep time needed: 5 minutes
2. Prior to class create an open space for play. If you are indoors, put chairs around the perimeter of the room. If you are outside, find an open space to play that is free of debris or obstacles.

**Time Needed:**

- ▶ Directions: 2 minutes
- ▶ Activity: 5 minutes
- ▶ Debrief: 15 minutes

**Activity Directions:**

- ▶ Have the participants stand in a circle. Include yourself in the circle.
- ▶ Shuffle your deck of cards and give one to each participant. Ask them not to look at the face of the card. As you explain the directions, ask the participants to hold their card so the face is down toward the floor.
- ▶ Tell them that in a moment you are going to ask them to place that card to their forehead. They are not to look at their own card, but everyone else can see their card.
- ▶ Instruct them that you are going to be intentionally vague with the directions. Figuring out what to do is a part of the game.
- ▶ This activity involves the players mingling around the room, holding their card on their forehead, and treating each other based on the face value of the cards that they see. Inform the group that they do not have the resource of their voice.
- ▶ Then ask them to place their card to their forehead and say, "Please treat each other based on the face value of the card that you see. Ready, Go."

▶  The mingling begins and there is some slight confusion at first. Some participants are uncertain how to treat others.
  ☐  Some typical behaviors are:
    ♦  The royalty cards are usually bowed down to, given high fives, and generally treated very well. Most cards want to "hang out" with the high cards. Usually royalty cards start grouping together.
    ♦  The middle cards are pretty much ignored. They sometimes get a "so-so" hand motion demonstrated to them or a shrug of the shoulders.
    ♦  The low cards are treated many different ways. Some get a dismissive hand gesture; some get the letter "L" sign on a forehead depicting "Loser." Some low cards will get a pretend kick their way or dirty looks by others. Some will get a thumbs down motion. These behaviors are obvious and can look somewhat severe to onlookers. Often participants with low cards will form smaller subgroups and begin to back out of the middle of the mingling area.

▶  After about two minutes of mingling, without looking at their cards, ask the participants to separate into what group they think they are in, low cards, middle cards, or high cards. Players place themselves based on how they were treated. When everyone is in a group, ask the participants to look around the room at the order of cards on each player's forehead, and then look at their own card.

---

**Facilitator Script:** "Let's form a circle to hear the directions for our first game. *(Hand each person a playing card.)* I'm going to hand each one of you a playing card. Please don't look at it and hold it so it is face down. If you accidentally peek, then trade cards with a neighbor so you don't know what card you have. In a minute, but not yet, I'm going to ask you to place that card on your forehead so everyone else can see what card you have, but you don't know what your card is. Now I'm going to be intentionally vague with the directions. Figuring out what to do is part of the game. Once I ask you to put that card on your forehead, I want you to mingle around the room and interact with one another. I want you to treat each other based on the playing card you see on their forehead. Again, I'm going to be vague on purpose, you need to figure out how to treat people based on the card they have on their forehead. You also do not have the resource of your voice, so please do not talk during the game. Go ahead and place that card to your forehead now and begin."

---

**Debriefing Sequence:**

Start with the low cards and ask them these questions:

- What were some behaviors that were done toward you that led you to believe you had a low card?
- How quickly did you realize you had a low card?

Then move to the middle cards and ask them these questions:

- What were some behaviors that were demonstrated toward you that led you to believe you had a middle card?
- How long did it take you to realize what value of card you had?

Then move to the high cards and ask these questions:

- What were some behaviors that were demonstrated toward you that led you to believe you had a high card?
- How quickly did you realize you had a high card?

The next round of questioning starts with the high cards, then moves to the middle cards, and then moves to the low cards. Ask each group this question:

- After you realized what value of card you had, did it influence the way you played the game?
- What were some specific behaviors you did toward others because of the value of card you had?

The responses to this question are pretty profound. Typically the royalty cards report that they treated others poorly because they had the power. It's interesting to watch the royalty cards get bowed to and the "2" cards get pushed away and treated poorly. During the activity the participants with the low cards will usually back out of the middle of the mingling area. This can lead to a great discussion on one's willingness to fully participate in a group if they are being treated poorly.

- Did anyone with a low card find themselves backing out of the activity?
- How does this relate back to the real world?
- How does this relate to recovery and wellness?

This activity also leads to a great discussion on who places value on you.

- What happens when people feel left out?
- Isn't the "2" card sometimes the most valuable card when playing blackjack and you have a 19?

▶ How would the activity be played differently if there were no royalty cards in the deck?

▶ If you were running a race wouldn't you rather be second than tenth?

These are great topics of discussion for diversity, cultural norms, and society in general. People of all abilities can play.

**NOTE:** This game can bring up some interesting emotions that you may have to deal with. These are the teachable moments! Some teachable moments are more powerful than others for different people. Keep a watchful eye over all your players. Make sure they all leave the activity with their self-esteem intact.

**Recovery/Wellness Metaphor:** Even today there is such a negative stigma associated with people in recovery. Words like junkie, addict, and alcoholic conjure up such negative associations. Sometimes we degrade others in order to make ourselves feel better. This powerful activity allows us to see what happens when we treat each other based on perceived values. Having a discussion on worth can be a powerful follow-up and how worth is different than value.

# Promenade Tag

**Group Size:** 8–50

**Purpose:** To allow participants the opportunity to trust a partner. Metaphorically think about what obstacles they might encounter and how they can turn away from them.

**Props Needed:** None

**Activity Preparation:**

1. Prior to class create an open space for play. If you are indoors, put chairs around the perimeter of the room. If you are outside, find an open space to play that is free of debris or obstacles.

**Time Needed:**

- ▶ Directions: 5 minutes
- ▶ Activity: 10 minutes
- ▶ Debrief: 5 minutes

**Safety:** No running aloud. A slow walking pace is recommended. This activity requires a certain amount of trust. If participants become reckless, trust building could be compromised. Keep a close watch and call out those partners that are going too fast or are colliding with others.

**Activity Directions:**

- ▶ Have the participants stand in a circle. Include yourself in the circle.
- ▶ The objective for this activity is to work together with a partner coordinating movements around the room without making contact with any other pairs of participants.
- ▶ This tends to work better with larger groups, but can be done with small groups as well. For smaller groups, restrict the size of the playing area. If the space is too large, pairs may find the activity less challenging—tighter quarters seems to make this one play better. Lively background music makes this one even more fun!
- ▶ Phase 1: Creatively pair up participants and ask the partners to stand side-by-side and hold hands in a square dancer's "promenade" position—left hand to left hand, right hand to right hand holding like you're shaking hands. (See picture.)
- ▶ Without letting go of hands, have the pairs practice rotating their bodies 180 degrees. This rotation is done by one partner pushing one hand and pulling with the other. This double action forces the partners to face in the opposite direction. After each pair

understands how to perform the 180, spread the pairs out around the playing area. On the "Go" start (or when you start the music), have pairs move forward in a straight line. As the pairs move they will encounter other pairs or other obstacles like walls. Before making contact with any obstruction, the pair must perform their 180 degree turn calling out, "Turn Around!" while reversing direction. After the reverse, the pair proceeds forward again in their new direction until they come to another obstruction that requires a 180. As mentioned above, the smaller the playing area, the greater the number of switches and changes. Play for three minutes. Call "freeze" to stop the action or simply turn off the music.

► No running allowed. A slow walking pace is recommended.
► CAUTION: This activity requires a certain amount of trust. If participants become reckless, trust building could be compromised—keep a close watch.
► Phase 2: (Need a photo of this position.) To take this experience to a deeper level, proceed to Phase 2, which has a higher risk level and is a trust progression.
► Connect pairs together so they are facing in opposite directions. Standing side-by-side, right shoulder to right shoulder. They will connect right hand to left hand and left hand to right hand.
► Before moving, assign participants a number, Participant #1 and Participant #2. During the first round, the pairs will move in the direction Participant #1 is facing. Participant #2 will not be able to see where they are going. During the second round, the pairs will move in the direction Participant #2 is facing. Participant #2 will be able to see what the pair just missed. You should see the increase in the trust factor.

**Facilitator Script:** "Please find a partner and come stand in a circle to hear the directions for our first game. We're going to play a game called Promenade Tag. Has anyone ever danced a promenade before? Here's how it will work. You're going to stand shoulder to shoulder with your partner, and connect your left hand to your partner's left hand, then your right hand to your partner's right hand holding like you're shaking hands. (*Demonstrate this with a partner.*) Next, you are going to walk forward with your partner. (*Demonstrate this.*) If the two of you encounter another group of people, or an obstacle of any kind you are going to call out, 'Turn around!' and then reverse direction by pushing with one hand and pulling with the other hand, like this. (*Demonstrate this.*) Let's practice this. Connect hands with your partner, and practice the turn. It will take a few tries for it to feel right. (*Pause for a few moments while the group practices this skill.*) Does everyone feel like they understand the movement? We're going to play this first round for three minutes. Anytime you get close to another group of people or an obstacle, call out 'Turn around!' and then reverse direction. Are there any questions? (*Pause for questions.*) Let's begin."

Phase 2: "OK, let's get back into a circle. How did everyone do? Did you get better at your turns? Next, we are going to increase the trust factor of this game by altering your physical position with your partner. Stand next to your partner and connect your right shoulder with your partner's right shoulder. *(Demonstrate this with a partner.)* You will be facing different directions. Connect your right hand to your partner's left hand, and your left hand to your partner's right hand. *(Demonstrate this.)* Between the two of you, you will decide who is going to walk forward first. The other partner will be walking backward. The person walking backward will have to trust that their partner will not walk them into any obstacles. Just like the last game, when the partner walking forward gets close to another group of people or an obstacle, they will call out 'Turn around!' and then reverse direction by pushing with one hand and pulling with the other. *(Demonstrate this.)* You will need to practice the turns again, as it is a little different process than Phase 1. Let's practice this now. *(Pause while the group practices.)* We will have a slow pace for this round. This round will last for about two to three minutes, then we will switch roles so you can experience both walking forward and taking care of your partner, as well as walking backward and trusting your partner. Are there any questions?"

## Debrief:

► What did you enjoy about this activity?
► In what ways did you have to trust your partner?
► What were some feelings that came up for you?
► In this game, there were times that you were walking backwards and you had to trust that your partner was watching out for you, so you didn't run into any obstacles or people. They helped you turn around and go the other direction so you didn't get hurt or collide with anyone. How can you relate to this?
► Each time you were about to run into an obstacle, you had to say, "Turn around!" What is the significance of this for you?

**Recovery/Wellness Metaphor:** Recovery asks us to develop healthy trusting partnerships in which we walk the path of recovery together. These partnerships can come in the form of a recovery ally, sponsor, mentor, peer support specialist, therapist, counselor, or fellow peer in recovery. We have the opportunity to learn to ask for help and remember we are not alone.

**Role of Facilitator:** Safety and speed monitor.

# Protector Destroyer

**Group Size:** 12–50

**Purpose:** Help participants identify who their Protector might be in the real world, as well as what (or who) are the things that could represent their Destroyer.

**Props Needed:** None

**Activity Preparation:**
1. Prep time needed: 5 minutes
2. Prior to class create an open space for play. If you are indoors, put chairs around the perimeter of the room. If you are outside, create some kind of boundaries about 100 feet by 100 feet. You can use soccer cones or any other items you can locate to visually designate the play area.

**Time Needed:**
- ▶ Directions: 5 minutes each round, 15 minutes total
- ▶ Activity: 2 minutes each round, 6–7 minutes total
- ▶ Debrief: 5–10 minutes each round, 15–30 minutes total

**Set-Up:** None

**Safety:** It is important that you have participants walk during this game. Stress this point. Often people are not looking where they are going because they are looking for the people in the roles of their Protector and their Destroyer. If people are running, then collisions are more dangerous and could lead to injuries. If people are walking there is less risk of hard collisions.
- ▶ Physical—Risk of collisions if pace is not controlled.

**Activity Directions:**
- ▶ Have the participants stand in a circle. Include yourself in the circle.
- ▶ Round 1: Instruct the group to look around the circle and secretly pick one person that will represent a "Destroyer" in the game. Secretly means they are not to tell the person that they have chosen them.
- ▶ Next instruct the group to secretly pick a different person that will represent a "Protector" in the game.
- ▶ Tell them that when you say "Go" everyone will start walking around in the middle of the room/boundary area. They must keep their "Protector" between themselves and their "Destroyer" at all times.

- ▶ Play for two to three minutes.
- ▶ Debrief Round 1.
- ▶ Round 2: Instruct the group to look around the circle and secretly pick one person that will represent "Addiction" in this round. Secretly means they are not to tell the person that they have chosen them.
- ▶ Next instruct the group to secretly pick a different person that will represent a "Protector" in this round.
- ▶ Tell them that when you say "Go" everyone will start walking around in the middle of the room/boundary area. They must keep their "Protector" between themselves and their "Addiction" at all times.
- ▶ Play for two minutes.
- ▶ Debrief Round 2.
- ▶ Round 3: Instruct the group to look around the circle and secretly pick one person that will represent "Addiction" in this round. Secretly means they are not to tell the person that they have chosen them.
- ▶ Next instruct the group to secretly pick a different person that will represent a "Friend in Recovery" in this round.
- ▶ The participant will play the role of "Protector" in this round.
- ▶ Tell them that when you say "Go" everyone will start walking around in the middle of the room/boundary area. Since they are the "Protector" they must keep themselves between their "Friend in Recovery" and their "Addiction" at all times.
- ▶ Play for two minutes.

**Round 1 Facilitator Script:** "Let's form a circle to hear the directions for our first game. What I'd like you to do is look across the circle from where you are standing and secretly choose someone that is going to be your 'Destroyer' in this game. When I say secretly, it means I do not want you to tell them that you have chosen them. Just keep that person in your mind as your Destroyer. Everyone have someone picked? Good. Next, I need you to secretly pick a different person that is going to be your 'Protector' in this game. Again, when I say secretly, don't tell them you've chosen them, just pick someone quietly. Everyone have their Protector picked? Great. Next I want you to notice the boundaries I have set up for this game.

*(Indoor version):* Please stay within the boundaries of this room and on the front side of the chairs. We do not want people to trip over the chairs so we can keep everyone safe.

*(Outdoor version):* See the boundary indicators I have placed? Please stay within the boundaries.

What we are going to do is mingle around within the boundaries by walking. While you are mingling, you must keep your Protector physically between yourself and your Destroyer at all times. *(Demonstrate this concept with your hands. Hold up your index finger on your left hand that would represent the Protector, hold up your index finger on your right hand that would represent the Destroyer. Move them both around and imitate walking around keeping your Protector finger in between yourself and your Destroyer finger.)* This is a walking game. Please do not run so we do not collide with other participants. Are there any questions? Remember, keep your Protector between yourself and your Destroyer at all times, and keep your pace to a walking pace. Ready, Go!

*(Play the game for about one to two minutes. You will notice lots of giggling and walking around. The movement of the participants might look like a school of fish maneuvering around one another.)*

*(After a few minutes of play, loudly say—)* OK, you may stop! *(You may need to say this a few times for everyone to hear.)* Please go and thank the two people who played your Protector and your Destroyer and then get back into a circle."

### Round 1 Debrief:

► How did it feel when your Protector was not in-between yourself and your Destroyer?

► Was it difficult to keep your Protector between yourself and your Destroyer?

► Did you come up with any strategies to help make you successful in the game?

► Let's think about the two roles in this game and relate them back to the real world. Who might be someone that is your Protector in the real world?

► Who or what might represent your Destroyer?

► What can you do if your metaphoric Destroyer gets too close to you, and your Protector is not nearby?

**Round 2 Facilitator Script:** "We're going to play this game again, however this time we are going to change the roles a little bit. Like last time, I want you to look across the circle from where you are standing and secretly choose someone that is going to be your 'Protector' in this game. Everyone have someone picked? Good. Next, I need you to secretly pick a different person that is going to be your 'Addiction' in this game. Again, when I say secretly, don't tell them you've chosen them, just pick someone quietly. Everyone have someone picked to represent their 'Addiction'? Great. Same boundaries exist for this round. What we are going to do is mingle around within the boundaries by walking. While you are mingling, you must keep your 'Protector' physically between yourself and your 'Addiction' at all times. Remember, this is a walking game. Please do not run so we do not collide with other participants. Are there any questions?

*(Play this round for about ninety seconds. You will notice this round being a little more somber. The movement of the participants will still look like a school of fish maneuvering around one another.)*

*(After a few minutes of play, loudly say—)* OK, you may stop. Please go ahead and get back into a circle."

## Round 2 Debrief:

- ▶ How was this round different than Round 1?
- ▶ Were your emotions different in this round? How were they different?
- ▶ How did you react when your Addiction got close to you?
- ▶ Let's talk about the role of the Protector in this round. Did your Protector's movement help you or hurt you with trying to keep away from your Addiction? How is this like real life? What are the dangers of placing too much emphasis on someone else protecting you from your addiction?

**Round 3 Facilitator Script:** "We're going to play this game one more time, and change the roles again. Like last time, I want you to look across the circle from where you are standing and secretly choose someone that is going to be 'Addiction' in this game, not necessarily your addiction, just the role of 'Addiction.' Everyone have someone picked? Good. Next, I need you to secretly pick a different person that is going to be your 'Friend in Recovery' in this round. Again, when I say secretly, don't tell them you've chosen them, just pick someone quietly. Everyone have someone picked to represent their 'Friend in Recovery'? Great. You are going to play the role of the 'Protector' in this round. You must keep yourself in between 'Addiction' and your 'Friend in Recovery' at all times. Same boundaries exist for this round. What we are going to do is mingle around within the boundaries by walking. While you are mingling, you must keep yourself physically between your 'Friend in Recovery' and 'Addiction' at all times. Remember, this is a walking game. Please do not run so we do not collide with other participants. Are there any questions?"

*(A very interesting movement phenomenon will occur in Round 3 that is strikingly different than the other rounds. You will notice in Round 1 and Round 2 the movement will be very scattered and spread out. In Round 3, all of the participants will rush to the middle and it will resemble a "mosh pit" of people.)*

**Round 3 Debrief:**

- How was this round different than Round 2?
- Were your emotions different in this round? How were they different than the other rounds?
- How successful were you at keeping your Friend in Recovery away from Addiction?
- Were you Protecting someone that didn't want protection?
- Did you feel you were successful?
- Was your strategy to place yourself closer to your Friend in Recovery or closer to Addiction? What are the pros and cons to both strategies?
- How does this relate back to the real world?
- What takeaways will you have from this experience?

**Recovery/Wellness Metaphor:** Help participants identify who their Protector might be in the real world, as well as what (or who) are the things that could represent their Destroyer.

**Role of Facilitator:** Safety monitor, both physically and emotionally. Control the pace of the game by stating, "Walk please!" multiple times during the game if necessary.

# Serenity Prayer Shuffle

**Group Size:** 5–25

**Purpose:** Help participants to embody the serenity prayer as a tool for recovery, create group cohesion, help participants see what they can control and what they can't.

**Props Needed:**

1. 1 10-foot rope
2. 1 50-foot rope
3. serenity shuffle scenarios
4. 1 Can Change and 2 Cannot Change pages to label circles

**Activity Preparation:** Prep Time Needed: 10 minutes

1. Print off serenity shuffle scenarios
2. Print off pages with Can Change and Cannot Change printed on them
3. Prior to class create an open space for play. If you are indoors, put chairs around the perimeter of the room. If you are outside, find an open space to play that is free of debris or obstacles.

**Time Needed:**

▶ Directions: 5 minutes
▶ Activity: 25 minutes
▶ Debrief: 15 minutes

**Set-Up:**

1. Lay out inside circle with the 10-foot rope.
2. Lay out outside circle with 50-foot rope.
3. Label inside circle as Can Change.
4. Label outside circle as Cannot Change.

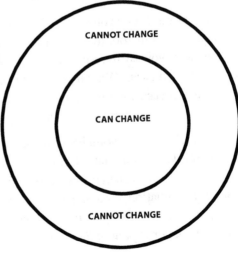

## Activity Directions:

- ▶ Have the participants stand around the outside circle.
- ▶ Explain activity is about putting the lessons of the serenity prayer into practice.
- ▶ Have participants move to the circle they believe is most fitting for each scenario read.
- ▶ Have a mini debrief after each statement to help reinforce learning.
- ▶ Conclude activity with a final debrief.

**Facilitator Script:** "Let's gather around the outer circle to hear the directions for today's group. As you can see, we have two circles. The outer circle is labeled as Cannot Change and the inner circle is labeled as Can Change. We are going to put the lessons of the serenity prayer into practice. Remember there are things in life we cannot change and there are things that we can. In a moment, I am going to read a statement, phrase, or scenario and then ask you to move to the circle which best represents whether or not you feel it falls into the category of things you can change or things you cannot change. Once you are in place we will discuss why you chose the circle you are in. Does anyone have any questions? *(once questions are answered you can move on)*

OK, here is the first scenario. You are in rehab and your roommate decides he doesn't want to stay so he leaves. Do you feel this is something you can or cannot change? Move to the circle that best represents your ability to change the situation. *(You might have to reread the scenario more than one time. Once everyone is in place, process their positioning. Pick a participant.)* Why did you choose Cannot Change? *(If there is a participant in the Can Change)* Why did you choose Can Change?

*(From time to time remind group that there are no wrong answers.)*

Great, let's reset, everyone back to the outside. Now listen to the second scenario. You are in rehab and your roommate decides he doesn't want to stay. Do you feel you can or cannot change what you say in response to this? Move to the circle that best represents your ability to change the situation. *(You might have to reread the scenario more than one time. Once everyone is in place, process their positioning. Pick a participant.)* Why did you choose Can Change? *(If there is a participant in the Cannot Change)* Why did you choose Cannot Change?

Great, let's reset, everyone back to the outside. Now listen to the third scenario. You are in rehab and your roommate decides he doesn't want to stay. Do you feel you can or cannot change what others do in response to this? Move to the circle that best represents your ability to change the situation. *(You might have to reread the scenario more than one time. Once everyone is in place, process their positioning. Pick a participant.)* Why did you choose Cannot Change? *(If there is a participant in the Can Change)* Why did you choose Can Change?

Great, let's reset, everyone back to the outside. Now listen to the fourth scenario. You are in rehab and your roommate decides he doesn't want to stay, do you feel you can or cannot change what you do in response to this? Move to the circle that best represents your ability to change the situation. *(You might have to reread the scenario more than one time. Once everyone is in place, process their positioning. Pick a participant.)* Why did you choose Can Change? *(If there is a participant in the Cannot Change)* Why did you choose Cannot Change?

*(While it might be tedious, it is important to go through each of the four related scenarios to help reinforce what we can and cannot change.)* Good job everyone!

OK, here is the next scenario. You are in a grocery store and all of a sudden you find yourself in the middle of the wine aisle. Do you feel you can or cannot change your reaction to this? *(You might have to reread the scenario more than one time. Once everyone is in place, process their positioning. Pick a participant.)* Why did you choose Cannot Change? *(If there is a participant in the Can Change)* Why did you choose Can Change?

*(From time to time remind group that there are no wrong answers.)*

Great, let's reset, everyone back to the outside. Now listen to the next scenario. You are in a grocery store and all of a sudden you find yourself in the middle of the wine aisle. Do you feel you can or cannot change your response to this? Move to the circle that best represents your ability to change the situation. *(You might have to reread the scenario more than one time. Once everyone is in place, process their positioning. Pick a participant.)* Why did you choose Can Change? *(If there is a participant in the Cannot Change)* Why did you choose Cannot Change?

Great, let's reset, everyone back to the outside. Now listen to the next scenario. You are in a grocery store and all of a sudden you find yourself in the middle of the wine aisle. Do you feel you can or cannot change others' reactions to this? Move to the circle that best represents your ability to change the situation. *(You might have to reread the scenario more than one time. Once everyone is in place, process their positioning. Pick a participant.)* Why did you choose Cannot Change? *(If there is a participant in the can change)* Why did you choose Can Change?

Great, let's reset, everyone back to the outside. Now listen to the next scenario. You are in a grocery store and all of a sudden you find yourself in the middle of the wine aisle. Do you feel you can or cannot impact others' reactions to this? Move to the circle that best represents your ability to change the situation. *(You might have to reread the scenario more than one time. Once everyone is in place, process their positioning. Pick a participant.)* Why did you choose Can Change? *(If there is a participant in the Cannot Change)* Why did you choose Cannot Change?

*(You can continue with another scenario or if the group is getting the gist of the exercise move on to debriefing.)*

Awesome job everyone. Give yourselves a hand. *(start to clap).* Now let's talk about this for a minute." *(Debrief)*

### Debrief:

1. What did you notice about this activity?
2. What did you learn as a result of this activity?
3. Now that you know this, what is the implication for your life?
4. So how does this knowledge affect your current frustrations in life?
5. What are other scenarios that this can apply to?
6. What is challenging to accept about the things we cannot change?
7. What is challenging about the responsibility to change the things we can?
8. What is the difference between being able to impact a situation and change it?

**Recovery/Wellness Metaphor:** So much of life's frustrations are based on energy spent in trying to change things we simply cannot change or in not changing the things we can change. Helping participants place their energy in the proper place will ease a lot of suffering.

**Role of Facilitator:** It is significant that the inside circle be marked Can Change as that is indeed most of what we can change is inside us, while most of what we cannot change is outside of us. This is another thing that is nice to debrief, is in general what we can change is inside and what we cannot change is outside.

**Variations:** Feel free to change the scenarios to best suit your participants' needs. For participants who are less mobile give them a place card with their name on it and ask them where they would like it placed. You can also have index cards with Can Change and Cannot Change on them that participants can hold up rather than have to move.

# CANNOT CHANGE

Created by Marc Pimsler

# CAN
# CHANGE

Created by Marc Pimsler

# SERENITY SHUFFLE SCENARIOS

**Facilitator Note:** The following statements should be read in order, emphasizing the different words in each statement.

### You are in rehab

You are in rehab and your roommate decides he doesn't want to stay, so he leaves. Do you feel you can or cannot change this?

You are in rehab and your roommate decides he doesn't want to stay. Do you feel you can or cannot change **what you say** in response to this?

You are in rehab and your roommate decides he doesn't want to stay. Do you feel you can or cannot change **what others do** in response to this?

You are in rehab and your roommate decides he doesn't want to stay. Do you feel you can or cannot change **what you do** in response to this?

### In a grocery store

You are in a grocery store and all of a sudden you find yourself in the middle of the wine aisle. Do you feel you can or cannot change your reaction to this?

You are in a grocery store and all of a sudden you find yourself in the middle of the wine aisle. Do you feel you can or cannot change **your response** to this?

You are in a grocery store and all of a sudden you find yourself in the middle of the wine aisle. Do you feel you can or cannot change **others' reactions** to this?

You are in a grocery store and all of a sudden you find yourself in the middle of the wine aisle. Do you feel you can or cannot **impact others' reactions** to this?

### At a sports event

You are in a sports event and all of a sudden you find yourself craving a beer. Do you feel you can or cannot change your reaction to this?

You are in a sports event and all of a sudden you find yourself craving a beer. Do you feel you can or cannot change **your response** to this?

You are in a sports event and all of a sudden you find yourself craving a beer. Do you feel you can or cannot change **others' reactions** to this?

You are in a sports event and all of a sudden you find yourself craving a beer. Do you feel you can or cannot **impact others' reactions** to this?

Created by Marc Pimsler

**REPRODUCIBLE**

# Spot It! Cards

**Group Size:** 5–50

**Purpose:** Icebreaker, Get to Know You, Journaling, Processing

**Props Needed:**

1.  Spot It! cards

**Activity Preparation:** There are a couple of ways you can set this one up.

**Facilitator Note:** All the cards have a common symbol with every card in the deck . . . but the group doesn't need to know that.

**Time Needed:**

▶   Directions: 2 minutes
▶   Activity: 5 minutes
▶   Debrief: 5 minutes

**Set-Up:** Gather group together

**Activity Directions:**

▶   Pass out one Spot It! card to each participant.
▶   Find a partner and find the common matching image on the cards.
▶   Using the first letter of the common image state an adjective that introduces yourself (e.g., common image is an ice cube adjective that introduces me could be "Interesting Marc").

**Facilitator Script:** "Hey everyone, gather around. Today we are going to start off with an icebreaker. We will use this card set called Spot It! Cards. Each card has one matching image to every other card in the deck. Your task is to meet a new partner and find the image you have in common. Once you find that image introduce yourselves using an adjective that starts with the same letter as your common image. For example, if your common image is an ice cube you might say 'I am Interesting _____ (*say your name*).' If your image is cheese you might say 'I am Cheery _____ (*say your name*).' Try and complete three rounds in five minutes. Any questions?"

**Debrief:**

- ▶ What did you notice about this icebreaker?
- ▶ What was fun about it?
- ▶ What was something you learned about a peer?

**Recovery/Wellness Metaphor:** It is very helpful to increase group cohesion by playing games with the cards. See below for some additional activities you can use the cards for.

**Role of Facilitator:** Make processing fun rather than painful.

**Variations:** See below our favorite Spot It! Card Activities. Some of these ideas were shared with us by High Five Adventure, and in their book, *Ubuntu Activity Guide*.

## Common Bond

Give a card to each person in the group. Challenge everyone to pair up and find a matching image on their cards. When they do find a match, have them try to find something else in their lives that they have in common, a common bond. Once they are successful, have them move on to a new person and repeat the activity.

## Blind Find

Give a card to each person in the group and ask everyone to find a partner. Tell the group that (on your signal) they should study their own card for twenty seconds. Time can be adjusted based on age and ability of participants. Then, tell participants to hold their cards up next to their heads (at your count) so that their partners can see the card but they cannot. Have them attempt to find the match by looking at their partners' cards and recalling what is on their own. To continue, players trade cards and find someone new to play with.

## Face-Off

Divide group into two teams. The two teams line up facing each other so that the front person on each team is face to face. Half the deck is given to the first person in the line of each team, single image sides up. On GO, the two players flip over the first card in their deck. Whoever finds the match first wins that person to their team. The next two in line for each team step up and take the deck of cards. Play until it stops—one team has all the players or it stops being fun.

## Championship Find

This is a fun, light-hearted, competitive (and noisy) activity. Give each person a card and ask everyone to find a partner. On your signal, have the partners turn over their cards and race to find the matching image. The person who finds the match first wins and takes the opponent's card. The person who lost joins the winner's "team" as an enthusiastic fan and cheerleader. Winners continue to play by finding another undefeated participant to play against, while their growing fan base cheers them on. Play until one person has all the cards and all the fans. Congratulations!

## Back-to-Back (or Face-to-Face)

Give a card to everyone in the group. Have the group get into pairs. Partners stand back-to-back while looking at their multi-image side. Partners alternate asking yes/no questions in attempts to figure out what the common image is on the cards. They may not say the names of any of the objects, only descriptive questions (Do you have something red? Do you have an animal?). When the partner pair are sure they have found the match, they can guess. Switch cards and switch partners.

**Variation:** With larger groups, it can get too loud to hear standing back-to-back. Have partners face each other, looking at the multi-image side so that their partner cannot see it.

## Journaling

Have each person choose a card from the Spot It! deck. Using the images on the card, have each person write a story or reflect on an experience they had. Journaling can be done individually and then shared with the group or the group can create the journal entry together.

## Circle Storytelling

Activity is adapted from *The Chiji Guidebook* by Chris Cavert & Steven Simpson. Have the group in a circle standing on a place marker or sitting in a chair facing out of the circle. The facilitator will be the first storyteller and does not have a spot or seat. Each person, except the storyteller, received one Spot It! card and holds with image side out so the storyteller can see the pictures clearly. The storyteller starts, like all good storytellers do, with the opening, "Once upon a time," and then starts to walk around the outside of the circle. He or she then adds to the story featuring particular cards being held up by the players in the circle.

For example, "Once upon a time, I was driving in my car and I saw a T-Rex dinosaur walking down the road." When the car and T-Rex images are called, the players holding cards with that image get up and follow the storyteller around the circle. The story might continue, "When I stopped to pick up the clown that was hitchhiking who was holding an ice cube."

This adds players holding cards that have clown and ice cube to the storyteller's circle. When the storyteller is finished they are to state "The end" at which time everyone in the parade (storyteller and followers) is required to find a seat or place marker. The player left without a seat is the next storyteller.

Before starting a new story, pass out new cards to each player then begin again.

Spot It! cards can be purchased online. We suggest getting them from training-wheels.com

# Switch, Change, Rotate

**Original Source:** *The Empty Bag*, by Dick Hammond and Chris Cavert

**Group Size:** 8–50

**Purpose:** To allow participants the opportunity to feel overwhelmed while performing routine tasks.

**Props Needed:** None

**Activity Preparation:**
1. Prep time needed: 0–5 minutes
2. Prior to class create an open space for play. If you are indoors, put chairs around the perimeter of the room. If you are outside, find an open space to play that is free of debris or obstacles.

**Time Needed:**
- Directions: 5 minutes
- Activity: 10 minutes
- Debrief: 15 minutes

**Activity Directions:**
- Have the participants get into small groups of four to five people each, then stand in a single file line, one person right behind the next.
- You will be giving the group three different commands, and each command has a different action.
- Switch: The person at the front of the line and the person at the back of the line switch places.
- Change: The entire group changes direction 180 degrees.
- Rotate: The person at the front of the line rotates to the back of the line.
- Let the group practice each command as you are describing it.
- Once the group has practiced, inform them of one more command, "Move." When the group hears this, they will start slowly walking around the room in their small groups. While they are walking, you will call out one of the three commands, "Switch," "Change," or "Rotate."

► After the first few commands, increase the difficulty by calling out two to three commands at a time.

► Debrief the game.

**Facilitator Script:** "I need everyone to get into small groups of four to five people each. Then form a single file line, one person right behind the other facing me. *(Wait until everyone is in a group.)* Great! What's going to happen next is, I'm going to call out a few commands. The commands will be Switch, Change, or Rotate. Each one of those three words has a different action that goes with them. For example, if you hear me call out the word 'Switch!', then the person at the front of the line and the person at the back of the line are going to switch places. So, Switch! *(Let the group practice this.)* Great job! Now middle people, you need to know this command, too, because you are going to have a turn in the front of the line in a minute. Now the next command you might hear me call out is 'Change!' If you hear the word Change then the entire group is going to Change direction 180 degrees. So, Change! *(Wait until the group has practiced this. Now call out 'Switch!' and let them practice this command again. Then call out 'Change!' so they are facing you again.)* Great job! You are doing well. OK, the last command you might hear me call out is 'Rotate!' If you hear me call out 'Rotate' then the person at the front of the line will Rotate to the back of the line. Ready? Rotate! *(Wait for them to complete this.)* Rotate! *(Do this command twice so someone from the middle will now be at the front of the line.)* Switch! *(Let the new line leaders practice this since they are new to the front of the line.)* Change! *(Again, let them practice.)* And Change one more time. *(Wait for them to complete this.)* OK, great! How are we doing? Is everyone catching on? The four or five of you in your line are a little team. You need to work together to help everyone do the correct action with the correct command. Do you think you have them down? Let's practice one more time, because I'm going to make it harder here in just a minute. If you hear me call out Switch the person at the front of the line and the person at the back of the line will Switch places. If you hear me call out Change then the entire group will change directions 180 degrees. And if you hear me call out Rotate, then the person at the front of the line will Rotate to the back of the line. *(Have them practice these while you are saying them.)* OK, now to spice things up a bit, I'm going to add one more command. If you hear me call out 'Move,' then you and your group will start slowly walking in your line around the room. As you are walking, I am going to call out Switch, Change, or Rotate, so your group needs to do the correct action with the correct command while slowly walking, OK? Any questions? If not, then 'Move!' *(The group will start walking. Start slow, with one command.)* Switch! *(Wait for all groups to execute this command correctly.)* Change! *(Wait for all groups to execute this command correctly.)* Rotate! *(Wait for all groups to execute this command correctly. Now, we start to spice things up a bit . . .)* Switch, Change! *(Give two commands at once. There will be some hesitation and visible signs of being overwhelmed. Give them a moment, they will figure it out. Let all groups complete these two* commands before moving on.) Rotate, Rotate! *(This lets the groups have new line leaders, and lets those in the middle advance to the front.)* Change, Switch! *(Wait for all groups to execute this command correctly.)* Rotate, Change! *(Wait for all groups to execute this command correctly. Now we are going to spice things up even more . . . )* Switch, Change, Rotate! *(Note the laughter and 'screams' of disbelief. Wait for all groups to execute this command correctly.)* Rotate, Rotate, Change! *(Wait for all groups to execute this command correctly.)* Switch, Change, Rotate! *(Make sure all teams are keeping up. If they are struggling with three commands, reduce the number of commands back to one or two.)*

*(Continue play for three to four more call announcements, then say,)* And stop! Give yourselves a round of applause for a job well done! Please come and make a big circle here next to me." *(Now debrief the game.)*

---

## Debrief:

- ► How did your group do?
- ► What were some strategies you came up with in the moment to be successful?
- ► What went through your mind when I started calling out more than one direction?
- ► Did you ever feel like you were overwhelmed?
- ► How does what you experienced in this activity relate back to the real world?
- ► Who is in your support team that are helping you "make the right moves" in your recovery?

**Recovery/Wellness Metaphor:** Here is a story you can tell at the end of the debriefing session.

"One time we took a recovery group on a retreat in Jackson Hole, WY. This group consisted of people who had relapsed several times, and openly admitted they were good at setting goals but not always achieving them. *(Ask the group this question)* When you are climbing a mountain, what could one of the goals be? *(Usual answer: To get to the top.)* Right! To get to the top. Well, since this group had admitted they were good at setting goals and not always achieving them, we did this activity on the trail right before we got to the summit. If you've ever been hiking up a large hill or mountain, you know that the last few feet up to the summit are usually some of the hardest. As the group was doing the Switch, Change, Rotate activity, the facilitators would always say 'Change!' right before we got to the top. Then they would walk a long way down the mountain, while Rotating and Switching. Then eventually we would 'Change' again and they would start walking back up the mountain. Then again, right before they got to the top we said 'Change' one more time. Then they would Switch and Rotate back down. Eventually they summitted, and the view was amazing. The debrief was very powerful, and each of them had a new appreciation for setting and achieving their sobriety goals.

# Tell a Story Cards

**Timeline:** Before Lesson

**Group Size:** 8–50

**Props Needed:**
1. Picture cards, or cut pictures out of a magazine. You could also print a variety of pictures from Google images or use a collection of postcards.

**Activity Preparation:**
1. Prep time needed: 20–30 minutes
2. You will need to prepare at least 24–30 pictures for every 4 participants in your group.

**Activity Directions:**
- ▶ Have the participants get into groups of 4.
- ▶ Give each group 24–30 photo cards.
- ▶ Instruct the group that each person is to make up a silly story by turning over picture cards and incorporate the picture they see into the story.
- ▶ Each participant should use at least 6 pictures in their story.
- ▶ When the first participant is finished, they should pass the stack of pictures to the next participant and they can either build on the story that was started or start over with a new story.

**Time Needed:** 30 minutes

**Facilitator Script:** "I need everyone to get into groups of four and then listen to the directions for our first game. *(Wait until everyone is in a group.)* Great! What's going to happen next is, I'm going to bring each group a small stack of picture cards. Each person is going to get an opportunity to make up a silly story using the stack of picture cards. The story will start by turning over the first picture. When you see the picture you must start making up a story about what you see. Then, when you turn over the second picture, you must incorporate that picture into the next part of the story. Keep turning over pictures and keep adding onto your story. Then when you feel like your story is done, or when you have turned over at least 6 pictures, then you may give the stack of pictures to the next person. They can either build on the story the first person started, or start a new story of their own. Each person will get an opportunity to make up a story. Are there any questions?"

## Debrief:

- ▶ What was it like making up your own story?
- ▶ What was one of the most creative surprises that popped up in one of the stories you heard?
- ▶ How is this activity like creating our own story out in the real world?
- ▶ What "cards" or options do you need if you were creating your own deck of story cards?

**Variation:** You can choose to end the activity here, or take it to a much deeper place. Have a second set of cards that are addictions related. Pictures of jail cells, drug paraphernalia, alcohol bottles, and other items that correlate to addiction. We recommend using clip-art pictures of these items so they do not trigger anyone. Allow participants to peer over pictures and then choose the photos that would help them tell their story. Include some blank cards so participants could draw images that they cannot find on the cards you provide. Debrief this experience after each participant shares.

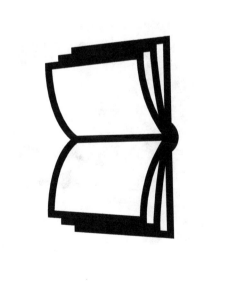

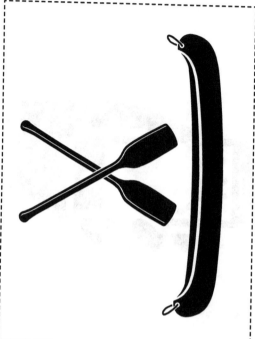

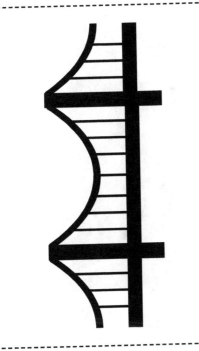

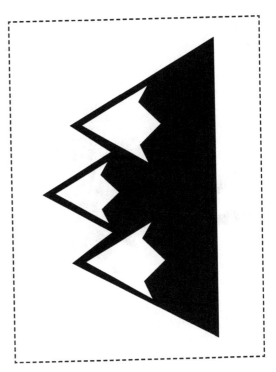

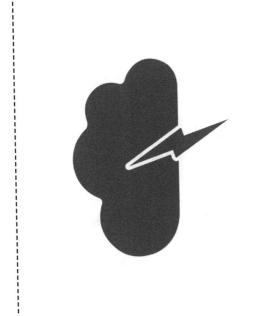

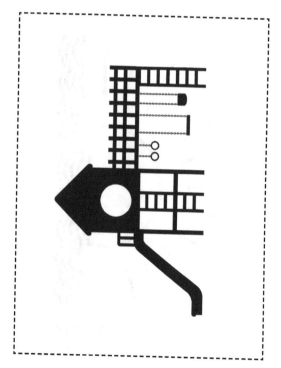

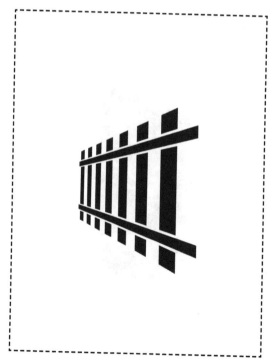

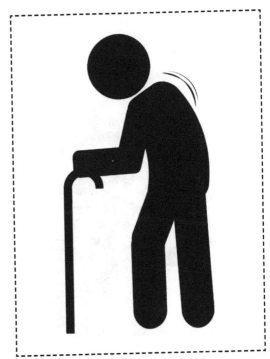

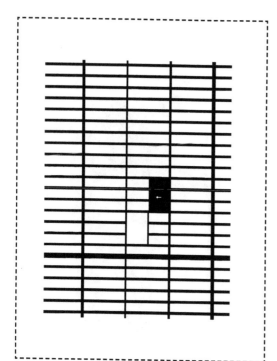

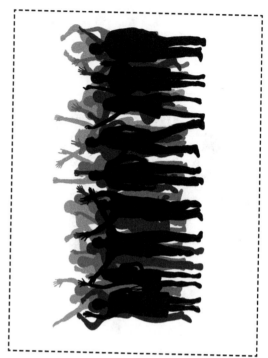

# Toxic Waste

**Group Size:** 5–25

**Purpose:** Increase frustration tolerance, problem solving, communication skills, group cohesion, and increase mindfulness skills.

**Props Needed:** 2 small hackey sacks, 1 50-foot boundary rope, 6 pieces of 15 foot webbing, various sizes of bungee cords, 2 bandanas, 2 hacky sacks, 1 bucket.

**Activity Preparation:** You can rename this activity to fit the needs of your group. Use your own discretion.

## Things to Set Up:
- ► Create a circle with the 50-foot rope.
- ► Place the bucket upside down in the center of the circle.
- ► Place the two hackey sacks on top of the bucket.
- ► Take one piece of webbing and make a circle with it. Place the circle about 30 feet from the large circle.
- ► Leave all other props in a pile on the outside of the circle.

## Time Needed: Total time 50 minutes
- ► Directions: 5 minutes
- ► Activity: 30 minutes (depending on how long it takes group to complete task)
- ► Debrief: 15 minutes

**Activity Directions:** (Please change these to fit the needs of your group.) Instruct the group that they must build a toxic waste removal device and move the toxic waste/hackey sacks to a secure place (the webbing circle). You may put as many restrictions on the group as you would like, or let them tell you how hard they would like the activity to be.

## Possible Restrictions:
- ► The balls must remain on the top of the bucket at all times.
- ► The bucket may not be scooted across the floor.
- ► Only the props provided may be used to transfer the toxic waste.
- ► The boundary ropes cannot be moved.
- ► If the hackey sacks fall off the bucket, the group must start over.
- ► You must be at least eight feet away from the toxic waste at all times.

▶ The only people that may touch the props are participants with blindfolds.
▶ When you are touching the props you lose your voice.

It's up to you and the ability level of your group! Ensure you have designated a "secure place" for the toxic waste to be deposited.

**Facilitator Script:** "Hey everyone today you have a critical mission. Today it is your job to ensure the safety of our space. As you can see there is a roped-off area. This area has been determined to be the toxic wasteland known to be hazardous to your health. In fact, if any body part crosses over the boundary line then you instantly die. The only thing that is able to cross over the boundary are these tools *(point to the pile of approved items)*. Of course I am wearing a safety suit that will allow me to reset the mission if the group needs to start over. Your mission is to remove the toxic waste from the center of the affected area and deliver them to the safety zone over here *(point to safety zone at least six feet away from the toxic wasteland)*.

Here are important things to keep in mind *(list off the restrictions you have chosen for this group)*.

The task is over and safety will be restored once the bombs are placed in the safety zone."

**Debrief:**
▶ What was this activity like for you?
▶ Describe the specific steps taken.
▶ How did the group work together to accomplish the task?
▶ What would you have done differently?
▶ How did the group communicate?
▶ What was frustrating about this activity?

**Recovery/Wellness Metaphor:** Show that we can work together to create creative solutions to our problems. What toxic waste do you need to remove from your life? How difficult is it to remove yourself from toxic environments? What tools do you need readily available to help you remove these toxic things from your environment?

**Variations:** Add possible restrictions to increase the difficultly level of the task.

# Traffic Jam

**Activity Source:** Silver Bullets

**Group Size:** 10–20

**Purpose:** Learn about trust, support, and coaching by setting and unsetting mousetraps.

Activity Trust level = High Risk (if going all the way through to minefield. Trust level can be modified by stopping before minefield).

**Props Needed:**
1. Enough place markers (plastic squares) for each person to have one plus a middle space.

**Activity Preparation:** Have a clear space so participants can line up with enough personal space between them.
1. Line up enough spots for each player and one extra middle spot.

**Time Needed:** Total time 1 hour or so.
- ► Directions: 5 minutes
- ► Activity: 45 minutes (depending on how long it takes for participants to solve the problem)
- ► Debrief: 15 minutes

**Safety:**
Physical—Make sure group takes this activity seriously as this can be a very frustrating experience for some participants. Pay attention to the emotional tone of both the individuals as well as the collective whole. This activity might increase anxiety or frustration; however, it will also give participants an opportunity to work through their feelings.

**Activity Directions:**
Each person occupies one of the "spaces" with an empty space in the middle (half group on one end, half on the other). Have everyone face the center spot. Using the following moves, people on the left side of center must end up in the places on the right side, and vice versa.

**Legal moves:**

1. A person may move into an empty space in front of him/her.
2. A person may move around a person who is facing him into an empty space.

**Illegal moves:**

1. Any move backward.
2. Any move around someone facing the same way you are (i.e., you are looking at their back).
3. Any move which involves two persons moving at once.

This can be a very frustrating event for some groups. It may need to be halted at some point and then debriefed. *(See next page for solution.)*

---

**Facilitator Script:** "Gather around everyone. Today you are challenged to solve a problem known as a traffic jam. First I need you to count off by twos. *(Have group separate into the 2 groups.)* OK, all ones line up on the spots over here and twos you are going to line up on the spots over here. Your challenge is to get everyone in your group to the spots on the other side, without making any illegal moves.

The legal moves are:

1. A person may move into an empty space in front of him/her.
2. A person may move around a person who is facing him into an empty space.

The illegal moves are:

1. Any move backwards.
2. Any move around someone facing the same way you are (i.e., you are looking at their back).
3. Any move which involves two persons moving at once.

Any questions? *(Let group ask questions.)* Has anyone done this activity before? *(If there are participants that have done this before you might encourage them to not take a leadership role in solving the problem.)*

OK, here we go and remember you can start over at any time." *(Make sure to let participants know when they are making an illegal move.)*

*(See the solution on the next page.)*

---

**Debrief:**

- ▶ What was this activity like for you?
- ▶ What strategies did you use to cope with the stuck points?
- ▶ How many people got frustrated during this activity? Why?
- ▶ How did the group communicate during the problem-solving stage?
- ▶ How did the group respond to the emerging leaders?
- ▶ How did the group deal with having to start over?
- ▶ How is this puzzle like recovery? Work? Home?
- ▶ What do you want to remember about this activity?

**Recovery/Wellness Metaphor:** Show how we often have far more courage and strength than we might initially think we have. Discuss how to work through frustration tolerance and how they responded to leaders emerging in the group. Talk about how the road to recovery isn't always laid out in a simple A to Z format. It can be tricky and sometimes hard to navigate.

**Role of Facilitator:** Emotional safety, monitor frustration levels.

**Where to Find It/How to Make It:** Spaces can be made by cutting up a tarp or even using copy paper. You can also purchase a full set of plastic place holders at Training Wheels, www.trainingwheelsgear.com.

# Traffic Jam Solution for Eight Participants

You can practice this solution sitting at a table. Put sticky notes on the table representing your spots, then use pennies and paper clips as your two different teams. Feel free to label these with the names of the people below to help you understand the correct stepping sequence of this activity.

## STARTING LINE-UP

| Jane | Sue | Deb | Ann | 0 | Bob | Carl | Greg | Paul |
|------|-----|-----|-----|---|-----|------|------|------|

1. Ann moves forward.

| Jane | Sue | Deb | 0 | Ann | Bob | Carl | Greg | Paul |
|------|-----|-----|---|-----|-----|------|------|------|

2. Bob moves around Ann.

| Jane | Sue | Deb | Bob | Ann | 0 | Carl | Greg | Paul |
|------|-----|-----|-----|-----|---|------|------|------|

3. Carl moves forward.

| Jane | Sue | Deb | Bob | Ann | Carl | 0 | Greg | Paul |
|------|-----|-----|-----|-----|------|---|------|------|

4. Ann moves around Carl.

| Jane | Sue | Deb | Bob | 0 | Carl | Ann | Greg | Paul |
|------|-----|-----|-----|---|------|-----|------|------|

5. Deb moves around Bob.

| Jane | Sue | 0 | Bob | Deb | Carl | Ann | Greg | Paul |
|------|-----|---|-----|-----|------|-----|------|------|

6. Sue moves forward.

| Jane | 0 | Sue | Bob | Deb | Carl | Ann | Greg | Paul |
|------|---|-----|-----|-----|------|-----|------|------|

7. Bob moves around Sue.

| Jane | Bob | Sue | 0 | Deb | Carl | Ann | Greg | Paul |
|------|-----|-----|---|-----|------|-----|------|------|

8. Carl moves around Deb.

| Jane | Bob | Sue | Carl | Deb | 0 | Ann | Greg | Paul |
|------|-----|-----|------|-----|---|-----|------|------|

9. Greg moves around Ann.

| Jane | Bob | Sue | Carl | Deb | Greg | Ann | 0 | Paul |
|------|-----|-----|------|-----|------|-----|---|------|

10. Paul moves forward.

| Jane | Bob | Sue | Carl | Deb | Greg | Ann | Paul | 0 |
|------|-----|-----|------|-----|------|-----|------|---|

11. Ann moves around Paul.

| Jane | Bob | Sue | Carl | Deb | Greg | 0 | Paul | Ann |
|------|-----|-----|------|-----|------|---|------|-----|

12. Deb moves around Greg.

| Jane | Bob | Sue | Carl | 0 | Greg | Deb | Paul | Ann |
|------|-----|-----|------|---|------|-----|------|-----|

13. Sue moves around Carl.

| Jane | Bob | 0 | Carl | Sue | Greg | Deb | Paul | Ann |
|------|-----|---|------|-----|------|-----|------|-----|

14. Jane moves around Bob.

| 0 | Bob | Jane | Carl | Sue | Greg | Deb | Paul | Ann |
|---|-----|------|------|-----|------|-----|------|-----|

15. Bob moves forward.

| Bob | 0 | Jane | Carl | Sue | Greg | Deb | Paul | Ann |
|-----|---|------|------|-----|------|-----|------|-----|

16. Carl moves around Jane.

| Bob | Carl | Jane | 0 | Sue | Greg | Deb | Paul | Ann |
|-----|------|------|---|-----|------|-----|------|-----|

17. Greg moves around Sue.

| Bob | Carl | Jane | Greg | Sue | 0 | Deb | Paul | Ann |
|-----|------|------|------|-----|---|-----|------|-----|

18. Paul moves around Deb.

| Bob | Carl | Jane | Greg | Sue | Paul | Deb | 0 | Ann |
|-----|------|------|------|-----|------|-----|---|-----|

19. Deb moves forward.

| Bob | Carl | Jane | Greg | Sue | Paul | 0 | Deb | Ann |
|-----|------|------|------|-----|------|---|-----|-----|

20. Sue moves around Paul.

| Bob | Carl | Jane | Greg | 0 | Paul | Sue | Deb | Ann |
|-----|------|------|------|---|------|-----|-----|-----|

21. Jane moves around Greg.

| Bob | Carl | 0 | Greg | Jane | Paul | Sue | Deb | Ann |
|-----|------|---|------|------|------|-----|-----|-----|

22. Greg moves forward.

| Bob | Carl | Greg | 0 | Jane | Paul | Sue | Deb | Ann |
|-----|------|------|---|------|------|-----|-----|-----|

23. Paul moves around Jane.

| Bob | Carl | Greg | Paul | Jane | 0 | Sue | Deb | Ann |
|-----|------|------|------|------|---|-----|-----|-----|

24. Jane moves forward.

| Bob | Carl | Greg | Paul | 0 | Jane | Sue | Deb | Ann |
|-----|------|------|------|---|------|-----|-----|-----|

# Turning over a New Leaf

**Group Size:** 15–25

**Purpose:** Learn about trust, support, emotional regulation, and increase group cohesion.

**Props Needed:**

1. Plastic Tarp (Tarp size depends on group size)

**Activity Preparation:** Clear space so it is free of obstacles. You need several feet between tarp and walls or chairs.

**Safety:** Make sure group takes this activity seriously and keep safety in high priority. Facilitator should pay close attention to physical and emotional safety during this activity.

**Time Needed:**

- ▶ Directions: 5 minutes
- ▶ Activity: 15–30 minutes
- ▶ Debrief: 10 minutes

**Activity Directions:**

- ▶ Have participants all stand on tarp
- ▶ Tell participants they are to turn over the tarp without touching the group around them

---

**Facilitator Script:** "OK, everyone come on over. First off we need to stand on the tarp. *(With the entire group standing on the tarp)* Your mission is to turn the tarp completely over without touching the ground around the tarp. For safety reasons, there is to be no stacking of people. Everyone must have at least one foot on the tarp with their own weight being supported by that foot. Are there any questions?"

---

**Debrief:**

- ▶ What was that activity like?
- ▶ What was challenging about it?
- ▶ Did you ever want to give up?
- ▶ What did it take to complete the task?

**Variation 1:** See how many times the group can fold the tarp in half without touching the ground.

**Variation 2:** See how many times the group can fold the tarp in half without losing contact with the tarp.

The activity changes with your wording. See if the group can figure out the differences.

# Two Truths and a Lie

**Group Size:** 5–50

**Purpose:** Fun icebreaker to create group cohesion.

**Props Needed:** None

**Activity Preparation:** Need some space to sit/stand around room.

**Time Needed:** Total time 15 minutes
- ▶ Directions: 2 minutes
- ▶ Activity: 8 minutes (depending on how long it takes group to complete task)
- ▶ Debrief: 5 minutes

## Activity Directions:
- ▶ Separate into teams of four
- ▶ You will make three comments about yourself. Two of these things will be true and one will be a lie/fib.
- ▶ The other three group members must decide which is the lie.

**Facilitator Script:** "Hey everyone we are going to get started with a brief icebreaker. Today I would like you to get into groups of four. It is best to be in groups with people that you don't know as well. I would like you to introduce yourself to the other group members by making three comments about yourself. Here is the thing, two of the comments need to be true and one will be a lie. It will be up to the other group members to determine which is the lie. Once the lie has been called out, the next member can introduce themselves. Go around until all members have had the chance to introduce themselves. Any questions?"

## Debrief:
- ▶ Was it difficult for you to come up with your lie?
- ▶ What made this activity fun?
- ▶ How does honesty relate to recovery?
- ▶ Was it difficult to tell the lie?
- ▶ How did you go about determining which was the lie?

**Recovery/Wellness Metaphor:** This activity is a fun way to create group cohesion. It can also be a fun way to start to talk about honesty in recovery.

**Role of Facilitator:** Make sure participants keep their comments brief rather than go in too much depth or take up too much time.

**Variations:** When working with younger groups we suggest that their fib could be a true story with a different ending. Go for Two Fibs and the Truth. This activity is a good way to open the topic of not telling the truth and the effects it has.

# UFO Ball
## *The Value of Connection*

**Group Size:** 1–225

**Purpose:** To demonstrate the value of connection.

**Props Needed:** UFO ball

**Activity Preparation:** Test out your UFO ball to make sure it is working properly.

**Time Needed:** 8–10 minutes

**Safety:** For participants with pacemakers, please have them observe. There is a non-shocking electric current that passes through each participant.

**Activity Directions:**
- ▶ Invite your group to stand or sit in a circle.
- ▶ Conduct a brief discussion on the value of connection. Why is it important? What are the benefits of being connected to a group or an individual?
- ▶ As the facilitator, hold the UFO ball in your left hand and touch one of the metal plates with your left index finger. Ask 'Bob', the person on your left, if he will demonstrate the activity with you. Invite him to touch the other metal plate on the UFO ball with his right index finger without physically touching you (meaning, no skin-to-skin contact between the two of you).
- ▶ Now describe to the group that you may not know very much about 'Bob', your partner, but you both work at the same organization (which is represented by the UFO ball). Explain that when you make a connection with 'Bob' exciting things can happen. At this moment reach up with your right hand and touch Bob's left hand. The moment you make physical contact with Bob's left hand the UFO ball will light up and make noise.
- ▶ Notice the "Ooooh's" and "Ahhhh's" that erupt from the group.
- ▶ This is a wonderful tool used to teach the value of connection in your team.
- ▶ Next, disconnect hands with Bob and invite the entire group to hold hands with the person standing next to them in the circle.
- ▶ Once everyone is connected hand-to-hand, have Bob touch the metal plate on his side of the UFO ball, and you touch the other metal plate. The ball will immediately light up and start making noise again. If one person disconnects hands from the

person next to them, the ball will immediately stop making noise. This is a powerful metaphor to debrief the effects on a team when someone is not fully committed or not giving 100 percent.

▶ The largest group we have experimented with was 225 people and it worked!

**Facilitator Script:** "Please form a circle. What I have here in my hand is called a UFO ball. It looks like a ping-pong ball, but it has two metal plates on it, and when a connection is made between these two plates, the ball lights up and makes noise. *(Demonstrate this. Turn to the person next to you.)* Now Bob, would you help me for a moment? Will you please place your right index finger on the metal plate closest to you? *(Have Bob do this.)* Great, thank you. Now I'm going to place my left index finger on the other metal plate. *(Demonstrate this.)* The ball isn't lighting up yet because we haven't completed our connection. Now, I just met Bob a few weeks ago, but I'm going to guess that the more connections I make with Bob, really cool things will start to happen. *(As you are saying this, reach out your right hand and gesture that Bob should do the same thing with his left hand.)* Bob, if you would reach out and touch my hand with your left hand. *(The moment he touches you the ball will light up and go off.)* Isn't that cool?! I bet each new connection I make with Bob more cool things will happen. *(Demonstrate this by connecting and reconnecting with Bob's hand multiple times in a row.)* Now, let's see if each one of us in the circle has made some sort of connection in today's meeting. Please hold hands with the person on your left and right, and let's see if we can get the connection to go all the way around the circle. *(Disconnect from the person to the right of you. As soon as you see that everyone has connected, touch the metal connector on the ball and then touch hands with the person on your right. The moment you connect with them, the ball will light up and go off. There will be some Oooooh's and Ahhhhh's from the group.)* Isn't that cool!? This is a great metaphor around if everyone is connected to the same mission, vision, or values of our group, then really cool things can happen. But if someone disconnects from the group, it has an effect on everyone else. Someone test it out, because you know you want to. *(Allow for a few people to connect and reconnect.)* It works just like Morse code. This is also a good metaphor around working your treatment plan. *(Disconnect from the group. Make the ball light up all by yourself.)* You can have a connection with yourself. If you are connected to yourself, your treatment plan, your exercise goals, your relationships, your *(insert topic here)*, then we can have more meaningful relationships with others. After all, how can we expect to connect with others when we do not have a connection to ourselves? Plus, the attitudes and energy we bring to our external connections will have an effect on those around us. If someone is committed to being connected to their treatment plan, they can have a more positive impact on their family or their team."

**Variation:** Use the UFO ball in a one-on-one debriefing session. Use the metaphor around connecting to your treatment plan.

**Debriefing Topics:**

- ▶ In what ways are we connected to each other?
- ▶ How can we cultivate the connections on our team?
- ▶ When someone disconnects from the team, how does it affect the others?
- ▶ Describe a time when you felt disconnected.
- ▶ How can we keep a healthy level of energy in our team?

**Where to Find It/How to Make It:** Purchase from the Training Wheels online store, www. trainingwheelsgear.com. It is often carried in science stores and other novelty shops.

# Wizards and Gelflings

**Activity Origin:** Karl Rohnke

**Group Size:** 8–15

**Purpose:** An energizer.

**Props Needed:**
1. A softball that would not hurt if you were to get hit with it.
2. Boundary Markers

**Activity Preparation:**
1. Prep time needed: 5 minutes
2. Prior to class create an open space for play. If you are indoors, put chairs around the perimeter of the room. If you are outside, find an open space to play that is free of debris or obstacles.
3. Place boundary markers in a large area that the group will have space to run around. If you have more than fifteen participants, create two areas for play that are near one another. You will need one ball per play area.

**Time Needed:**
▶ Directions: 2 minutes
▶ Activity: 10 minutes
▶ Debrief: 5 minutes

**Activity Directions:**
▶ Have the participants stand in a circle. Include yourself in the circle.
▶ In the universe (as defined by the boundaries of this game), there are two forces at work. Each force is represented by a unique species of beings. As is often the case when two species co-exist, there is tension and competition. The first species is the Wizards. Wizards tend to be pretty serious because they are always thinking—creating spells, calculating formulas, analyzing experiments, chanting ancient rituals . . . you know the type. They like their work a lot and don't like to be distracted. Choose one or more participants (pending group size) to be wizards.

▶ On the other hand, Gelflings love to have FUN (with a capital F!). They frolic, fantasize, sing, dance, merrily enjoying themselves without a care in the world. Well, almost not a care. They must watch out for Wizards. All remaining participants are automatically gelflings.

▶ Wizards have a fixated mindset about Gelflings. See a Gelfling, freeze it! NOW!! Wizards constantly try to freeze Gelflings by touching them with their magic ball (the soft ball you have selected).

▶ As soon as a Gelfling is frozen, it immediately reacts to the suspension of its ability to frolic by putting their hands up in the air and emitting the Universal Gelfling Distress Call: A very high pitched wail, "Help Me, Help Me, Help Me . . ." The physical motion of hands in the air emphasizes this distress chanting out ever so annoyingly, "Help Me, Help Me, Help Me . . ." is the universally recognized Gelfling symbol for "help." This call repeats itself over and over until at least two unfrozen Gelflings surround their frozen partner, joining hands and turn a circle around that person calling out, "Be free Gelfling, Be FREE!" At this joyful juncture, the frozen Gelfling is free to frolic once again.

▶ Wizards hate to see all their cryogenic work undone, so they get particularly upset as Gelflings become unfrozen. Wizards exhibit extra amounts of serious freezing energy when Gelflings congregate around a frozen partner.

▶ There are two ways this game can end. One is the Wizard can freeze all of the Gelflings. The other is for the Gelflings to freeze the Wizard. This takes place when FOUR Gelflings congregate around a frozen Gelfling, turn a circle around them, and call out, "Be free Gelfling, Be FREE!!" It can be quite a challenge to get four Gelflings around a frozen Gelfling without a Wizard taking serious notice.

---

**Facilitator Script:** "Let's form a circle to hear the directions for our next game. *(Wait until everyone is in a circle.)* Great! What's going to happen next is, we're going to play a game that has two types of species in it. In this universe, there are specific boundaries. Does everyone see the marker cones that I have placed out? Everyone must stay within these boundaries. In this universe there are two forces at work and each force is represented by a unique species of beings. As is often the case when two species co-exist, sometimes there is tension and competition between the two. The first species is the Wizards. Now Wizards tend to be pretty serious because they are always thinking—creating spells, calculating formulas, analyzing experiments, chanting ancient rituals . . . you know the type. They like their work a lot and don't like to be distracted. So in a minute, but not yet, we will choose one person to be the wizard. On the other hand, the other type of species is called Gelflings. Now Gelflings love to have FUN—with a capital F! They frolic, fantasize, sing, dance, merrily enjoying themselves without a care in the world. Well, almost not a care. They must watch out for Wizards. All remaining participants are automatically Gelflings. Now the Wizard has a fixated mindset about Gelflings. See a Gelfling, freeze it! NOW!! The Wizard will constantly try to freeze Gelflings by touching them with their magic ball (the soft ball you have selected). As soon as a Gelfling is frozen, it immediately reacts to the suspension of its ability to frolic by putting their hands up in the air and emitting the Universal Gelfling Distress Call: A very high pitched wail that goes like this, 'Help Me, Help Me, Help Me . . .' *(Demonstrate this action and noise.)* If you are a frozen Gelfling, you have to repeat this over and over until at least two unfrozen Gelflings can surround their frozen partner by joining hands and turn a circle around that person calling out, "Be free Gelfling, Be FREE!" *(Demonstrate this with two participants.)* At this joyful juncture, the frozen Gelfling is free to frolic once again. Now the Wizard will **hate** to see their cryogenic work undone, so they get particularly upset as Gelflings become unfrozen. Wizards exhibit extra amounts of serious freezing energy when Gelflings congregate around a frozen partner, which means they will probably be guarding the frozen Gelfling. If the Wizard tags anyone trying to free a Gelfling while they are chanting 'Be Free Gelfling Be Free!', then the originally frozen Gelfling remains frozen and the person who was tagged is also now frozen. So there are two ways this game can end. One, the Wizard can freeze all of the Gelflings. The other is for the Gelflings to freeze the Wizard. This takes place when **FOUR** Gelflings congregate around a frozen Gelfling, turn a circle around them, and call out, 'Be free Gelfling, Be FREE!!' It can be quite a challenge to get four Gelflings around a frozen Gelfling without a Wizard taking serious notice. Are there any questions before we begin?"

---

**Recovery/Wellness Metaphor:** Now if we break this down a little bit, we can take parts of the fun game of Wizards and Gelflings and relate it to recovery. What if the Wizard represented drugs and alcohol? Each time the Wizard tagged someone with the ball, that could represent each time we see a friend relapsing. If all of us are Gelflings, it is our duty to help others when they need help. So each time a Gelfling raised their hands in the air and said "Help me, Help me, Help me!", it was our duty to go and try and give them the help they needed to rid their lives of drugs and alcohol. The phrase "Be free Gelfling be Free!" could represent that the purpose of a sponsor or friend is to help someone know the freedom and forgiveness they can find in recovery. And what would happen if the Wizard froze all of the Gelflings? We need to all be on the lookout for each other so that we can go and help free them from harmful things they might be doing in their lives.

**Debrief:**

The intent of this game is to be an energizer; however, if you choose to debrief this activity with a recovery and wellness metaphor, here are some questions you could use:

- ▶ If you were to think about the roles of this game and relate them to the real world, who might the wizard represent? Who would the Gelflings be?
- ▶ What if the Wizard represented drugs and alcohol?
- ▶ Have you ever tried helping someone that was calling out for help, but outside influences prevented you from helping?

**Where to Find It/How to Make It:** We recommend the Knobby Gertie ball as the magic orb for this game. This ball can be found on Amazon or at other specialty toy stores.

# Symbolic Learning

# 1st Things 1st

**Group Size:** 5–50

**Purpose:** Increase awareness, increase organization and time management life skills, introduce tool, and practice using tool.

**Props Needed:**
1. Paper
2. Pen
3. 1st Things 1st Handout

**Activity Preparation:**
1. Print off enough handouts for each participant.

**Time Needed:** 45–90 minutes
- ► Directions: none
- ► Activity: 45 minutes
- ► Debrief: 15–30 minutes

**Set-Up:** Print off enough handouts for all participants. Ensure a hard surface to write on, this can either be tables or clipboards.

**Activity Directions:**
- ► Explain the purpose of having a written agenda.
- ► Explain the correlation to PAWS and how writing things down in early recovery is especially helpful.
- ► Introduce 1st things 1st tool.
- ► Have group members complete their sample 1st things 1st sample week.

**Facilitator Script:** "OK everyone, let's gather 'round and find a seat. Today we are going to go over a creative way to help you deal with PAWS or Post-Acute Withdrawal Syndrome. As you may know this can last anywhere from 18 months to 5 years into abstinence from alcohol and other drugs. One of the ways that PAWS can affect you is in your ability to maintain an optimum level of organization. Post-Acute Withdrawal is the brain's adjustment to the absence of alcohol and other drugs. When our brains are used to the presence of alcohol and other drugs it sometimes takes a while for them to get used to the absence of them. PAWS affect things like sleep, physical coordination, memory, and organization.

The 1st Things 1st tool can be a way to help you with organization. Here is the handout we will be looking at today. *(Pass out the handout.)*

Notice on the right-hand side of the page there are a couple of To Do lists. There are Have to's, Need to's, Want to's, as well as a space for you to write out your meetings and reminders.

Here is how the lists work.

The Have to's are agenda items with a specific time sensitivity or heightened priority.

These are things like appointments, school assignments, medication refill dates, and work shifts. These items cannot easily be changed or have a high recovery oriented priority. A high recovery oriented priority is something that must be done within the next twenty-four hours in order to support your overall well-being, for example; Call Probation Officer by 5 p.m. today.

The Need to's are agenda items with a moderate or flexible time sensitivity, moderate priority, or everything else.

These are things like 12-step meetings, sponsor time, homework time (school or therapy), and running errands. These items can be juggled around and do not have to be completed within the next twenty-four-hour time frame. An example of this would be schedule an evaluation within the next two weeks. Another example of this might be evening and morning recovery practices like prayer and meditation. These are need to's because we need to do them, but they can be moved around depending on the Have to's of the day. Something to be aware of is that Need to's become Have to's when they are postponed long enough; watch out for procrastination.

The Want to's are agenda items that are fun, pleasurable, and promote self-care.

This is the fun stuff. Some of these items include going to fellowship, working out, going on a hike, crafting, and anything that brings you joy and reduces stress. It is important to have enough want to's sprinkled throughout the week so that getting through the Have to's and Need to's don't seem so hard.

The Meetings section is a place where you can put down the weekly meetings you plan on attending, or maybe a new meeting you would like to remember to try out. This section can also be used for pop-up meetings like a doctor appointment or even reoccurring appointments like a therapist appointment.

The Reminder section can be a great place to write down things you don't want to forget like homework, calls you need to make, or anything else you want to keep in the forefront of your mind.

On the left-hand side of the handout you will find a weekly schedule. The first column is a place where you can start and end your day based on what works for you. The rest of the columns are places where you can plot out a schedule that allows you to start marking things off your Have to, Need to, and Want to lists.

Are there any questions about the hand out?

*(Once questions have been answered)* Great, let's take about twenty minutes to start to fill out the 1st Things 1st list.

*(Be sure to give time warnings when you are halfway and three-quarters of the way through the allotted time. Also, it might be useful to see if anyone needs individual help during this time.)*

OK great, who would like to share what they wrote down?" *(Give participants time to share if they wish. Be sure to leave time to debrief.)*

## Debrief:

- ▶ What was challenging about this activity?
- ▶ Which section was easiest/hardest to do?
- ▶ How did you feel about presenting your 1st Things 1st week?
- ▶ What did you think as you listened to your peers present theirs?
- ▶ What is the difference between recovery oriented Have to, Need to, and Want to versus addiction oriented Have to, Need to, and Want to?
- ▶ What actions bring you closer to recovery or closer to relapse?

## Recovery/Wellness Metaphor:

**Role of Facilitator:** There are three lists on the 1st things 1st agenda Have to, Need to, and Want to. It is important to have all sections completed and then go in and plot them on the agenda. Start out plotting the Have to's as there is not any flexibility with Have to's. Then go to the Need to's, as there is more flexibility with them. Pay attention to complete Need to's in time before they become Have to's. In other words if I have a Need to—that is get my medication refilled—and I keep postponing it, eventually it will become a Have to when my medication runs out.

**Variations:** This can be done in individual sessions or as homework.

# 1st things 1st

Have to – Agenda item with a specific time sensitivity or heightened priority

Need to – Agenda item with a moderate or flexible time sensitivity, moderate priority, or everything else

Want to – Agenda item that is fun, pleasurable, and promotes self-care.

**WEEKLY SCHEDULE**

| TIME | MON | TUES | WED | THURS | FRI | SAT | SUN |
|------|-----|------|-----|-------|-----|-----|-----|
|  |  |  |  |  |  |  |  |
|  |  |  |  |  |  |  |  |
|  |  |  |  |  |  |  |  |
|  |  |  |  |  |  |  |  |
|  |  |  |  |  |  |  |  |
|  |  |  |  |  |  |  |  |
|  |  |  |  |  |  |  |  |

Source information for worksheet Created by Marc Pimsler

# To Do

**Need To**

**Have To**

**Want To**

**Meetings**

**Remember**

Source information for worksheet Created by Marc Pimsler

**REPRODUCIBLE**

# The Bison and the Cow

**Group Size:** Any

**Purpose:** To explore how one deals with confrontation, stress, or any disturbance.

**Props Needed:**

1. The Bison and the Cow story

**Activity Preparation:**

1. Prep time needed: 5 minutes
2. The activity can be accomplished in any setting: individual or group setting.

**Time Needed:**

- ▶ Directions: Facilitator will read script, or have a group member read the story.
- ▶ Activity: 10–20 minutes, with discussion.
- ▶ Debrief: 10 minutes; may be longer with a larger group.

**Set-Up:**

- ▶ The activity can be accomplished in any setting: individual or group setting.
- ▶ Participants may be seated in a classroom or gathered around in a circle.

**Activity Directions:**

- ▶ Have participants find a seat or gather together; they may be seated in classroom style or in a large circle.
- ▶ Explain the purpose of the activity.
- ▶ Read Facilitators Script, complete handout toward end of activity.

---

**Facilitator Script:** "Let's gather around. I would like to tell you the story of the Bison and the Cow. Now as you listen consider how you approach the storms in your life. Picture this, you are standing out in an open pasture. You look up at the sky and see an ominous looking storm headed your way. The clouds are dark and threatening, the wind is whipping around you uncontrollably. There are blinding flashes of lightning and deafening claps of thunder. In the field with you are two types of animals, a cow and a bison. Both of these animals weather storms very differently. When a storm is brewing, the Cow's strategy is to turn from it and run in the opposite direction. The Cow is trying to get away from the storm as quickly as possible, trying to outrun the storm. The longer it tries, and the closer the storm comes, the more the Cow runs frantically to avoid it at all costs, running over anything in its way. As it runs it expends more energy running away, and gets more and more tired. Cows are not very fast. Trying to get away, they end up running with the storm as it catches up and overtakes the Cow. The intention is to get away from the storm but the outcome is the Cow spends most of his time in the storm.

The Bison is used to living on the Great Plains, and used to storms coming up quickly. When the storm comes, the Bison turns to face into the storm, heading straight into it so it can get through it. The Bison is accepting of the changes in weather, and is steadfast in its purpose. It is strong, standing its ground and pressing forward. It knows that while there is a storm, it too will pass, and the more it leans into the storm the quicker it will go through it. The Bison's intention is to get through the storm and the outcome is just that.

Today we are going to discuss how we approach confrontation and disturbance. Take a minute to reflect on confrontation. What is the purpose? What might be going on when we are met with confrontation? *(Give participants a little time to reflect on their response to confrontation or what they have observed in either self or others.)* It is normal for people to have fears, worries, or anxieties about what might happen in recovery. This discussion is about how we deal with those fears, worries, or anxieties. Let's consider a storm that is on the horizon. When we see a weather storm coming, what do we see? *(Give participants a chance to describe: dark clouds, rain, wind, weather changes, etc.)*

When confronted with challenges or storms, do you run away to seek shelter and get exhausted doing so, or do you lean in and remain steadfast, knowing you will find your way through it? Which are you more like: the Cow or the Bison?

Some would say that we are either about to enter a storm, are in the storm, or have just come through a storm. Life is not always easy. Problems and challenges will always come. Take time to complete your handout at this time."

## Debrief:

- ▶ What was your experience as you listened to the story?
- ▶ What thoughts were you aware of?
- ▶ Storms are inevitable. How do you approach a storm? Are you more like the Cow or the Bison?
- ▶ If you are more like the Cow, what qualities do you have for dealing with a storm? How do these qualities help you or challenge you?
- ▶ If you are more like the Bison, what qualities do you have for dealing with a storm? How do these qualities help you or challenge you?

- ▶ If you are more like a Bison, in what specific challenges might you be more like a Cow?
- ▶ If you are more like a Cow, in what specific challenges might you be more like a Bison?
- ▶ Are there other ways to deal with a storm? How will those ways help or challenge you?
- ▶ What did you learn about one another?
- ▶ What can you do to help others face a storm, or change their approach to their storm?

**Recovery/Wellness Metaphor:** Storms are part of life. It is in how we approach a storm that we learn more about our character or ability to weather the storm. When a storm or challenge comes, we can run from it, but eventually it will be something for us to deal with. If left undealt with, by avoiding or running, it may eventually become hurtful to us, or to others. While it may seem uncomfortable to approach a challenge head-on, with plans and support, we can weather a storm in a way that we may get through it quicker than avoiding it.

**Role of Facilitator:** Take time to debrief the story with participants, helping them explore the different ways to confront a storm. You may explore with them how they see others as well as themselves in the process. Finally it may be helpful for them to look at the benefits and consequences of holding firm to their approach, if it is the Cow, and what steps they will take to be more like the Bison.

**Variations:** When exploring how to deal with confrontation or challenges through the metaphor of a storm, the facilitator can use a specific example to explore. For example, some may perceive one type of challenge difficult, for example, changing jobs; another may embrace the challenge. Using specific examples—vocation, education, relationships, medication compliance, physical health, emotional health, nutrition—explore how the participants weather various storms.

# Facing Challenges: the Bison versus Cow Approach

What challenges am I most likely to face head-on?

What challenges am I most likely to shy away from?

What do I need to get through my challenge like a Bison, quicker and in better shape, than the Cow?

# Body Part Debrief™

**Created By:** Michelle Cummings. Also found in *A Teachable Moment*, by Cain, Cummings and Stanchfield.

**Group Size:** any

**Purpose:** To reflect using the metaphors of the body. The Body Part Debrief activity is a great activity for both new and seasoned facilitators. It is simple enough in nature that groups of any age will use it with ease. The body parts have a "coolness" factor to them that fosters a safe environment for people to talk. If you are having a hard time getting your participants to share or reflect, this activity will help.

**Props Needed:** Images or tangible items shaped like body parts.

**Activity Preparation:**
1. Prep time needed: 10–20 minutes if making your own.

**Time Needed:**
- ▶ Directions: 2 minutes
- ▶ Debrief: 15–30 minutes. Depending on the size of your group. Allot 1 minute per person.

**Activity Directions:**
- ▶ Invite your group to sit or stand in a circle.
- ▶ Frontload the debriefing conversation by identifying each body part and giving an example of the type of answer someone could give.
- ▶ Have each member of the group share a take-away from the day.

---

**Facilitator Script:** "Today to close our program we are going to use an activity called The Body Part Debrief. You'll notice here in the center of the circle there are several body parts. I want you to think about what you have experienced today, and relate a notable experience to the metaphor of one of the body parts you see here. *(Share an example for each part you have in the center of the circle. Additional examples below.)* For example, if you were to choose the brain, you might share with the group something new you learned about yourself or someone else in the group. If you choose the heart, you might share a feeling you experienced, or something you took to heart. With the hand you might acknowledge or give someone a hand for a job well

**213**

done, or discuss something that you learned tonight that will support or lend a hand to your recovery. If you choose the stomach you might share something that pushed you outside your comfort zone or something that took guts for you to say or do. The foot might represent a new direction you'd like to see yourself go. I'd like each person to share at least one time. I don't care who goes first. I'd like you to come to the middle, pick up the part you are using, share your thoughts, then put the part back in the center. That way someone else could use that same part when it is their turn. Are there any questions on what we are doing? *(Pause for questions.)* Let's begin. Who would like to go first?"

**Facilitator Note:** If you have a large group or are short on time, have participants share with a partner first. Then ask for four to five people to share with the large group. This way everyone gets an opportunity to debrief, and allows for a large group experience as well.

Examples for each metaphoric part:

### Eyes
- What is something new that you saw in yourself or someone else today?
- What vision do you have for yourself/the group?
- What qualities do you see in yourself?
- How did you see yourself interacting within the group?

### Stomach
- Describe something that took guts for you to do.
- What pushed you outside your comfort zone?
- What sick feelings have you felt before?
- Was something hard for you to stomach?
- Name a few things that might take a while to digest.

### Brain
- Describe something new that you learned about yourself, another participant, or the group.
- What thoughts do you have about what you learned today?
- What did you learn through your experience?

### Heart
- Describe a feeling that you experienced.
- What things come from the heart?
- What means a lot to you?

## Hands

- ▶ In what way did the group support you?
- ▶ Describe someone you would like to give a hand to for a job well done.
- ▶ How did you lend a hand during the activity?

## Ears

- ▶ Describe something you listened to.
- ▶ What was a good idea you heard?
- ▶ Describe something that was hard to hear—did you receive constructive feedback or not-so-constructive feedback?

## Smiley Face

- ▶ Describe something that made you smile or laugh.
- ▶ What are some of your positive attributes?
- ▶ What are some positive attributes of the group?

## Feet

- ▶ What direction would you like to see yourself/the group go?
- ▶ Have you ever stuck your foot in your mouth and said something you wished you wouldn't have?

## Lips

- ▶ Have you ever said anything that has hurt someone's feelings?
- ▶ Give an example of when your actions spoke louder than your words.
- ▶ Is there anything you would like to say to the group?

## Human Bone

- ▶ What strengths do you have?
- ▶ Have you ever come close to a breaking point?
- ▶ Have you ever felt broken?

## Spine

- ▶ What is the backbone of your company/family/organization?
- ▶ What took a lot of backbone to do?
- ▶ What took courage to say out loud?

## Nose

- ▶ Did you stick your nose into someone else's business?
- ▶ What about that performance really stunk? What would you have changed?

**Where to Find It/How to Make It:** Training Wheels has a few sets of The Body Part Debrief activity to choose from, www.trainingwheelsgear.com. These parts are made of stress-reliever material. You could also print photos or clip art images of body parts.

# Breaking Up Is Hard to Do

**Group Size:** 5–20

**Purpose:**

- ▶ Recognize that early recovery is a lot like breaking up with a partner.
- ▶ Create a step forward in the healing process.
- ▶ Physically create some separation between us and our addiction.

**Props Needed:**

1. Paper
2. Pen

**Activity Preparation:** Prep time needed: 5 minutes to gather pen and paper

**Time Needed:**

- ▶ Directions: 5–10 minutes
- ▶ Activity: 20 minutes
- ▶ Debrief: 15 minutes

**Set-Up:** It would be helpful to have a hard surface for participants to write on, like a table or clipboard.

**Activity Directions:**

- ▶ Provide a piece of paper and pen for each participant.
- ▶ Each person is to write a goodbye letter to their addiction, drug of choice, or preferred way of acting out.
- ▶ Give participants about twenty minutes to write the letter.
- ▶ Have members read their letter out loud.

---

**Facilitator Script:** "Gather 'round everyone. Some of you may have noticed that engaging recovery can, in some ways, be similar to breaking up with a long-term relationship. We know that before we can start a new relationship we have to truly end the last one, otherwise that is called cheating.

In this session, we are going to write a breakup letter to addiction or, if you would like, specifically your drug of choice. *(This also works well for process addictions or acting out behaviors.)* In your letter, be sure to cover the following components in order to make the greatest impact.

- ▶ Acknowledge all that you liked about your addiction/DOC/acting out
- ▶ Thank it for serving its purpose and honor the role it served
- ▶ Tell it what no longer works for you
- ▶ Review all the reasons you can no longer stay together
- ▶ Be kind but be clear this has got to end!

We will take about fifteen to twenty minutes to complete the letter. Don't overthink this and let it come from your heart. Does anyone have any questions?

*(Give participants about twenty minutes to complete the letter. Make sure to give time warnings when they are halfway and three-quarters of the way through the allotted time.)*

Great, we find that it is really beneficial to the process to read the letters out loud. In many ways, it makes it more real. Who would like to go first?" *(Go around the circle or ask for volunteers.)*

## Debrief:

- ▶ What was it like to think of your addiction as a relationship?
- ▶ What emotions did you notice when you wrote the letter?
- ▶ What story were you telling yourself about this relationship?
- ▶ Does this story match your experience?
- ▶ Did you hear the voice of your addiction revolting against the breakup?
- ▶ How does misplaced loyalty show up in this relationship?
- ▶ What is hard about leaving your addiction behind?
- ▶ What is easy about leaving it behind?

**Recovery/Wellness Metaphor:** We are so involved with our addictions that it is very much like being in a relationship. Especially when you think of the time, energy, money, and other resources we put into them. Doing this activity is a nice way to create some intentional space of separation.

**Role of Facilitator:** Support participants in thinking of their addiction as a meaningful relationship that they are seeking to end. Some participants find this activity funny and that is OK, although when taken seriously, it can be a very powerful experience especially when you add the aspect of burning the letter.

**Variations:** Have group members read the letter outside and then burn the letter in a fire pit or some other safe place. Doing so will add symbolism and be a ceremonial way of truly letting go. Another variation is that this can be done as an individual session. This can also be separated into two distinct processes: (1) the writing of the letter (can also be homework) and (2) the reading/burning of the letter.

# The Butterfly Story

**Group Size:** Any

**Purpose:** To increase awareness of one's response to another's struggle.

**Props Needed:**
1. The Butterfly story—can either be copied as a handout or projected on a screen.

**Activity Preparation:**
1. Prep time needed: 5 minutes
2. The activity can be accomplished in any setting: individual or group.

**Time Needed:**
- ▶ Directions: Facilitator will read The Butterfly story, or have a group member read the story.
- ▶ Activity: 10 minutes, with discussion.
- ▶ Debrief: 10 minutes; may be more with a larger group.

**Activity Directions:**
- ▶ Have participants find a seat.
- ▶ If you are projecting the story onto a screen, have participants face the projected image or story.
- ▶ Explain the purpose of the activity.
- ▶ Read Facilitato's Script and The Butterfly story.

**Facilitator Script:** "Hey everyone, gather 'round so we can get started with today's group. Let's take time to listen to the story of The Butterfly.

**The Butterfly Story:**

A man found a cocoon of a butterfly. One day a small opening appeared. He sat and watched the butterfly for several hours as it struggled to squeeze its body through the tiny hole. Then it stopped, as if it couldn't go further. So, the man decided to help the butterfly. He took a pair of scissors and snipped off the remaining bits of cocoon. The butterfly emerged easily but it had a swollen body and shriveled wings. The man continued to watch it, expecting that any minute the wings would enlarge and expand enough to support the body, neither happened! In fact, the butterfly spent the rest of its life crawling around. It was never able to fly. This is what the man, in his kindness and haste, did not understand: The restricting cocoon and the struggle required by the butterfly to get through the tiny opening is nature's way of forcing the fluid from the body into the wings so that it would be ready for flight. Sometimes struggles are exactly what we need in our lives. Going through life with no obstacles would cripple us. Without our struggles we could never be as strong as we could have been and we would never fly.

Today's activity is designed to explore the role of struggle in a process of change. We can all identify with the experience of struggling and wanting things to be easier. Some of us might have questioned why we have to struggle so much. When we think about struggle, either our own or someone else's experience, we may become uncomfortable. It may feel like we need to jump in and help them through the struggle, instead of allowing them the time and space to go through their own process on their own terms. Or maybe we wished someone could come and save us from our struggle.

Take a moment to think about how going through struggles and obstacles in your life might have made you much stronger than had you not gone through them. *(Either have the group process personal examples of this lesson or debrief the story.)*

## Debrief:

▶ What did you notice as you listened to the story?
▶ What thoughts were you aware of as you listened to the story?
▶ What are some of the challenges one faces when observing someone else's struggle?
▶ What might be getting in your way when you look at your own struggle?

**Recovery/Wellness Metaphor:** Sometimes we wish or wait for a knight in shining armor to come and rescue us when we experience struggle. Recovery is about perseverance and leaning into the discomfort. Another way of looking at this story is when observing someone else's process of change, sometimes this may make us uncomfortable. We may choose to jump in without thought and take action for or give solutions when it would be best for them to do it for themselves. There is strength in the struggle of growth. Sometimes all we need to do is put one foot in front of the other and walk through it.

**Role of Facilitator:** Take time to debrief the story with participants, helping them explore what perceptions or actions that may keep them out of balance when observing their struggle or the struggle of another. Through the metaphor of the story, encourage participants to explore and identify their internal response, and outward expression toward others who may struggle. Assist participants to explore the consequences and benefits of over-functioning for others.

**Variations:** This can be accomplished in individual sessions.

# Change Debrief

**Source:** *Setting the Conflict Compass*, by Michelle Cummings and Mike Anderson

**Group Size:** 5–50

**Purpose:** Processing Tool

**Props Needed:**
1. Object in the shape of an Egg
2. Object in the shape of a Carrot
3. Object in the shape of a Coffee Bean
4. Object in the shape of an Ice Cube

**Activity Preparation:**
1. Prep time needed: 5 minutes
2. Prior to class make sure you have all your props.

**Time Needed:**
- ▶ Directions: 2 minutes
- ▶ Activity: 10 minutes
- ▶ Debrief: 15 minutes

**Set-Up:** Gather the group together so that they can hear the story and process how it relates to change.

**Activity Directions:**
- ▶ Have the group gather around to discuss.
- ▶ Pull out one prop at a time and ask the group to discuss what happens when the item is placed in a "hot water" situation. Frontloading the metaphors that accompany each part is important to the level of depth participants will share.

---

**Facilitator Script:** "Hey everyone, gather around. Today we are going to look at how food has a lot to teach us about being in Hot Water situations. A hot water situation can be how we respond to change, anger, or any other aspect of life. Let's imagine that this is a boiling pot of water (*point out a chair or table that can represent a boiling pot of water, so that when you place* *the objects on it they are in the boiling pot of water).* Let's discuss what happens to each object when it is placed in a hot water situation.

*(Pull out the egg)* What happens to the egg in a hot water situation? *(Let the group come up with suggestions)* Yes! When the Egg is placed in a hot water situation the outside stays the same but the inside changes and becomes hard. Sometimes we can look like we have our game face on but on the inside we are becoming hardened by the experience. If the egg is left in boiling water too long it will crack or explode.

*(Pull out the carrot)* What happens to the carrot in a hot water situation? *(Let the group come up with suggestions)* Yes! A carrot will turn soft and change itself dramatically when placed in hot water. We all know people who turn to mush and do whatever the "hot water" wants them to do when faced with a change.

*(Pull out the rock)* What happens to the rock in a hot water situation? *(Let the group come up with suggestions)* Yes! When a rock is placed in a pot of boiling water, it will sink to the bottom and not change. How does this change style affect the environment? When making soup, having a rock in the pot doesn't have much affect on the rock but it sure can spoil the soup.

*(Pull out the ice cube)* What happens to the ice cube in a hot water situation? *(Let the group come up with suggestions)* Yes! Like the others there are pros and cons to being an ice cube. What are the cons? A cube of ice can lose itself in the hot water situation. What are the pros? A cube of ice can diffuse the situation and cool things down.

*(Pull out the coffee bean)* What happens to the coffee bean in a hot water situation? *(Let the group come up with suggestions)* Yes! A coffee bean certainly does change and adapt to the situation and will leave the hot water even better as a result of the heat. One way to respond to change is by being energized and influential when change occurs."

## Debrief:

► What do you think is your typical change stage when first faced with a new change?
► Does this stage encourage or prevent a conflict with others?
► How do you approach others who have different perspectives and opinions about the change?
► Describe the positive aspects of knowing what change stage each individual is in.

**Recovery/Wellness Metaphor:** Often, individuals will go through each stage in a changing environment. Use the props as a timeline to describe a person's journey through the change.

Here is a story that could be a good topic of discussion to use with The Change Debrief.

## IN THE TEST KITCHEN OF LIFE

A young woman was complaining to her father about how difficult her life had become. He said nothing but took her to the kitchen and set three pans of water to boiling. To the first pan, he added carrots; to the second, eggs; and to the third, ground coffee. After all three had cooked, he put their contents into separate bowls and asked his daughter to cut into the eggs and carrots and smell the coffee. "What does this all mean?" she asked impatiently.

"Each food," he said, "teaches us something about facing adversity, as represented by the boiling water. The carrot went in hard but came out soft and weak. The eggs went in fragile but came out hardened. The coffee, however, changed the water to something better."

"Which will you be like as you face life?" he asked. "Will you give up, become hard, or transform adversity into triumph? As the "chef" of your own life, what will you bring to the table?"

**Where to Find It/How to Make It:** Training Wheels sells a set of stress reliever parts for this activity. There are five parts packaged in a tidy 7 × 9-inch mesh envelope. The stress relievers are all made of polyurethane, latex free.

**Purchase from the Training Wheels store:** Setting the Conflict Compass, Change Debrief

You can also source all of these items from your kitchen and backyard. We recommend hard-boiling the eggs before you bring them to your group!

**Suggestion:** If you are trying to encourage everyone to be like the coffee bean and be energized about the new changes, you could send everyone home with a bag of coffee beans encouraging them to be energetic change agents.

# Coping Skits

**Group Size:** 5–30

**Purpose:** Promote teamwork, identification, enactment of coping skills, and social perspective-taking.

**Props Needed:** Ten to Twelve props per group that participants can use to dress up or accessorize their character in their skits (e.g., hair ornaments, hats, beaded necklaces, badges, cups, pens or pencils, deck of cards, sunglasses, toothbrush, doll, toy cell phone, book, etc.).

**Activity Preparation:**
1. Prep time needed: 15–30 minutes to gather props for skits

**Time Needed:**
- ▶ Directions: 5 minutes
- ▶ Activity: 20 minutes for development of skit; 5 minutes each group to enact their skit for larger group to view
- ▶ Debrief: 10 minutes

**Set-Up:** Find a space that is free from debris and where the groups can form, come up with their storyline, accessorize their character, and practice their skit.

**Activity Directions:**
- ▶ This activity requires participants to work as a team to develop and enact skits pertaining to personally relevant problems and ways of coping with those problems.
- ▶ Give each group a bag filled with four to five props. Instruct participants that they must do the following:
  - ☐ Use as many of the props in their skit as possible.
  - ☐ Assign each member of the group a role in the skit.
  - ☐ Include at least two scenes in their skits: one portraying a problem situation and one portraying functional or healthy ways of coping with the problem. Remind them to think about the different coping skills that they are learning in their individual and group counseling.
- ▶ Give the groups the freedom to develop the skit in their own creative, playful, and personally meaningful fashion.

- ▶ Allow the groups about eight to ten minutes to develop and rehearse their skit.
- ▶ Then, have the groups present their skit to one another. While one group is performing, ask the other groups to figure out the problem being portrayed and the coping mechanisms used to handle the problem. Invite the observing group to suggest other strategies for coping with the problem.

**Facilitator Script:** "Let's form a circle to hear the directions for our Activity: Coping Skits. First, we will count off to identify our groups. *(Have participants count off or otherwise separate into smaller groups.)* Now that you are in your assigned groups, you are going to create skits. This activity is called Coping Skits. Your objective is to create a skit using all the props you have been given. All members of the group need to have a role. In your group think about a problem that you might encounter or one that you have previously encountered that might challenge your recovery. Now thinking about your coping skills, you will demonstrate a coping skill or solution for the problem through your skit. You will have twenty minutes to develop and practice your story line. When we reconvene you will enact your skit for the entire group."

## Debrief:

- ▶ What was the experience like for you? Was it fun?
- ▶ Was it easy or difficult for your group? How so?
- ▶ Did you like how your group performed? Why or why not?
- ▶ What could your group have done to work better as a team?
- ▶ Have any of you been in the situations that you acted out in the skit?
- ▶ What did you learn from the skit about coping with problems?
- ▶ What did you learn about others in the group?
- ▶ What was it like playing different roles (e.g., counselor, security officer)? Do you see now how they might feel about you? How so?
- ▶ What thoughts/feelings came to mind when you were doing this activity?
- ▶ How can this activity help you change your behavior, both here or at home?
- ▶ How does this activity help you become the kind of person you want to be? Or, does it get in the way, or make it more difficult in some way? Why?

**Recovery/Wellness Metaphor:** This is a fun way to reinforce skills already learned while simultaneously creating group cohesion. Participants are encouraged to be as creative as they can in their problem-solving skills.

**Role of Facilitator:**

- ► Keep groups on task for developing their skit. If they get stuck, or shy about their part acting in the coping skit, coach them with ideas to help them with moving forward. Encourage groups to keep it fun, appropriate, yet simple.
- ► Keep an eye on the class as they observe each group. There may be a lot of laughter as participants enact their skit. There may also be valuable information, lessons learned, or coping skills you are attempting to reinforce for the larger group.

**Variations:** Use a specific problem area instead of leaving it up to the group. Use internal characters to visualize the "voices in my head."

**Where to Find It/How to Make It:** Props can be acquired anywhere—toy stores, garage sales, Goodwill, and party stores are a few of our favorites.

**Source:** Adapted from Yurkovic and Sherman, 2009.

# Crunch Time

**Group Size:** 5–25

**Purpose:** Teach mindfulness in a fun way, create group cohesion.

**Props Needed:**
1. Hot Water
2. Fragrant Tea Bags
3. Ice
4. Hot/Cold Cups

**Activity Preparation:**
Prep time needed: 15 minutes prior to class
1. Gather ingredients
2. Heat up the water for tea

**Time Needed:**
- ▶ Directions: 5 minutes
- ▶ Activity: 30 minutes
- ▶ Debrief: 15 minutes

**Set-Up:** Lay out props so that participants have access to them. It is recommended to have participants circled around a table.

**Activity Directions:**
- ▶ Have the participants gather around the props and have a seat
- ▶ Walk participants through visualizing making a cup of tea. Prompts below.
- ▶ Invite participants to take a cup of hot water and a tea bag
- ▶ Mindfully make tea
- ▶ Mindfully smell and taste tea
- ▶ Invite participants to take a cup of ice
- ▶ Mindfully taste and crunch ice
- ▶ Go back and forth
- ▶ Debrief

**Facilitator Script:** "Welcome everyone, please have a seat around this table. Today we are going to have some fun with mindfulness. Anyone have experiences with mindfulness training? *(Process previous experiences, briefly.)* Today we are going to try something a little different. The truth is you can do anything mindlessly. In fact, many people spend most of their lives mindlessly. The opposite is true as well, you can do anything mindfully. You can be mindful while brushing your teeth, eating, walking, driving, or having a conversation. Another word for mindfulness is awareness. The goal is to just be with the experience rather than trying to fix, fade, or run from it. So today we are going to practice increasing our awareness with some mindfulness training.

Let's start with making a cup of tea mindfully. Everyone needs a cup of hot water and a tea bag. *(Help participants to get their cup of hot water and tea bag.)* First, see if you can feel the sensation of holding a hot cup. See if the hot water has a scent. Look at the water and notice the color. Now open the package the tea bag is in. Breathe in the aroma of the tea bag. See what you notice within yourself. Now take the tea bag and put it into the water. Watch . . . Listen . . . Smell . . . use all of your senses to really pull in the experience of the moment. For the next minute allow the tea to steep while just looking into the cup. See what you notice as you sit with your cup of tea. *(Allow a minute to pass.)*

Now in a moment you will taste your tea. Notice what you feel within yourself physically, emotionally. Notice the thoughts going through your mind as you anticipate drinking your tea. Raise up the cup and take a big breath in through your nose to really get a sense of the aroma of the tea. Close your eyes and taste the tea. Notice the sensation of the liquid in your mouth before you swallow it. Swallow the tea. See if you can notice the hot liquid as it makes its journey down. With your eyes closed, sit a moment before taking another sip. Notice any desire to move faster or a yearning for another taste. Stretch out the moment, especially if you are craving another sip on any level. Play with that space and see what that feels like. When you are ready you can open your eyes and take another sip. Then, once again take a moment to sit with what your experience is right here, right now.

OK, let's add in another experience to the mix. Everyone take a cup of ice. *(Pass out cups with ice in them to all participants.)* Now see what you notice within yourself. Lift the cup of ice to your nose, take a deep breath in through your nose and see what you notice. Can you feel the cool air? Does it have a scent? See if you can sense the cool of the ice through the cup as you hold it. Take one of the pieces of ice and hold it in your hands. Notice your attention and reactions. Take a piece of ice and put it in your mouth. Notice what that is like. If you want, you can crunch the ice and eat it. Notice the sound and sensation. As you swallow the ice see if you can follow its journey as it makes its way down.

Go back to your tea. Take another sip of the hot tea and see if you notice anything different between the hot tea, the ice, and now the hot tea again. Play with the sensations and things you notice. Go back and forth and see what you notice in your physical, mental, and emotional experiences. Let's take five minutes to go between the two.

Great job everyone!"

## Debrief:

▶ What did you notice in that experience?

▶ What was a challenge?

▶ What did you enjoy?

▶ How can this relate to wellness and recovery?

▶ Would you be willing to make mindfulness a part of your daily practices?

**Recovery/Wellness Metaphor:** The more we are able to increase our awareness, the greater our ability to be in the moment with mastery.

**Role of Facilitator:** Help guide the process and keep the group on task.

**Variations:** Feel free to make adjustments for population. For example, if you cannot use hot tea consider using ice tea and switching from sweet tea to unsweetened tea.

**Where to Find It/How to Make It:** Local store

# Feeding the Two Wolves

**Group Size:** 5–50

**Purpose:** Increase awareness, recognition of how beliefs, thoughts, and actions either propel us forward or backward.

**Props Needed:**

1. Feeding the Two Wolves story—can be copied as a handout or projected on a screen.

**Activity Preparation:**

1. Prep time needed: 5 minutes

**Time Needed:**

- ▶ Directions: Facilitator will read "Feeding the Two Wolves" story, or have a group member read the story.
- ▶ Activity: 10–20 minutes, with discussion.
- ▶ Debrief: 10 minutes; may be more with larger group size.

**Set-Up:**

- ▶ The activity can be accomplished in any setting: individual or group.
- ▶ Participants may be seated in a classroom style set-up or seated in a circle.

**Activity Directions:**

- ▶ Explain the purpose of the activity.
- ▶ Read Facilitator's Script and *The Story of Two Wolves*.

---

**Facilitator Script:** "Alright everyone, come and have a seat. I wanted to share a story with you today. It is a wise old tale known as the Story of the Two Wolves. There once was a wise old grandfather and his young grandson walking through the woods. The grandson was going on about his experiences in school and how he sometimes struggled to listen and get his homework done on time. Grandfather listened patiently to all the struggles he was experiencing. The boy was complaining that he just didn't understand why he was always getting into trouble. Then all of a sudden they came across a clearing. The grandfather put his hand out to stop the boy in his tracks.

The boy looked up to see in the clearing two wolves in the process of a showdown. They were snarling at each other and it looked like at any moment they would pounce into an epic battle. The boy looked with fascination and the grandfather took the moment to explain the scene to him. The grandfather said, "we have this same scene going on within us every day. The dark wolf is our anger, resentment, lies, superiority, pride, and shame. This wolf only seeks to hurt us and all those around us. This wolf is also known as the voice of our addiction and it seeks to take us down.

The other wolf is the light wolf. It is happy, joyous, and free. It is hopeful, serene, humble, kind, generous, faithful, and authentic. This wolf only seeks to help us and those around us. This can also be known as the voice of recovery and it seeks to lift us up."

The boy listened deeply to his grandfather as he watched the scene unfold in front of him. As the tension mounted both inside the boy as well as the two wolves, he turned to his grandfather and said, "which one will win?" The grandfather smiled and said, "Whichever one you feed."

You see, we feed the wolves through every action we take. We feed the wolves through every thought and belief we have. When we do the right thing, we feed the light wolf. Every time we go to a meeting, call a sponsor, reach out and ask for help, we strengthen the light wolf while starving the dark one. Every choice we make and every step we take feeds a wolf. It is up to us to ask moment to moment which one am I feeding."

---

**Debrief:**

- ▶ What was your experience as you listened to the story?
- ▶ What thoughts were you aware of?
- ▶ What are some of the challenges one faces about feeding one wolf compared to the other?
- ▶ What might be getting in your way when you look at the bigger picture?
- ▶ What are the pros and cons of feeding each wolf?
- ▶ Which wolf are you feeding?
- ▶ What are two small steps you will focus on to strengthen your recovery and wellness?

**Recovery/Wellness Metaphor:** Clients who are struggling with their addiction or mental illness, and even those in early recovery, can sometimes experience an internal battle of negative versus positive thinking. From a change perspective, there is a belief that we attract that which we focus on. When one is only focused on the negative, it can lead to a gloomy outlook and feelings of hopelessness. On the contrary, when we help others focus on the positive, we give them permission or an opportunity to consider all possibilities.

**Role of Facilitator:** Take time to debrief the story with participants, help them explore their perceptions or thinking errors that may keep them off track from their recovery. Explore with participants their challenges, what is useful to support their recovery, wellness, or desired outcomes and what is not; and what may keep them stuck by holding onto their challenges versus letting go. Also explore with them what they may need to embrace their perceived challenges or thinking errors, and possibly gain an openness of acceptance or surrender. By moving from being stuck in one's challenges to embracing their possibilities, participants can explore what is needed to surrender in order to move forward.

**Variations:** This can be accomplished in individual sessions or given as homework.

**Reference:** *The Story of Two Wolves* is adapted from Virtues from Live, http://www.virtuesforlife.com/two-wolves/

# The Fences and Wells Analogy

**Group Size:** Any

**Purpose:** To increase awareness of choices in the real world, and placing importance on recovery and wellness.

**Props Needed:**
1. The Fences and Wells Analogy—can either be copied as a handout or projected onto a screen.

**Activity Preparation:**
1. Prep time needed: 5 minutes

**Time Needed:**
- ▶ Directions: Facilitator will read the Fences and Wells Analogy, or have a group member read the story.
- ▶ Activity: 5 minutes.
- ▶ Debrief: 10 minutes; may be more with a larger group.

**Set-Up:**
- ▶ The activity can be accomplished in any setting: individual or group setting.
- ▶ Participants may be seated in a classroom style set-up or in a circle.

**Activity Directions:**
- ▶ If you are projecting the story on to a screen, have participants face the projected image or story.
- ▶ Explain the purpose of the activity.
- ▶ Read Facilitator's Script and The Fences and Wells Analogy.

**Facilitator Script:** "Hey everyone, gather around so we can get started with today's group. Let's take time to listen to 'The Fences and Wells Analogy.'

**The Fences and Wells Analogy:**

Most farmers in the U.S. build fences around the land where their animals roam as a way of keeping their livestock in and the livestock of neighboring farmers out. But in many rural communities around the world fencing is not an option, either because of the cost or the expansiveness of the region. In many of these places, such as several ranches across Australia, farmers use wells instead. They sink a bore and create a well in order to provide a precious water supply in the middle of the outback. It is assumed that livestock, although they will stray, will never roam too far from the well . . . lest they die. As long as there is a supply of clean water, the livestock will remain close by. If you think about this in terms of wellness and recovery, these fences and wells mean different things to each individual. For some, meeting regularly with people who support you is like a well of water to which we are drawn to quench our thirsts, rather than viewing it as a boundary that keeps me in. For others, they need strict boundaries, like fences, in order to stay clean. The reality is that we need both. For an addict to survive in the outside world is to both commit to building a fence or a boundary around their actions: they follow the recommendations of the professionals in their lives, follow the law, and work a program of recovery. These are like fences or boundaries that they choose to live in. However, they must also learn to understand the center of it all, and see that Wellness is like a well of water, more attractive and refreshing than the addiction they are entangled in. In this way we must tap into our own passions and see what fills our wells. What nourishes us? What ignites our passions?

In recovery, it is critical to have a combination of both fences and wells. We need to place obstacles to relapse while also creating a life worth living. The fences are obstacles to relapse while the well allows us to live a life we can get excited about.

Take a moment to think about what would represent your fences, and what would be your wells." *(Either have the group process personal examples of this lesson or debrief the story.)*

## Debrief:

- ► What did you notice as you listened to the story?
- ► What thoughts were you aware of as you listened to the story?
- ► What is an obvious fence in your life?
- ► What might represent a well for you?
- ► What is difficult about this analogy? (That it's different for each person.)

**Recovery/Wellness Metaphor:** In recovery it is critical to have a combination of both fences and wells. We need to place obstacles to relapse while also creating a life worth living. The fences are obstacles to relapse while the well allows us to live a life we can get excited about.

**Role of Facilitator:** Take time to debrief the story with participants, helping them explore what would represent a fence (hard boundary) or a well (something that supports them) in their life. Through the metaphor of the story, encourage participants to explore and to identify their internal response and outward expression toward others. Assist participants to explore the consequences and benefits of each.

**Variations:** This can be accomplished in individual sessions.

# The Gem Story

**Source:** *A Teachable Moment*, by Cain, Cummings and Stanchfield. Story by Rich Allen, Impact Learning

**Group Size:** Any

**Purpose:** A story you can tell to talk about the "gems" of learning they got from the program.

**Props Needed:**
1. The Gem Story
2. Small glass stones, enough for every participant.

**Activity Preparation:**
1. Prep time needed: 5 minutes
2. The activity can be accomplished in any setting: individual or group setting.

**Time Needed:**
1. Directions: Facilitator will read script or have a group member read the story.
2. Activity: 10–20 minutes, with discussion.
3. Debrief: 10 minutes; may be more with larger group size.

**Set-Up:**
1. The activity can be accomplished in any setting: individual or group setting.
2. Participants may be seated in a classroom or gathered around in a circle.

**Activity Directions:**
- ► Have participants find a seat or gather together—they may be seated in classroom style or round circle group.
- ► Tell the story. Be animated in your delivery. The more memorable you make the story, the more impactful the stones will be for the participants.
- ► Adjust the story as you need to make it your own and to have meaning for your participants.
- ► As you are telling the story, pass out a few stones when you get to the part about when he discovers he has diamonds, rubies, etc.
- ► Then after you finish the story, pass out the rest of the stones. You'll be amazed at how many people were concerned that they weren't going to get a stone like the first three did—even adults.

▶   To close the story, talk about how you hope the participants were able to pick up a few "gems" during the program and that they will value them like precious stones.

▶   Read Facilitator's Script—complete handout toward end of activity.

**Facilitator Script:** "Let's gather around. I am going to read you *The Gem Story*. *(Place a few glass stones in your pocket before beginning the story.)*

## The Gem Story

A traveler was on a long journey. Each morning he got up and traveled along his path. One morning he woke up and set out again on his journey. However, he soon noticed that on this particular morning the path appeared to be getting more and more narrow. He began to grow concerned that he had taken a wrong turn, and decided that he would ask the next person he saw that morning if he was indeed on the correct path. But no one else was on the path that morning. He walked and walked, and it wasn't until noon that he encountered the first person he had seen all day. He entered a clearing in the woods, and there at the far side of the clearing sat a very old man. This old man had long, flowing white hair, and a white beard, and had his eyes closed.

The traveler was quite excited to see the old man. He hurried up to him and asked: "Excuse me, but I was traveling along the path this morning, and it began to get very narrow, and I started to wonder if I was on the right path. Can you tell me? Am I going the right way?" The old man just sat there in silence, his eyes still closed.

The traveler tried again, but could get no response. Finally, in frustration, he started to leave. He was at the far side of the clearing when he heard a sound, and he turned around. The old man had opened his eyes, and was staring straight out in front of him. And when he spoke he said, very softly: "You're on the right path. Keep going."

But the traveler was at the far side of the clearing, and wasn't sure if he had heard correctly, so he asked the old man to repeat himself. The old man did say something, but this time it was something quite different. This time he said: "Gather what you find before you cross the river." And then he closed his eyes once again.

Now, the traveler had heard this last part quite clearly, but he was confused—what did it mean? But he could get nothing more from the old man, and finally the traveler did leave, continuing on the path as before.

It was hot on the path that day, and the traveler grew sweaty, tired, and thirsty. And the path, while growing ever more narrow, was still visible enough to follow. Finally, late in the afternoon, the traveler turned a corner and found in front of himself a river. He was so excited! He ran down to the river, drank some of the water, and used more water to wash himself. When he was fully refreshed he started to wade to the other side, but as he took his first step the words of the old man came back to him, and he paused.

"What did he say?" the traveler asked himself. And then he remembered the words: "Gather what you find before you cross the river." "Did he mean this river?" wondered the traveler. "Ah, he was crazy!" and he began to move again. But the words of the old man were echoing so strongly in his mind that he found himself backing up to the bank of the river. He looked around.

"If I was going to gather something" he asked himself, "what would I take here?" He looked around, and saw trees, shrubs, and pebbles by the river's edge—but nothing of any value. But the words of the old man were so strong in his mind that he said:

> "This may be the strangest thing I have ever done, but . . ." and he bent down and picked up some of the pebbles and put them in his pocket. (*Shake the stones you have in your pocket. Loud enough that the group can hear them.*) Then he waded across the river and continued traveling. However, at the far side of the river he soon lost his way and traveled aimlessly until he found another path to follow several hours later. He knew he could now never retrace his steps back the way he had come.

Late that night the traveler slept by the side of the road. He woke up in the middle of the night, but did not know what had awakened him. Then he realized that he had rolled over on the pebbles in his pocket, and he shook his head.

"That old man was crazy," he said aloud. "I don't know why I picked these up!"

He reached into his pocket and took out the pebbles. He was in the act of throwing them away when suddenly the moonlight shone down on what he held in his hand, and he paused.

"No," he said. "It can't be!"

Because what he was holding in his hand were no longer mere pebbles. Now they were diamonds, rubies, sapphires, and emeralds—precious gems of all kinds. (*Hand a glass stone to three to four people listening to the story.*) And he realized what had happened—they had been precious gems all along, but when he had first picked them up they had been covered in dirt, and in his pocket they had rubbed against each other so that the dirt had come off and he could see them for what they were.

And then the traveler said the most important thing of all. He said:

"Oh. OH! I wish I had gathered more pebbles, before I crossed that river!"

*(Debrief the story, make sure everyone goes home with one glass stone. Have them name what their 'gem' of learning is with the group.)*

## Debrief:

- ▶ What was your experience as you listened to the story?
- ▶ What thoughts were you aware of?
- ▶ What do you think is the purpose of the story?
- ▶ What are some pebbles from your life?
- ▶ How can you look at them as gems now that you are in recovery?
- ▶ What are some "gems" of learning you can apply to recovery and wellness?
- ▶ If you were to take one of these stones home with you, what is one "gem" you have learned in class?
- ▶ What would you tell others about your recovery?

**Recovery/Wellness Metaphor:** So often in life we look at the things in our past as annoying pebbles. Especially in addiction we have done some messed up things and very often people have done messed up things to us. Through the process of recovery, we learn that these pebbles actually become gems when washed in the river of recovery. Some negative experiences from our past can be like walking with a pebble in our shoe causing us pain each step we take. By entering in recovery we get to take out our pebbles and look at them differently trying to find the gem hidden within.

**Role of Facilitator:** Take time to debrief the story with participants, helping them explore what some of the gems of learning they have learned in their recovery.

# Grief Timeline

**Group Size:** 1–30

**Purpose:** Explore grief in an expressive way, to create group cohesion. Create a pathway for healing and to normalize the grieving process.

**Props Needed:** Art supplies, drawing paper, Grief Timeline Handout.

**Activity Preparation:** Familiarize yourself the with activity and Stages of Grief. Remain observant of participant's expression of grief. Important for facilitator to remain supportive and non-judgmental of a participant's expression of grief. With larger groups it may be helpful to have co-facilitators in the event someone needs some individual time.

**Prep Time Needed:** 10 minutes. Have art supplies, drawing paper, and Grief Timeline Handout at each table for participants. Participants can gather into groups.

## Time Needed:
- ▶ Directions: 10 minutes
- ▶ Activity: 20–25 minutes
- ▶ Debrief: 15–20 minutes

## Set-Up:
- ▶ This activity may be best sequenced after the group has developed some rapport.
- ▶ The activity can be accomplished in any setting: individual or group.
- ▶ Participants may be seated in a classroom or gathered around in a circle.

## Activity Directions:
- ▶ Have enough supplies and Grief Timeline Handout for each member of the group.
- ▶ Create a safe, supportive, and creative space for members to explore their grief.
- ▶ Give members 20–30 minutes to do the activity.
- ▶ Invite participants to share their timeline with one another and the group.

**Facilitator Script:** "Let's gather around and take a look at the table. Before you are art supplies, drawing paper, and a Grief Timeline handout. Today's activity is doing a Grief Timeline. In the recovery/wellness journey, there may be many losses: loss of personal time, loss of trust, of one's drug of choice, of one's image of how life would be, the self-image created in addiction or in chaotic choices in life, of loss of one's lifestyle. One may experience a loss of hopes and dreams, of one's spiritual connection. We may have had deaths occur.

It's important to acknowledge that in the reality of death, grief, and loss, that grieving is a normal process. The response is a very personal and individual one. The renowned psychiatrist Elisabeth Kübler-Ross (1926–2004) wrote extensively on death and dying and the grief process, *On Death and Dying* (1969). Let's explore the Five Stages of Grief developed by Kübler-Ross:

Stage 1: Denial—a conscious or unconscious refusal to accept the facts. 'There is absolutely no way this could be happening!'

Stage 2: Anger—emotional expression; outward or inward; a person can be angry with self or others, the person who died. 'How could they do this (to me) (to themselves)? I cannot believe I am even having to deal with this too!'

Stage 3: Bargaining—or seek to negotiate a compromise or different outcome. 'I promise. I quit today. If you help me stay quit from these drugs/alcohol or behaviors, I will never (*fill in the blank*) again.'

Stage 4: Depression—sadness over the loss; emotional acceptance without personal attachment. 'I hate this disease—everyone around me has died or left me. I am all alone. My family has disowned me—they will never trust me or love me again. I don't even know who I am anymore.'

Stage 5: Acceptance—emotional attachment to the loss and objectivity. 'This disease is killing me. I just don't know what else to do. I have got to do something right now or I will be another statistic just like the others.'

For this next part, we are going to dig a little deeper about how grief and loss show up in our journey. There are times when grief or loss is not dealt with. Sometimes we just shove it to the inner recesses of our mind, block it out intentionally or unintentionally. However, if we leave it alone, never dealing with it, grief or loss has a funny way of coming to the surface in the most unexpected times of our life.

This activity is designed to explore grief in an expressive way, to normalize the grief process, and create a supportive pathway for healing.

On the Grief Timeline handout you have an arrow that faces to the top of the page. You are going to create a grief timeline from today as far back as you choose. I want you to think about your active addiction/illness and your recovery/wellness journey.

On the left side of the page you will write down the events that represent grief/loss, all that has been lost and when the loss occurred. Try to plot events in sequence from bottom (oldest events) to top (most recent). You can write the year, or month/year if multiple events happened in one year. Or you can also use your age to help you keep track of when the loss occurred. For example: Best friend died, 5/2015.

Also be sure to enter on your timeline: Sobriety/Wellness date.

On the right side of the page write the Stage of Grief associated with each loss. This does not have to be exact. I encourage you to just think about the event, how you experienced the event or getting the news at that time, and how that experience is associated with a grief stage.

Let's take about twenty minutes to write out your timeline.

Now, I encourage you to share your timeline with your group members.

Now that you have shared with one another, is there anyone who would like to share their timeline with the class?"

## Debrief:

► What was hard about this activity? What was easy?

► What might it feel like to be free from grief?

► What emotional sensations did you experience?

► What physical sensations did you experience?

► What is liberating about this activity?

► What events did you identify with in the Acceptance Stage of Grief?

► What tools/resources were important for you to achieve acceptance?

► What have you learned about yourself as you identify the stages of grief and your events?

► What do you need to move forward in your identified stage of grief to the next stage?

► What one action step will you put in place to help you in your healing process?

**Recovery/Wellness Metaphor:** It is interesting that grief and loss is one area that can be universally uncomfortable or difficult for people to accept or manage. This activity is designed to normalize the grieving process, and encourage a supportive pathway for healing.

**Role of Facilitator:** Introduce and guide the activity. Remain observant of participant's reaction or response to their timeline or that of others, and to participant's expression of grief. Remain supportive and non-judgmental of a participant's expression of grief.

**Variations:** Participants may clip pictures from magazines and make a collage of their timeline in the form of a vision board.

**Source:** Adapted from "Grief Cycle Model" first published in *On Death and Dying*.

# GRIEF TIMELINE

On this side of the arrow, using one word or phrase, list events that represent grief or loss to you and write the date. Oldest date at bottom of arrow. Most recent at top of arrow.

On this side of the arrow, write the Stage of Grief associated with each loss: Denial, Anger, Bargaining, Depression, Acceptance.

Source information for worksheet created by Diane Sherman

REPRODUCIBLE

# Group Guidelines

**Group Size:** 5–50

**Purpose:** Participants set up their own guidelines to create safety and ownership. This can be a great icebreaker and way of starting out a program.

**Props Needed:**
1. Large piece of paper or whiteboard
2. Markers

**Activity Preparation:**
- ▶ Prep time needed: 5 minutes
- ▶ Prior to group draw a circle and in the middle of it write "Group Members." Then separate the paper into four quadrants. Label Quadrant 1 "Do." Label Quadrant 2 "Do Not." Label Quadrant 3 "Are." Label Quadrant 4 "Are Not."

**Time Needed:**
- ▶ Directions: 2 minutes
- ▶ Activity: 10 minutes
- ▶ Debrief: 5 minutes

**Set-Up:** Hang up paper so group members can get to it and fill out the quadrants.

**Activity Directions:**
- ▶ Have the participants fill out the group guidelines.

**Facilitator Script:** "Hey everyone we are going to start group today by setting up group guidelines. We all know rules are made to be what?!? *(Most groups will shout back 'Broken.')* That's right, broken. SO we aren't going to establish rules, we are going to establish guidelines because guidelines are meant to keep us on track. As you can see here *(point to paper)*, using the prompts in each quadrant, I would like you to fill this out with what you think will help keep our group on track. The prompts are Group Members Are, Are Not, Group members Do, Do Not. Once we get everything written down we will review it and see what you have come up with. I would like everyone to write at least one thing on the board.

*(Give participants a couple of minutes to complete the task.)* OK, has everyone written something on the board? Great! Now let's see what you came up with. Can I get a volunteer to read what we have? *(Or if you prefer you can read it to the group.)*

Does anyone want to add anything or feel like we are missing anything?" *(Make sure important things like confidentiality, safety, respect, no cell phones, and other general housekeeping items have been captured in a general way. If not then you might suggest the group add something.)*

## Debrief:

- ▶ How do rules and guidelines differ? How are they the same?
- ▶ What was it like to come up with the group guidelines?
- ▶ Was there anything you wanted to suggest but talked yourself out of?
- ▶ Is there anything up there that you think should not be?

**Recovery/Wellness Metaphor:** "Rules are meant to be broken" is a common slogan amongst our population. Creating group guidelines allows the group to take ownership and buy into the process. Remember guidelines help keep us on track.

**Role of Facilitator:** Help support the group in making sure everyone's voice is heard and respected. Make additional suggestions to the group if they miss out on key guidelines.

## Variations:

**Where to Find It/How to Make It:** We have found the large size post-it note paper to be the most effective. Be aware that some markers will bleed through onto the wall. You might consider doubling up on the paper.

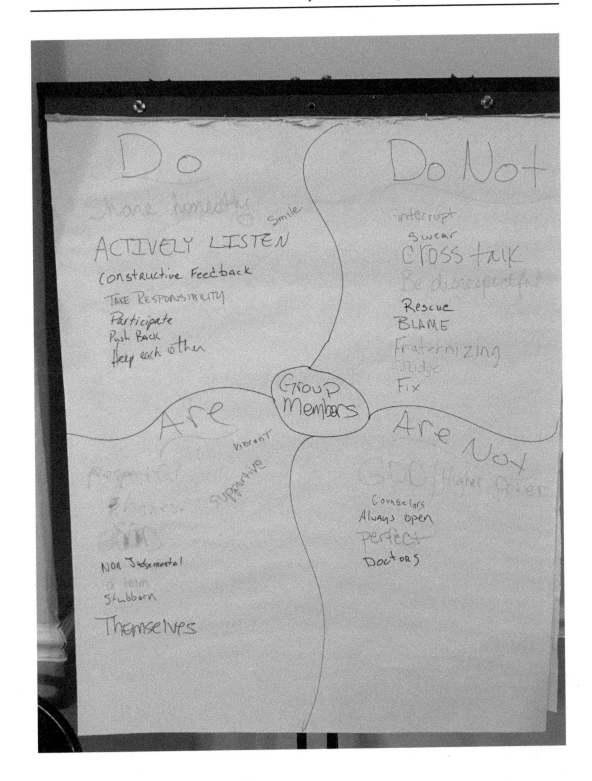

**Do**

Share honestly ♡ Smile
ACTIVELY LISTEN
Constructive Feedback
TAKE RESPONSIBILITY
Participate
Push Back
Hear each other

**Do Not**

Interrupt
Swear
Cross talk
Be disrespectful
Rescue
BLAME
Fraternizing
Judge
Fix

**Group Members**

**Are**

Vibrant
Supportive
Aggressive
Honest
SILLY
Non Judgemental
a team
Stubborn
Themselves

**Are Not**

GOD/Higher Power
Counselors
Always open
Perfect
Doctors

# Growth Zone

**Source:** Activity generously provided by Swami Jaya Devi Bhagavati of Kashi Atlanta

**Group size:** 5–25

**Purpose:** Normalizes fear, creates joyful acceptance of being imperfect, promotes courage

**Props Needed:** Growth Zone Practice Handout

**Activity Preparation:** Prep time needed: 5 minutes prior to class
1. Become familiar with concept of Growth and Comfort Zones
2. Print handout with identified practices

**Time Needed:**
- ▶ Directions: 5 minutes
- ▶ Activity: 45 minutes
- ▶ Debrief: 15 minutes

**Set-Up:** Have participants gather around tables or provide clipboards.

**Activity Directions:**
- ▶ Have the participants sit comfortably
- ▶ Read *The Growth Zone*
- ▶ Discuss reading
- ▶ Introduce Growth Zone practices

**Facilitator Script:** "Have a seat everyone. Today we are going to talk about a different aspect of the change process called the Growth Zone. What do you think of when you hear the words Growth Zone? *(allow for group discussion)* Listen to this reading and see what you think.

## The Growth Zone
by Swami Jaya Devi Bhagavati

We live in a world infatuated with perfectionism. In many ways, we strive to do better, be better, and constantly "do the right thing." We want to be good and to earn our worth through right action. But we often end up placing our self-worth outside of ourselves, in our work, our appearance, or our relationships. We lose sight of the fact that we are loved and lovable exactly as we are, that we do not have to do anything to earn love, we only have to remember that we are love.

When we are young, we are exposed to a variety of different learning experiences. We take many different classes in school. Some of us play a wide range of sports, sing in choir, play an instrument in band, write poems and essays, act in the school play, paint or draw in art class. We have the courage to try new skills regularly because we ourselves are new, and opening ourselves to untested experiences seems normal. We often test and stretch beyond our comfort zone in an exuberant and exploratory manner. We reach out to the world with a child's natural sense of joy and curiosity.

Inevitably, the time comes when we try something unfamiliar—like roller skating or playing the tuba—where we find no natural skill or expertise within us. We may fall in front of our peers in a messy, clothes-over-the-head heap. We may experience fear, embarrassment, humiliation, or shame. Others may laugh at our expense or judge us. In these moments, we come smack up against our imperfection, our humanity, and our vulnerability. How we deal with these perceived shortcomings has a powerful impact on our self-worth. If we are raised to expect and display perfection, we often lose sight of the playful arena just outside our comfort zone, which I call the Growth Zone.

Your Growth Zone is just beyond the perimeter of your comfort zone. You access it by working your growing edge, by opening yourself to explore new ideas, experiences, and concepts. You access growth by opening your heart and becoming emotionally available and present. People often avoid their growth zone by over-emphasizing the feeling of emotional safety, by wanting to remain comfortable, or by staying in ruts of thought or behavior. What is safe is not always what is fulfilling, kind, or joyful. It is not always what is most creative or most conscious.

In recovery, you want to create a realm of safety for your physical, mental, and emotional well-being, but not at the cost of authentic vulnerability. Because you are human, you have the ability to live with your heart open, where you are available to experience love as a way of being in the world. This is an elemental quality shared by all humanity. When you stay hidden inside your comfort zone, you limit your experience of love and deep, satisfying connection with other people.

Finding and experiencing your comfort zone is a wonderful thing. As children, when we feel comfortable, we often feel loved, safe, and relaxed. We can feel at peace with ourselves. Our comfort zone is elemental to our well-being and can be filled with creative, simple, satisfying experiences. But as adults, our comfort zone is rarely where we grow.

We must access courage to fulfill the longing of our hearts. Taking up the tools of courage and curiosity, we begin to grow when we stretch beyond what we already know. We grow when we step into uncertainty, into unfamiliar territory. We grow when we reach into the dark ground of our creativity and explore. We grow when we make ourselves vulnerable. We grow when we try something new, when we can laugh at our insecurities and ourselves. We grow when we normalize our fears, when we expose them with love and acceptance. This awakens our joy of being alive and our ability to connect with other, equally fallible humans. It softens our inner hearts and rekindles our sense of humor. When we can love and accept who we are with all our mistakes and successes, we overcome shame. We are okay with who we are. We are okay with being us, with loving and failing and getting up and trying again. We embrace our messy, imperfect nature. We try not to judge ourselves or anyone else too harshly. We open to the wild, sacred dance of all of life but mostly we choose love anyway. We choose love over fear, expansion over contraction, joyful exploration over unworthiness. Choice by choice, moment by moment, we lay down our fears, take up our courage, and love anyway.

© 2016 Kashi Atlanta

What thoughts come up for you as you reflect on this reading? *(Allow for group discussion, if necessary use debrief prompts to spark conversation.)*

Here is one of the Growth Zone practices. *(pass out the circling up handout)* We are going to do a Growth Zone Practice called Circling Up. Take a moment to reflect on what you just learned. What would you say is inside of your comfort zone? List the items that make up your current Comfort Zone. When you have completed that, fill out the items that can be found in your Growth Zone. Feel free to be as creative as you can. There are no wrong answers. These are things that you currently believe are just outside of your edge of comfort. We have found it beneficial to start with items that are just outside of your comfort zone rather than starting with things that are way outside of your comfort zone. Does anyone have any questions?" *(Address participant questions.)* *(This activity can be done in group or as homework to be reviewed in the next session. Be sure to leave time to debrief the activity.)*

## Debrief:
- What thoughts come up for you as you reflect on this reading?
- How do you know when you are in your comfort zone?
- How do you know when you are in your growth zone?
- What does it take to move from your growth zone to your comfort zone?
- What keeps you in your comfort zone?

**Recovery/Wellness Metaphor:** By naming and claiming the comfort zone we are more likely to gain access to the growth zone.

**Role of Facilitator:** Provide education on the concepts of the comfort zone and the growth zone. Guide participants in the growth zone practices.

**Variations:** Here are some additional Growth Zone Practices as given by Swami Jaya Devi

- ► List five things you are currently bad at or have room for improvement. Now select one that you are willing to do. This practice is geared toward normalizing fear while creating joyful acceptance of being imperfect.
- ► List five things that expand you, that make you feel more alive. Select one you are willing to do and try it out. This practice is excellent and creates courage.
- ► Oops Mantra. Don't try to cover up your mistakes, embracing them is where you grow the most. Don't try to defend or be right, just apologize well and be good at being wrong. Doing this normalizes "doing bad" without "being bad." This practice creates a sense of self-worth by separating actions from the actor.
- ► Practices to reclaim self-worth: Repeat the following mantra. Breathing in "I am loved, I am love" breathing out "I am loved, I am love."

**Resources:** For more information and teachings by Swami Jaya Devi, please visit the Kashi Atlanta Website at www.kashiatlanta.org

## GROWTH ZONE PRACTICE—CIRCLING UP

Take a moment to reflect on what you just learned. What would you say is inside of your Comfort Zone? List the items that make up your current Comfort Zone. When you have completed that, fill out the items that can be found in your Growth Zone. Feel free to be as creative as you can. There are no wrong answers. These are things that you currently believe are just outside of your edge of comfort. We have found it beneficial to start with items that are just outside of your Comfort Zone rather than starting with things that are way outside of your Comfort Zone.

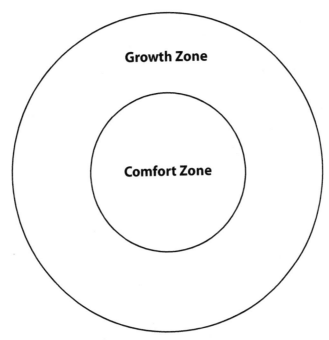

Once you have an exhaustive list filling both your Comfort Zone and Growth Zone, select one item in your Growth Zone that you are willing to try.

I am willing to try _____.

I will ask _____ for help when _____.

I intend to start this practice _____.

I will ask _____ to hold me accountable by saying/doing _____.

**REPRODUCIBLE**

# I Am Grateful

**Group Size:** 5–50

**Purpose:** Increase coping skills, neurocognitive restructuring, enhance positive thinking

**Props Needed:**
1. I Am Grateful handout
2. Pens

**Activity Preparation:**
1. Prep time needed: 5 minutes
2. Prior to class make sure that facilitator has enough pens and handouts for each participant.

**Time Needed:**
- ▶ Directions: 5 minutes
- ▶ Activity: 25 minutes
- ▶ Debrief: 15 minutes

**Set-Up:** It would be helpful to have a hard surface for participants to lean on while writing such as tables or clipboards.

**Activity Directions:**
- ▶ Provide pens and handout to group.
- ▶ Explain what gratitude is and how it can benefit someone in recovery.
- ▶ Ask group to fill out each section of the handout with as many items as the section calls for. Don't leave any spaces blank.

**Facilitator Script:** "OK everyone, have a seat. Today we are going to do a gratitude practice. Research shows having a gratitude practice has the power to not only change our patterns of thinking, but actually changes the structures of our brains. Most of us spend the day doing the opposite of a gratitude list. We are so used to focusing on what is wrong with us, our situations, and the world around us. A gratitude practice causes us to focus on what is right with us, our situations, and the world around us. Each time we have a thought it creates a groove within our brains and the more we have it the more this groove is reinforced. This practice is about creating a new groove that can be even more useful in our daily lives.

People in recovery have a long history of using a gratitude list as a way of changing our perceptions. Now science is catching up with the recovery movement. Gratitude can help you when you are stuck in recovery, when you are down, as well as when you are feeling hopeless. There is a universal principle that you will experience more of what you focus on. For example, the more you focus on what is negative the more you will experience negativity; however, the more you focus on the positive the more you experience positivity.

Your challenge today is to come up with a list of things you are grateful for. I suggest doing twenty-five things for twenty-five days! It is a fun way to change our brains together. This might be more challenging than you might initially think. Use the "I am Grateful" handout as a springboard into your gratitude practice.

So let's take the next twenty minutes or so to fill out the I am Grateful handout. Go through each section and make sure that you have an answer for each one.

*(Give participants twenty minutes to fill out the handout. Make sure to give them warnings when they are halfway through their allotted time and another warning when they are three-quarters through with their time. When 90 percent of the participants are completed with the handout it might be OK to move on to the next part.)*

Great job everyone! Who would like to share what they have? *(Let participants volunteer, unless you have enough time to go through everyone then it would be OK to go around the circle. This is a facilitator preference. Also consider after each participant shares clapping to reinforce the participant's willingness to be vulnerable.)* OK, who's next?

So what was this activity like for you?"

---

## Debrief:

► What was your initial reaction to hearing we are doing a gratitude list today?
► Have you ever done a gratitude practice before? What was it like?
► Were there any sections that were easy to fill out?
► What sections were harder to fill out than others?
► Are you willing to do the twenty-five things for twenty-five days challenge?

**Recovery and Wellness Metaphor:** When we can open our minds to the realization that there are things right within us, our situations, and the world we start to automatically respond differently. When we do a gratitude practice the filters through which we see the world literally change.

**Role of Facilitator:** Create a quiet space so that participants can have the space that they need to do the gratitude practice. Create a space that allows room for creativity.

**Variations:** If you don't have access to a printer you could give participants blank sheets of paper and ask that they come up with a list on their own. This can be more challenging as participants find it easier to have prompts such as those on the "I am Grateful" handout.

**Where to Find It/How to Make It:**

# I am Grateful . . .

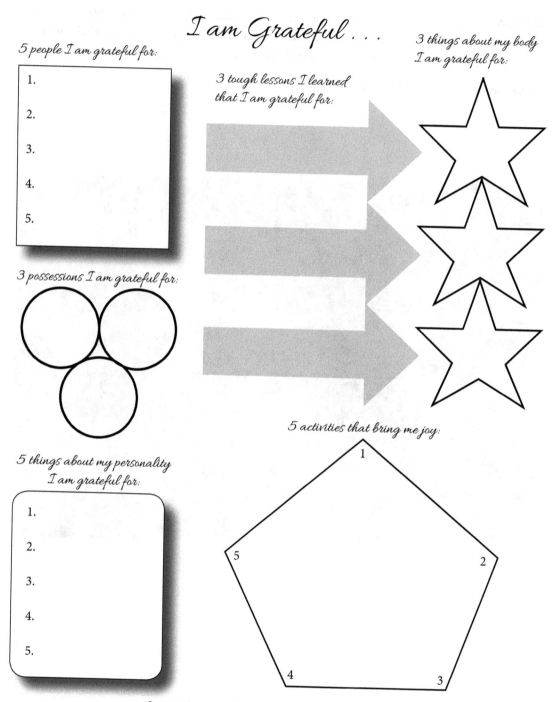

5 people I am grateful for:

1.
2.
3.
4.
5.

3 tough lessons I learned
that I am grateful for:

3 things about my body
I am grateful for:

3 possessions I am grateful for:

5 things about my personality
I am grateful for:

1.
2.
3.
4.
5.

5 activities that bring me joy:

1
5
2
4
3

Source information for worksheet Created by Marc Pimsler

# I Am Group Affirmations

**Group Size:** 5–25

**Purpose:** Increase sense of personal well-being, increase group cohesion.

**Props Needed:**

1. Brown paper lunch bags
2. Pens
3. "I am" handout
4. List of group members' first name and last initial

**Activity Preparation:** Prep time needed: 60 minutes

1. Prior to group, print off a list of first names and last initial of all members in the group.
2. Make enough copies of "I am" handout and cut it into slips so that each group member has a slip of paper for each of their peers.
3. In each bag place a pen, a list of group members' first name and last initial, and enough "I am" slips of paper to write an affirmation for each of their peers.
4. Using a larger marker label the bags with a participant's first name and last initial. Write large enough so the name can be seen and read from a distance.

So if there are ten group members total you will have ten bags each containing a pen, nine slips of paper, and a list of the ten group members' names in each bag.

**Time Needed:**

- ▶ Directions: 5 minutes
- ▶ Activity: 40 minutes
- ▶ Debrief: 15 minutes

**Set-Up:** Give each bag to the participant that it belongs to.

**Activity Directions:**

- ▶ Hand out pre-packaged bags to group members.
- ▶ Have a discussion about affirmations and how sometimes it is hard to come up with positive affirmations about ourselves.
- ▶ Tell participants they will find a list of names of all group members, blank slips of paper, and a pen in the bags provided.

▶ Their task is to write out one positive sentence that completes the sentence stem "I am . . ." for each of their peers.

▶ Reinforce this must be something positive and uplifting, as one day their peer might be having a bad day and come across their bag of affirmations. What they write down for their peer might be the thing that saves their life. Let them know we will be reading these out loud so please take it seriously and write legibly.

▶ Remember who you write each affirmation for, it might help to put their name on the back of the slip of paper.

▶ Once you have an affirmation slip for each group member you will deliver the affirmation into the bag of the person you wrote it for.

▶ Once this is done have group members read out loud the affirmations found in their bag.

---

**Facilitator Script:** "OK everyone, we are going to get started. Here is a bag for each of you. Inside your bag you will find a pen, a list of names, and several slips of paper. Here is what we are going to do. Many of us have a hard time thinking about what is good about ourselves. Or if someone asked you to create a list of self-affirmations we might struggle. So we are going to create affirmations for each other.

Take out the list of names from your bag. Find your name and cross it off. Does anyone not see their name listed? *(If there is a participant that doesn't have their name listed have everyone write their name on the list and apologize for overlooking it.)*

Your task is to complete the sentence stem 'I am' for each of your peers. So you might say something like 'I am always uplifting to my friends when they are down' or 'I am a prime example of a strong man in recovery.' Make sure that whatever you write is positive and uplifting. You never know, your peer might be having a bad day and come across their bag of affirmations. What you write down for them might be the thing that saves their life. Also we will be reading these out loud so please take it seriously and write legibly.

You will have about twenty minutes to complete the affirmations for your peers so don't overthink it. Once you have written everyone's affirmation please place their affirmation in their bag. Place your bag open on the floor in front of you so your peers can fill it with your affirmations.

*(Be sure to give time warnings when group is half and three-quarters of the way through the time allotted.)*

OK, great job everyone. Who would like to read their affirmations first?" *(You can either go around the room or accept volunteers.)*

---

## Debrief:

- ▶ What was it like to write the affirmations for your peers?
- ▶ What was it like to know that others are writing things about you?
- ▶ How did it feel reading your affirmations out loud?
- ▶ What did you think about what your peers said about you?
- ▶ Was there anything that was surprising?
- ▶ What was easy about this activity?
- ▶ What was challenging about it?

**Recovery/Wellness Metaphor:** This activity can be a powerful way to dismantle the negative sense of self. Previous participants have said they never knew others saw them this way as they were debriefing this powerful activity.

**Role of Facilitator:** Help to keep clients on track by managing the logistics and answering the questions. It is important to pay attention to ensure understanding from each participant. Make sure participants are taking it seriously as if something is negatively written it can have a negative impact to the participant reading the affirmation out loud.

**Variations:** Feel free to adapt sentence stems or purpose to fit population and goals of group. Facilitator may ask participants to write one affirmation about each person in the group on a post-it note. Then get up and while moving around, the participant with the sticky note will pat the one being affirmed on the back as if giving them a pat on the back, and sticking the post-it note affirmation to their clothing. Once everyone has all affirmations stuck to their back, ask participants to collect the affirmations from one participant from their back and hand them to that participant. Once each has their own affirmations, then each one will read aloud their own affirmations to the group.

**I am**

_____

_____

_____

**I am**

_____

_____

_____

**I am**

_____

_____

_____

**I am**

_____

_____

_____

**I am**

_____

_____

_____

Source information for worksheet Created by Marc Pimsler

# Junk to Jewels

**Source:** Adapted from *Quick Team Building Activities for Busy Managers*, Brian Cole Miller, Amacom, 2004.

**Group Size:** Any size.

**Purpose:** This is a great activity where participants pick from common office supplies to create an individual and a collective story of their recovery or wellness.

**Props Needed:** Various (and multiple similar) office or art supplies: paper clips different sizes, eraser, cups, coffee mugs, pens, pencils, color pencils, sticky-notes, Kleenex, highlighters of various colors, staple remover, scissors, stapler, pins, tacks, glue, glitter, stickers, calculator, bandana, blindfold, construction paper, etc. Any office or art supply will work.

**Activity Preparation:** Gather your own office supplies before you buy more. Collect them into a container or bag to keep them together. Display items on a table—spread out on a flat surface large enough for all participants to gather around. You can complete both parts of the activity—individual and collective. Complete the first part and have participants share their story. Then move on to the next part, the collective story, and have participants share their collective story.

**Prep Time Needed:** 10 minutes—set items out on table or flat surface.

**Time Needed:**

- ► Directions: 5 minutes
- ► Activity: 5–10 minutes
- ► Debrief: 15–25 minutes

**Set-Up:** This activity can be used at any point in sequencing.

**Safety:** Instruct participants to use care so they do not get hurt using or picking up any supplies.

**Activity Directions:**

- ► Gather the attention of participants. Explain that everyone is looking over the table with the office supplies.
- ► Thinking about your recovery or wellness process, select supplies that give a meaning to your personal path of recovery and/or wellness.

> ▶ Each person will pick something from the table that symbolizes their recovery or wellness path.
> ▶ Share with the group what the meaning of their symbol is.

---

**Facilitator Script:** "Let's gather around and take a look at the table. Notice there are various items that we would usually see in an office. Some of them are used to keep things together, some to erase, some to highlight, some to stick, some to remove something, some are containers to keep liquid or other things in. You can use your imagination for the use of each item.

For this first part of Junk to Jewels, I want you to think about your recovery or your wellness journey. What item before you represents your journey? What item speaks to you; symbolizes something important in your journey? Pick an item from the table and tell the group why you selected this item then have a seat. *(Facilitator gives participants an opportunity to share what they picked and what it represents. Also remove any remaining items from the table or flat surface.)*

Now that we have shared, let's return all the items you have chosen to the table. The next part of this activity is to create a group story. All the items on the table are those that you selected. They represent your individual story. Now you will create a collective story, one that includes everyone. Using all the items you picked, your task is to create a story using all items." *(Give participants time to come up with a collective story using all their items.)*

---

**Debrief:**
> ▶ What story does your item represent?
> ▶ What is the meaning of your collective story?
> ▶ What did you notice about yourself in picking your item? What did you notice about others' selections?
> ▶ If you picked something similar as another person, was your representation similar or different?
> ▶ Were you hesitant to pick something someone else chose? Why or why not?
> ▶ Why do you think similar items have different meanings?
> ▶ Why do you think different items have similar meanings?
> ▶ Did you learn something about yourself in someone else's item or story?

**Recovery/Wellness Metaphor:** It is an interesting activity in exploring the similarities and differences among participants in the group. There are many ways through and to recovery and wellness. Participants may become open in their thinking about their item or another's as each one shares their story.

**Role of Facilitator:** Introduce and guide the activity.

**Variations:**

- ▶ Participants can pick something that is representative to their family or the region where they grew up.
- ▶ They may pick something that represents a strength they see in themselves, or in one another.
- ▶ Participants may clip pictures from magazines and make a collage of their own story and their collective in the form of a vision board.

**Where to Find It/How to Make It:** Gather supplies and unused items from your cupboard, home, supply cabinet. Any items will do; gather a variety with lots of options for participants.

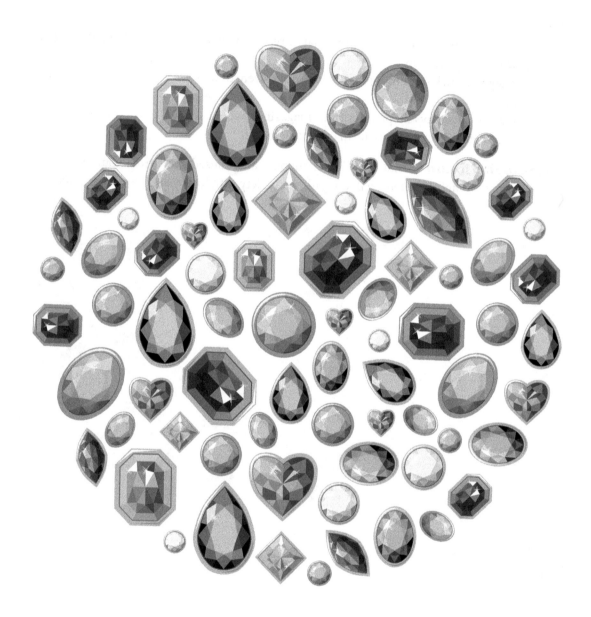

# Learner's Permit

**Source:** Inspired by Brene' Browns Permission Slips activity

**Group Size:** 5–25

**Purpose:** Increase authenticity, vulnerability, and group cohesion

**Props Needed:**

1. Pen
2. Learner's Permit Handout

**Activity Preparation:**

1. Prep time needed: 5 minutes
2. Prior to print off enough handouts for each participant to have one

**Time Needed:**

► Directions: 5 minutes
► Activity: 25 minutes
► Debrief: 15 minutes

**Set-Up:** It would be helpful to have a hard surface for participants to lean on while writing such as tables or clipboards.

**Activity Directions:**

► Explain the Learner's permit
► Provide pens and handout for each participant
► Give group 10–15 minutes to complete list (give a 5- and 2-minute warning)
► Have each member stand up and read their list

**Facilitator Script:** "Have a seat everyone. Most of us have had the experience of getting a learner's permit when we first started to drive. As you may know a learner's permit is the state's department of motor vehicles giving you permission to move forward in the process of learning to drive. Learning to drive is in many ways similar to the change process.

Obtaining a provisional license or learner's permit allows certain restrictions to be lifted from the driver, such as the times that they are allowed to drive, and the number of people allowed in the car. We often place restrictions on our own change process that need to be lifted in order to move forward. Restrictions can be rooted in old messages we heard like 'never let them see you sweat or you better stop crying or I will give you something to cry about.' These messages translate into decision rules about how we present ourselves to the world. We hide, fade, and deny our authentic self and experience. When we are hiding we are spending energy in risk management and image crafting that could otherwise be used toward growth and transformation. This activity is designed to lift the restrictions we bring to the process of change.

Many times when we are in a process of change we need to give ourselves permission to move forward. For a moment, think about some places where you might be stuck. Are you limiting your ability to be vulnerable, to connect with others, to be honest, or in your acceptance of where you're at? In order to move forward we have to first acknowledge where we are. Are there some reservations to the change process or things that might be standing in the way? For example, the desire to be right, or perfectionism might be obstacles to the change process.

Think about what it is that you need a permit to do. Is it a permit to be vulnerable, to laugh at yourself, to cry, to make a mistake, to grow, to leave old patterns behind, to feel the pain, or maybe it is to do the opposite of what the fear in your mind tells you to?

Let's take the next ten minutes to fill out our own learner's permit. What are ten things you give yourself a permit to do or be? Right above the blank lines you will see the sentence stem 'In the spirit of growth and change I (Fill in your name) lift the restrictions I brought to the change process and allow myself to . . .'

Write in the line what comes to mind. So I allow myself to cry, laugh, mess up, be imperfect, get it wrong, grow, heal, and love. Write down whatever comes to mind. First thought, best thought and don't overthink it.

*(Give participants ten minutes to complete this activity and make sure to give time warnings when they are halfway and three-quarters of the way through the allotted time.)*

OK, time is up. Good job everyone. Who would like to share first?" *(Go around the room until everyone gets a chance to share.)*

## Debrief:

- ▶ What was it like coming up with your list?
- ▶ Did you argue with yourself about writing certain items down?
- ▶ Was there anything that you thought about that you opted not to write down?
- ▶ What was your emotional tone as you were writing your list?
- ▶ Did you notice any physical sensations as you were writing your list?
- ▶ What was it like to read it out loud?
- ▶ What was your emotional tone as you were reading your list out loud?
- ▶ Did you notice any physical sensations as you were reading your list out lout?

**Recovery/Wellness Metaphor:** This activity can be a powerful tool for individual or group. It helps to give the participant space to remove obstacles and claim it publicly.

**Role of Facilitator:** Hold the space and allow participants to write down what comes to mind.

## LEARNER'S PERMIT

Obtaining a provisional license or learner's permit allows certain restrictions to be lifted from the driver, such as the times that they are allowed to drive, and the number of people allowed in the car. Oftentimes we place restrictions on our own change process that need to be lifted in order to move forward. Restrictions can be rooted in old messages we heard like "never let them see you sweat" or "you better stop crying or I will give you something to cry about." These messages translate into decision rules about how we present ourselves to the world. We hide, fade, and deny our authentic self and experience. When we are hiding we are spending energy in risk management and image crafting that could otherwise be used toward growth and transformation. This activity is designed to lift the restrictions we bring to the process of change.

In the spirit of growth and change I, _____ lift the restrictions I brought to the change process and allow myself to . . .

1. _____
2. _____
3. _____
4. _____
5. _____
6. _____
7. _____
8. _____
9. _____
10. _____

From this day forward until such time as I choose by the power vested in me I authorize this learner's permit to be true and withstanding.

_____        _____
Signature                                                          Date

Source information for worksheet Created by Marc Pimsler

# Me, Myself, and I

**Group Size:** Any size

**Purpose:** Increase group cohesion, icebreaker, increase self-awareness

**Props Needed:** Pens and handout.

**Prep Time Needed:** 5 minutes

**Time Needed:**
- ▶ Directions: 3 minutes
- ▶ Activity: 5–10 minutes
- ▶ Debrief: 5–10 minutes

**Set-Up:** Print out enough handouts for each participant to have one.

**Activity Directions:**
- ▶ Have enough pens and handouts for group members and pass them out.
- ▶ Each member will complete the sentence stems.
- ▶ Give group 20–25 minutes to complete and give 10-, 5-, and 1-minute warnings.

---

**Facilitator Script:** "It's time to think of Me, Myself and I. This activity is one where we will take time to get to know one another a little more. You have a handout called 'Me, Myself, and I.' Please complete each sentence stem on the handout. Some questions may be easier to answer than others. Some may be fun and silly. Allowing yourself to be vulnerable helps us create a space that is safe for all to share and to grow together. Take the next twenty minutes to complete the worksheet with your first thought. Don't overthink your response. Remember, the first thought is probably your best thought. I will give you a ten-minute warning to let you know that you should be at least halfway through the worksheet. If you are not halfway through, then you are probably overthinking it. *(Give participants about ten minutes and give them a warning time—then allow approximately ten more minutes to complete the rest of the worksheet.)*

Now that everyone has completed their worksheets, we will go around and share. At the table you are sitting, everyone share his or her number one response. When finished, then go on to number two, and so on, until we go through the entire worksheet."

---

**Debrief:**

▶ What was this experience like for you?

▶ What was easy about it?

▶ What was the hardest sentence to complete?

▶ What did you notice about yourself as you were completing the worksheet? As you are reading your answers out loud?

▶ What is something you learned about the group?

**Recovery/Wellness Metaphor:** It can be challenging and sometimes even scary to get to know others and be vulnerable, this activity can ease the tension in getting to know each other.

**Role of Facilitator:** This is an activity for participants to get to know one another. Some questions may be easier than others. Some questions may just be playful and fun. Guide the activity, encouraging participants to write down what first comes to mind and not critique themselves or their thoughts.

**Variation:** Change out questions to best serve your population.

## ME, MYSELF, AND I EXERCISE . . .

This exercise is a series of sentence stems, which are useful for group members to explore their self-concept. Finish each statement with whatever comes to mind; usually your first thought is the best. I encourage you to not edit or censor your initial thoughts. First thought, best thought.

1.  I am happiest when . . .

2.  In a group I am . . .

3.  When I'm alone at home I . . .

4.  Most people know . . .

5.  I get angry when . . .

6.  When someone tries to bully me I feel . . .

7.  What I most want in life is . . .

8.  I often find myself . . .

9.  People who know me well think I am . . .

10. I used to be . . .

11. It makes me uncomfortable when . . .

12. When people first meet me they . . .

13. In a group I am not afraid to . . .

14. When I'm on cloud nine I feel . . .

15. My biggest obstacle is . . .

16. Usually I don't like to talk about . . .

17. When people don't appreciate what I have done I feel . . .

18. I am most content when . . .

Source information for worksheet Created by Marc Pimsler

**REPRODUCIBLE**

19. When everyone is telling me what to do I feel . . .

20. When I am loved I feel . . .

21. I have never liked . . .

22. I trust those who . . .

23. I respect . . .

24. I feel irritated when . . .

25. From past experiences I believe teachers think I am . . .

26. My family thinks that I am . . .

27. I would consider it risky to . . .

28. When someone praises my work I feel . . .

29. I need to improve most in . . .

30. It makes me proud . . .

31. A good thing that happened recently was . . .

32. Since last year I have changed most in . . .

33. People seem to like my . . .

34. My biggest fear is . . .

35. I am most hopeful about . . .

36. My biggest trigger is . . .

37. My greatest dream is . . .

38. When I grow up I want to . . .

# Metaphor Cards

**Source:** *A Teachable Moment*, by Cain, Cummings and Stanchfield.

**Group Size:** Any

**Purpose:** Providing a tangible image upon which participants can attach their thoughts helps give their ideas substance and shape in profound depth. Participants seem to go more in-depth about their ideas and feelings when they attach their thoughts to a symbol or picture.

**Props Needed:** A collection of pictures on cards, minimum of 50 cards.

**Activity Preparation:**
1. Prep time needed: 30 minutes if you are making your own cards

**Time Needed:**
- ▶ Directions: 2 minutes
- ▶ Activity: 10 minutes
- ▶ Debrief: 15 minutes

**Activity Directions:**
- ▶ Invite the group to get into a circle.
- ▶ Spread the cards out before the group.
- ▶ Invite participants to pick a card that metaphorically represents where they are at in their recovery.
- ▶ Ask them to share their card with a partner. This allows them to process through their thoughts before sharing with the large group.
- ▶ Depending on time constraints, either invite each participant to share with the large group, or ask for four to five volunteers to share their story.

---

**Facilitator Script:** "You'll notice I have spread multiple picture cards on the floor (or table). What I'd like you to do is think about where you are at in your recovery journey, and pick a picture that would metaphorically match this place. *(Give an example.)* For example, I might choose this card that has a picture of a railroad track on it. For me, this might represent that I have come a long way, but I am focused on the future, pointed in the right direction. I also have a long way to go before I will feel like I have reached my destination. Peer over the different pictures on the floor (table) and choose one. Then partner with someone and share with them why you chose the card that you chose. Then we will share with the large group as well. Are there any questions on what we are doing?"

## Debrief:

▶ What were some thoughts that went through your mind when you were picking out a card?

▶ How did it feel to share your story?

**Variation:** As an introductory activity participants can choose the card that best represents a strength they bring to the group, or a goal they have for the day, course, or program.

**Variation:** As a pre-brief in the early part of a program, spread the cards out before the participants and have them pick a card that best represents where they are in their recovery at that moment.

**Variation:** At the very beginning of the day/program, spread the cards out before the group and have them pick a card that best represents where they are mentally coming into the day. Invite each participant to share their card with the rest of the group.

**Variation:** Ask participants to pick three pictures that would metaphorically tell the story of where they began, where they are now, and where they want to be.

**Recovery/Wellness Metaphor:** Very often we are challenged to simply tell our story when words escape us. Using these metaphor cards allows us to access the unconscious to tell our story in a way we might have never been able to in the past.

**Where to Find It/How to Make It:** Create your own cards by cutting out photos from magazines or greeting cards. Download images to create cards from public domain Internet websites.

Chiji Cards, Climer Cards, and Metaphor Cards are readily available from Training Wheels, www.trainingwheelsgames.com. Bookstores are a great place to find interesting images on postcards.

# My Coat of Arms

**Group size:** 5–25

**Purpose:** Increase insight and awareness, increase group cohesion, tell our story through symbols and metaphors.

**Props Needed:**
1. Coat of Arms handout
2. Art Supplies (Markers, crayons, colored pencils)

**Activity Preparation:**
1. Prep time needed: 15 minutes
2. Prior to class ensure that you have enough art supplies and handouts so that everyone has some.

**Time Needed:**
- ▶ Directions: 5 minutes
- ▶ Activity: 40 minutes
- ▶ Debrief: 15 minutes

**Set-Up:** It is helpful to make sure that participants have enough supplies spread throughout the room and a hard surface to lean on like a table or clipboard.

**Activity Directions:**
- ▶ Explain history and meaning of a coat of arms.
- ▶ Explain they will be creating their own personal coat of arms.
- ▶ Pass out coat of arms handout and art supplies to each member of the group.
- ▶ Ask members to draw a symbol or picture that represents each section as identified by the legend. Only use words for the motto.
- ▶ Give group about 15–20 minutes to complete the handout.
- ▶ Give a 10- and 5-minute warning to help keep them on time.
- ▶ Once they have completed each section have group members present their coat of arms to group.

**Facilitator Script:** "Gather 'round everyone we are going to go ahead and get started. Today we are going to do some work with the idea of creating our own coat of arms. Does anyone know what that is?

The coat of arms traces back to the eleventh century and was used by the ancient Romans as a way of sharing their history. Militaries, families, corporations, and individuals use the coat of arms to tell their history. To tell the story it usually includes different sections and a motto. Here is a handout in which you will create your own coat of arms.

*(Pass out both sheets of paper and hold up the handout.)* You should have two sheets of paper. One is the actual coat of arms that you will be creating and the other is the legend for what goes where. On the shield, I encourage you to draw pictures and use symbols, no words. And on the ribbon at the bottom, using words, write out your motto. In the top left section, you will draw out a symbol that represents your definition of recovery. In the top right section, you will draw out a symbol that represents something about yourself that makes you feel proud. In the middle left section, you will draw out a symbol that represents a hard lesson you learned. In the middle right section, you will draw out a symbol that represents one opportunity for growth. In the bottom left section you will draw a symbol that represents where you draw your strength from. In the bottom right section, you will draw out a symbol that represents your vision for the future. Finally, in the ribbon at the bottom you will write out your personal motto.

Use the legend as your guide in creating your coat of arms. You will have about fifteen to twenty minutes for this part of the activity. Don't overthink it and remember this is not an art contest.

*(Give group fifteen to twenty minutes to complete their coat of arms. Be sure to give time warnings when they are about halfway and three-quarters of the way through their allotted time.)*

Great job everyone! Our time is about up. Who would like to share what you created?"

## Debrief:

▶ What was challenging about this activity?
▶ Which section was easiest/hardest to do?
▶ How did you feel about presenting your coat of arms?
▶ What did you think as you listened to your peers present theirs?

**Recovery/Wellness Metaphor:** So often we are relegated to tell our stories only using words. By engaging the creative mind, we are able to access even deeper aspects of our story. The coat of arms is often used on the battlefield and often the process of recovery can sometimes feel like a battle. Leaning into this metaphor puts participants in the role of the hero of their story!

**Role of Facilitator:** Help to keep participants on task and know that sometimes doing art projects can bring up shame and other feelings of discomfort. Help to hold the space and keep the room quiet while participants are creating.

**Variation:** Feel free to adapt the sections of the coat of arms to fit your population, topic, and purpose of the group.

**Draw a symbol that represents:**

1. My definition of recovery is . . .
2. Something about myself that makes me feel proud is . . .
3. A lesson hard won was . . .
4. One opportunity for growth is . . .
5. I draw my strength from . . .
6. My vision for my future is . . .

**Write out:**

My personal motto is

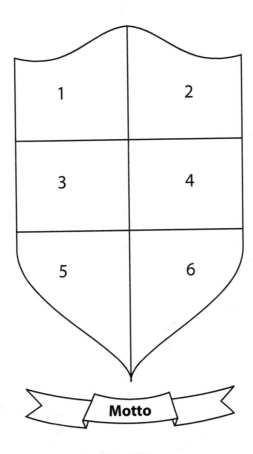

Source information for worksheet created by Marc Pimsler

# No Two Snowflakes

**Group Size:** 2–50

**Purpose:** To illustrate we all perceive directions differently.

**Props Needed:** One sheet of blank paper per person. One pair of scissors per person.

**Activity Preparation:**
1. Prep time needed: 5 minutes
2. Prior to class make sure you have all your props.

**Time Needed:**
- ► Directions: 2 minutes
- ► Activity: 5 minutes
- ► Debrief: 10 minutes

**Set-Up:** Give each participant an identical piece of paper and a pair of scissors. Ask them to hold the piece of paper in their hands and close their eyes.

**Activity Directions:**
- ► Participants may be seated for this activity.
- ► Give each participant an identical piece of paper and a pair of scissors. Ask them to hold the piece of paper in their hands and close their eyes for the duration of the activity.
- ► They are not allowed to ask questions during the activity. Ask the participants to sequentially do the following.
  - ► 1. Fold the paper in half and tear off the bottom right-hand corner.
  - ► 2. Fold the paper in half again and tear off the top right-hand corner.
  - ► 3. Fold the paper in half again and tear off the lower left-hand corner.
- ► After everyone has finished the three "tears" ask them to open their eyes, unfold their papers, and compare results.

**Facilitator Script:** "For this activity I need everyone to get a piece of paper and a pair of scissors, then have a seat in your chairs. (*Wait until everyone has completed this task.*) From this moment forward, you do not have the resource of your voice. You cannot ask me questions, but you must follow my directions. I also need everyone to close their eyes for the duration of the activity. Please stay seated in your chairs, and wait for my instructions. With your piece of paper, please fold the paper in half and tear off the bottom right-hand corner. *(Pause while they perform this task.)* Next, fold the paper in half again and tear off the top right-hand corner. *(Pause while they perform this task.)* Next, fold the paper in half again and tear off the lower left-hand corner. *(Pause again.)* Ok, you may open your eyes and unfold your papers!"

## Debrief:

▶   Compare your paper to someone sitting next to you. Are they the same? Why not?
▶   Didn't everyone hear the exact same instructions?
▶   Who did it the right way?
▶   What was left up to interpretation in this activity?
▶   How did ambiguity play a role in this?
▶   If you hear me say the words "shared mental model," what does that mean?
▶   If I have a mental model of what recovery looks like, why would it look different to you?
▶   How does this relate to what recovery looks like especially between the addict and the family?
▶   How does this apply to giving and receiving instructions for wellness?
▶   If I were to allow you to talk to each other during the activity, how do you think it would have changed the outcome?
▶   How does this relate back to the real world?

**Recovery/Wellness Metaphor:**
It is powerful to recognize that we can hear the exact same directions and yet have two very different outcomes. Sometimes our recovery looks different for our peers. Some go to two to three meetings a day while others go to two to three meetings a week. What is important is that what we do works for us.

**Role of Facilitator:** Guiding the process.

# Picture This

**Group Size:** 5–50

**Purpose:** To explore the differences in communication: what is heard, and what is said.

**Props Needed:**
1. Blank drawing paper.
2. Pens, pencils, markers.
3. If desired, can use art supplies—water paints, glitter, stickers, etc.

**Activity Preparation:**
1. Prep time needed: 5 minutes
2. Assemble supplies—paper and drawing/art supplies and have available to distribute to participants
3. Table or clipboard or sturdy surface for participants to draw/color
4. Allow enough space between participants so when they are drawing they cannot easily see one another's drawings—or have extra props to create a little barrier in-between participants.

**Time Needed:**
- ▶ Directions: 5 minutes
- ▶ Activity: 40 minutes (depending on size of group)
- ▶ Debrief: 10 minutes

**Set-Up:**
1. Tables and chairs—may be set up in classroom style or in a circle.
2. Place drawing paper and art supplies on tables, enough for each participant.

**Activity Directions:**
- ▶ Determine where in the discussion to introduce this activity.
- ▶ Have group pair up.
- ▶ Have each partner draw a simple picture.
- ▶ Then have partner A guide partner B to drawing the same picture that partner A created.
- ▶ Partner B is not allowed to see partner A's picture until after they are finished drawing their rendition.

**Facilitator Script:** "Let's gather around for this next activity. You may have noticed the paper and art supplies. Today we are going to explore differences in communication, and the way we will explore communication is through drawing. You might notice your reaction as I mention that we are going to draw today. We are not art critics, but we are using art as a symbolic way to explore communication—giving information to and receiving from others.

You will need a couple of blank pieces of paper—one to draw on for this first part, and you will need another blank piece of paper for the second part of our activity.

In this first part, I want you to draw something, anything that comes to mind. For example, it can be a person, place, animal or pet. It can be a place of serenity. A place that you like or remember, a place you have been to or want to go to. Something symbolic of the present or your past. It can be shapes or symbols. It can be anything at all. Be as simple or expressive as you choose.

Focus your attention on your drawing. I also want you to have enough space between one another so you don't see one another's drawings. If you need to move around the room to give more space in-between you and another, that is fine. We will take fifteen minutes for this first part."

(Instructor Note: *When 15 minutes has gone by, then interrupt.*)

"For this second part, you are going to partner up with someone. DO NOT let your partner see your drawing. Be sure to have another blank piece of paper to draw on."

(Instructor Note: *Allow participants to find a partner and be seated together.*)

"Now without showing your picture to your partner you will describe your drawing to your partner. You are to use words to describe your picture—but you cannot use the name. For example, if you have a mountain on your picture, then you will describe the shape without using the word *mountain*. If you have a fish on your drawing you will describe the shape, but you cannot use the word *fish* or words associated with a fish like *this is something that swims in the ocean*. You will also communicate where your partner is to draw the object(s) on the paper.

Decide who will be the communicator and who will be the receiver. We will take ten minutes for the first round, and then we will switch roles, and the communicator will become the receiver and will draw your partner's picture.

OK everyone. Let's gather back around in the entire group. Share your original drawing with your partner and let's see how close the pictures align."

### Debrief:

- ▶ What did you notice about yourself when given the activity instructions?
- ▶ Did you notice any judgment of yourself or others?
- ▶ What did you experience about yourself or your partner, when
  - ☐ giving instructions to your partner?
  - ☐ receiving instructions from your partner?
- ▶ What did you learn about yourself—are you a better communicator or receiver?
- ▶ What might get in your way of clear communication—either giving or receiving?
- ▶ What will you do to improve the area that represents a challenge—communicator or receiver?

**Recovery/Wellness Metaphor:** This is a great activity to explore different ways of communication, filters, perceptions, words. Also, a way to support that there are many ways to communicate, differences in approach or words, how they are interpreted or perceived—just like there are different ways into wellness and recovery. Sometimes we can choose to adapt to see or experience things different, and to value the journey of others as unique, and sometimes we have to know how to stay in our own lane.

**Role of Facilitator:** Allow participants to come up with their own drawing. Some may struggle with deciding what to draw, or may want specific directions/guidance. Resist this to allow them to find their own drawing.

**Where to Find It/How to Make It:** Art or office supply store.

# Reel Recovery

**Group Size:** Any

**Purpose:** To increase awareness of one's focus, adaptability, passion, desire, and continuous improvement.

**Props Needed:** None

**Activity Preparation:**
1. Prep time needed: 5 minutes
2. The activity can be accomplished in any setting: individual or group setting.

**Time Needed:**
- ► Activity: 10 minutes, with discussion.
- ► Debrief: 10 minutes; may be more with larger group size.

**Set-Up:**
- ► The activity can be accomplished in any setting: individual or group setting.
- ► Participants may be seated in a classroom style set-up or gathered around in a circle.

**Activity Directions:**
- ► Have participants find a seat—they may be seated in theater style or round circle group.
- ► If you are projecting the story onto a screen, have participants face the projected image or story.
- ► Explain the purpose of the activity.
- ► Read Facilitator's Script and Fly Fishing parallels.

---

**Facilitator Script:** "Hey everyone let's gather around so we can get started with today's group. Let's take time to listen to a story about a woman fly fisher.

I started fly fishing in 2009. I found fly fishing to be a lot tougher than I had expected and I nearly gave up after a few unsuccessful attempts. I usually pick things up very rapidly and I was astounded by how much there was to learn. I was hopelessly discouraged after my initial exposure found me overwhelmed by what seemed to be an endless array of complexities, dozens of casting techniques, and enough knots to hold Houdini captive.

But I kept pushing myself. Tried a new casting technique, tried a new fly, hired a guide to help mend my mistakes. Then one day I realized that I could improve my casting by focusing on my goals, adjusting my techniques, and following through with commitment—all things I instruct my clients to do to meet their goals.

When it dawned on me that I had found something that was pushing me outside my comfort zone, I got excited. I ask people to step outside their comfort zones on a regular basis. Finding something that did the same for me gave me new perspective, and an opportunity to find some parallels back to recovery.

There are several techniques in recovery that remind me of fly fishing: focus, adaptability, passion, desire, and continuous improvement.

Here are a few of my favorite parallels between recovery and fly fishing:

▶ You have to know when to untangle a knot and when to cut your losses. One time I was standing in the river untangling a horrible knot. For some reason I was hell-bent on untangling it instead of cutting off the fly and starting over. Suddenly something caught my eye, and when I looked down I literally had a fish swimming at my knees. Because I was so focused on untangling a knot, I missed the opportunities that were right in front of me. I think we do this in life as well. There are times we spend so much time focused on the mistakes we have made in the past, that we don't see the opportunities that are right in front of us.

▶ Conditions change—you have to be prepared to change with them. There's a saying in fly fishing: 'Don't fish yesterday's fish.' Just because you were successful doing something yesterday, or if one tactic worked for a week, or a month, or a year, that was then. You have to figure out the now. Tides change, weather changes, fish move. Try to look ahead to the next spot, where you can use the knowledge you gained at your old spot. That's how you repeat success.

▶ You have to want to get better or you will become complacent and frustrated.

▶ The last 10 percent of your backcast is the most important part of your cast. Most anglers work two to three times harder than they need to when trying to catch a fish. Most people work two to three times harder than necessary. Better results are necessary with less effort. Sometimes we miss the mark when we are trying to force it to happen. Working smarter rather than harder can be extremely useful.

Take a moment to think about how the lessons from the Reel Recovery story relates to things you have gone through or are currently going through." *(Either have group process personal examples of this lesson or debrief the story.)*

## Debrief:

- ▶ What did you notice as you listened to the story?
- ▶ What thoughts were you aware of as you listened to the story?
- ▶ What are one of the parallels you identified with?
- ▶ What might be getting in your way when you look at your own struggle?

**Recovery/Wellness Metaphor:** This story relates to several recovery slogans like cutting your losses related to knowing when it is important to walk away from people, places, and things that do not support your recovery. Conditions change relates to the slogan learning to live life on life's terms. We have to learn adaptability in order to manage life without using negative coping skills. Recovery is also about not resting on our laurels and the parallel about getting better rather than being complacent relates to that. Like the quote from the movie *Shawshank Redemption* "guess it comes down to a simple choice really, get busy living or get busy dying."

**Role of Facilitator:** Take time to debrief the story with participants, helping them explore what they relate to in the story.

**Variations:** This can be accomplished in individual sessions.

# Serenity Prayer Deconstructed

**Group Size:** 5–50

**Purpose:** Deconstruct the Serenity Prayer in a way that participants can use it as a tool for recovery

**Props Needed:**
1. Flip chart or whiteboard
2. Markers (different colors)
3. Serenity Prayer handout

**Activity Preparation:**
1. Prep time needed: 5 minutes.
2. Prior to class print off enough handouts for each participant.
3. Bring enough pens so that participants can make notes.
4. Familiarize yourself with the Facilitator Script.

**Time Needed:** 45–90 minutes
- ▶ Directions: none
- ▶ Activity: 45 minutes
- ▶ Debrief: 15–30 minutes

**Set-Up:** Prior to group, put chairs in a semi-circle around the whiteboard or flip chart. Familiarize yourself with Facilitator Script and concepts. Copy Serenity Prayer handout. You can write out Serenity Prayer on a flip chart unless you want a participant to do it.

**Activity Directions:**
- ▶ Have the participants find a seat facing the whiteboard.
- ▶ Review the Facilitator Script and introduce the Serenity Prayer as a tool for recovery.

---

**Facilitator Script:** *(Engage group by asking for a volunteer to write out the Serenity Prayer. Allow room to write in-between lines as well as have a second flip chart for the lists OR leave room on the board.)*

*(Pass out handout while prayer is being written on the board.)*

"The Serenity Prayer is said at almost every single 12-step meeting, sometimes twice. We say it unconsciously and most of the time completely unaware of its meaning and true potential to change our lives. The goal of this group is to break down the Serenity Prayer so that you can define it for yourself and see how it can be a tool for transformation. This is going to be very interactive so please jump in when you have a thought or question.

So let's take a look at the first word.

*(Underline God in a different color than it is written in.)*

This word seems to trip some people up. For some people they don't have any issues associated with this word. If you are one of those people that is fantastic and feel free to use it. For those of you that have a problem with this word or will not use this tool because of this word then by all means do not use it. In order for this tool to work you do not have to start out with this word. Again if you do not have any issues with this word use it, if you do then don't use it.

*(Underline the words grant me in a different color than it is written in.)*

Now we have grant me. What does grant me mean to you?

*(Allow group members to throw out what they think it means. Engage with members as they yell out answers.)*

Yes, we are asking for something. It implies we don't have something. What is it we do not have?

*(Allow group members to throw out what they think is missing until someone says serenity. Engage with members as they yell out answers.)*

YES, serenity. So this is how you know that it is time to use this tool—when you need some serenity. So what is serenity?

*(Underline the word serenity in a different color than it is written in. Allow group members to throw out what they think it means. Engage with members as they yell out answers. As soon as someone says peace—)*

YES, peace but it isn't like world peace, right? What type of peace is it?

*(Allow group members to throw out what they think it is.)*

Yes, inner peace or peace of mind.

*(Write Peace of mind on the board on top of the word Serenity.)*

*(Underline the word accept in a different color than it is written in.)*

Now we have the word accept. What does the word accept mean to you?

*(Allow group members to throw out what they think. Engage with members as they yell out answers.)*

Sometimes with this word it is easier to define what it is not rather than what it is. So in order to accept something do you have to like it? Do you have to agree with it? Do you have to give it your permission? NO, in order to accept something you do not have to like it, agree with it, or give it your permission. What you do have to do is simply say 'It is what it is.' In other words you do have to acknowledge it without trying to fix it, fade it, or hide it. You simply have to look at it and say it is what it is. I see you and I acknowledge that it is what it is, you are who you are.

*(Write It is what it IS on the board on top of the word accept.)*

It is usually really easy to accept things that we like and truly a challenge to accept things that we don't. Like when a drug dealer gives you a little bit extra it is typically not hard to accept that; however, when things don't go our way that is usually when we struggle against it.

*(Underline the word courage in a different color than it is written in.)*

Now we have the word courage. What does the word courage mean to you?

*(Allow group members to throw out what they think. Engage with members as they yell out answers.)*

OK, so does anyone remember the movie *Braveheart*? I know it is an old movie, but there is a scene where Mel Gibson is looking across at the opposing army and what does he notice? He notices that he is significantly outnumbered. He looks across at them and the camera zooms in on his face and there is a look of fear that slowly creeps across his face. What does he do next? Well, he paints his face blue which isn't the courageous act. What is the courageous act? He takes one step closer to his enemy. And that to me epitomizes courage. Taking that single step in the face of fear. In fact that is exactly how I define courage, the ability to take the next step especially in the face of fear. To put one foot in front of the other especially when you are afraid or unsure of your footing, that is a courageous act. Courage is not about winning the war it is about fighting in the battle. Courage is certainly not the absence of fear it is moving forward through it.

*(Write FEAR on the flip chart.)*

Does anyone know the acronym for FEAR? So in recovery we see that there are a couple of ways in which to deal with FEAR. There is the relapse oriented approach which says F everything and run and then there is the recovery oriented approach—Face everything and recover. Then there is also false evidence appearing real. So let's say I have been raised to believe that this is the color that represents red.

*(Point to a wall that is not painted red.)*

All my life the people that raised me told me this is what represents red. Then all of a sudden I run into you people and you tell me this color is. . . What would you say this color is? OK, so how will I experience you if you're telling me that this is white but everything in me says that it is red. I will experience suffering and will stay stuck until I am willing to change my perception, which takes tremendous courage, but more on that later.

*(Underline the word wisdom in a different color than it is written in.)*

OK, so now we have the word wisdom. What does the word wisdom mean to you?

*(Allow group members to throw out what they think. Engage with members as they yell out answers.)*

Yes, knowledge, but what type of knowledge, it isn't like book knowledge, what is it? It is knowledge gained from experience.

*(Write Exp. Knowledge on the board on top of the word Wisdom.)*

OK, so where do we get wisdom from?

*(Listen for someone to say our experience.)*

Yes, our experience. We can look at our past and if we are paying attention we can learn from our own experience. Now we don't want to live in the past because that is just depressing; however, when we visit the past it can become an incredible teacher.

*(Listen for someone to say the experience of others.)*

Yes, other people's experience. That is why we have a counselor and a sponsor and other people whom we trust that can help be our guides. Another powerful place to gain wisdom from is from people who just came back from a relapse. They have tremendous experience that we can learn from. Man, when someone comes back into the rooms of recovery from a relapse I am one of the first people to talk to them because I want to know what happened that led them out and what was so bad that it drove them back into recovery. That is tremendous wisdom that I can gain and I don't have to experience any of the pain.

*(Underline the words things I cannot change as well as the words things I can in a different color than they were written in.)*

OK, so now we have these things. Let's first look at the things I cannot change.

*(Draw a vertical line creating two columns. On the top of the left list write Can't Change and on the top of the right list write Can Change.)*

So what are some things that I cannot change?

*(Write out everything that people say. Create an exhaustive list. Things should include: weather, my past, the fact that I am an addict, my diagnosis, the fact that I am in rehab, my parents, other people's perceptions of me, other people's behavior, my exes, other people's opinions, how other people act, the rules of the treatment center, the laws of the land, my genes, my family, things I did while intoxicated . . .)*

*(NOTE: People might challenge that you can change some of these things which leads to a discussion on the difference between change and impact.)*

There is a big difference between having the ability to change something and having the ability to impact it. When we think of the word change you can replace it with the word control. I cannot control what another person does; however, I certainly can impact it. I can't control the future because of all the unknown variables that exist; however, I can certainly impact it. I cannot control the laws of the land; however, I can certainly impact it by becoming a legislator and fighting to create change in our country. In fact, we have such an impact on our environment that steps 8 and 9 were created just to help us address how our behaviors in the past have impacted others. But I simply cannot control or change how others receive those amends. OK, so what about our thoughts or feelings can we control or change?

*(Allow for some discussion on this.)*

So I believe that our thoughts and feelings are very much like a military sonar machine and we are the soldier at the screen. Let's say that you *(point to someone in the group)* are on my team and you come across my screen. What do I do? Well, I will probably just wave and have you pass by uninterrupted. But let's say that you *(point to another group member)* are not on my team and you come across my screen. What do I do? I call you, and you, and you, and we go after him. Now what is the difference?

*(Allow for some discussion on this.)*

The difference is in my response. While I cannot control what comes across my radar screen, I certainly can control what my response to that is. Well, I believe that our thoughts and emotions function in a similar way. I cannot control what initial thoughts or feelings arise; however, I can learn to control my responses to them. For example, I might have a thought 'Man, I'd like to get high.' What I do in response to having that thought is critical. I can think 'I have sixty days clean and I deserve to get high.' I can indulge the thought and make it grow in intensity and power by giving it my power. Or, when I have the thought 'Man, I'd like to get high,' I can follow it up with an action of calling my sponsor or telling on myself. This response diminishes the thought's power and intensity. So I cannot necessarily control my initial thoughts but I certainly can control my response to them. Let's put thoughts and feelings in the middle.

*(Allow for some discussion on this and write the words thoughts and feelings on the vertical line in the center.)*

The other thing I like to put in the middle is the present. Because there are so many unknown variables that affect the present moment that we cannot say we have full authority over it. But this leads us into a discussion of what we can change. Before we move on does anyone have anything else for this list of things we cannot change?

*(Allow for some discussion and if anyone thinks of anything else write it down.)*

OK, so what do you think goes on this list?

*(NOTE: Truly there are only a couple of things that can go here—my behaviors, my perceptions . . .)*

*(Allow group members to throw out what they think. Engage with members as they yell out answers. Be clear about what you write on this list. It is important to show visually that there are many more things we cannot change than there are things we can. So only write out my behaviors rather than list out all the different types of behaviors. For example, when someone, people, places, and things challenge that notion.)*

Can we really change or control people, places, and things? The truth is we can't; we can change who we hang out with but that is really changing where we show up which is our behavior. So while this is a popular slogan in recovery—to change people, places, and things—we truly can't do it. Is there anything else that we can change? What do you notice about these two lists?

*(Allow group members to throw out what they think. Engage with members as they yell out answers. Point to second list.)*

What does this list have in common? ME.

*(Circle all the MY's and write ME off to the side.)*

What does this list have in common? Not ME.

*(Write Not ME off to the side.)*

OK, good, so I believe that in any given twenty-four-hour period there is a limited amount of energy that a human being has to spend. Some of it we are able to direct and some of it we are not. For example, thank God we do not have to remember to remind our heart to beat, lungs contract, or cells divide. I don't know about you but I would have been dead a long time ago. But there is a significant amount of energy that is up to me to determine and direct how I choose to spend it. So who is good at math?

*(Write 80% × 0 = next to the first list of things we cannot change.)*

Let's say we spend 80 percent of our energy on the things we cannot change. What is the return on that investment? ZERO, correct.

*(Write 80% × 1 = next to the second list of things we can change.)*

Let's say we spend 80 percent of our energy on the one thing we can change—which is ME—what is the return on that investment? Eighty percent, correct. So, focusing all our energy trying to change the things we cannot is like banging our head against the wall wondering why we have a headache. That is truly insanity. But when we focus all of our energy on the one thing we can change—ME—that is when we are truly living skillfully. So, what are we supposed to do with this list?

*(Point to the first list of things we cannot change. Listen for someone to say Accept and write the word Accept on top of the list.)*

Yes, accept it. And what do we need in order to change this list?

*(Point to the second list of things we can change. Listen for someone to say courage and write the word Courage on top of the list.)*

Yes, we need courage, because change can be very scary. Again, we do not need to know how to finish the marathon we simply need the courage to take that next step. I believe that 90 percent of our frustrations occur when we are too busy having the courage to change something that in fact we cannot OR are too busy accepting something about ourselves that we should be changing.

*(Circle the word accept and draw a diagonal line across to the other list and then circle the word courage and draw a diagonal line across to the other list, creating a big X.)*

Clearly this creates chaos. In fact, change is so scary one of our primary defense mechanisms is creating chaos. Anyone remember the *Peanuts* character, Pigpen? He was the guy that every time he made a move there was a cloud of dust all around him. That cloud of dust is very much like the chaos we create. But what happened when he would stop moving, what did we see?

*(Listen for someone to say the dust settled.)*

Yes, the dust settled. And we saw him. That is what we call vulnerability and it is incredibly scary and comes with tremendous risk, because if you truly see me I risk getting hurt. The problem is that living a life in hiding I am already in pain, but at least the pain is my own and familiar. In fact, many times we don't change until the pain of staying the same outweighs the pain of change. That is why we need courage; the ability to put one foot in front of the other especially in the face of fear when we are looking to create change in our lives.

We have to get real clear about what to do with both of these lists. We need to accept the ability to say it is what it is with the things we cannot change and we need to beg for courage to change the one thing we can, which is ourselves.

So you can use the Serenity Prayer as a tool whenever you find yourself frustrated or disturbed. Simply make a list of all the things that you are frustrated about and determine which category they fall in—Things I cannot change or Things I can change. Once you know which list they go in, you know exactly what you need to do. When we can put things in their proper places, we have the freedom to choose skillful actions.

---

### Debrief:

- ▶ Is this a different way of looking at the Serenity Prayer?
- ▶ What came up for you as you listened to this?
- ▶ What can help you implement these concepts into your life?
- ▶ What might prevent you from implementing change in your life?
- ▶ How will you address these obstacles?

**Recovery/Wellness Metaphor:** Research indicates that stress is a significant contributor to returning to use. It is critical to support participants in adopting tools that help to reduce stress. This way of thinking and approaching problems will help participants to sort through their problems to see what category they fall in. Once participants know what category their problems fall, in they automatically know what to do about them.

**Role of Facilitator:** In this activity the facilitator takes on the role of guide. Be a guide rather than a teacher. Engage participants rather than lecture. Ask lots of questions and keep participants engaged by going around and distributing the participation amongst all members.

This is a more active role and the more familiar you are with the script the more effective you become.

**Variations:** The script can be adapted to suit your needs. Feel free to use the concepts without having to use the script once you are familiar enough with them. Adapt and apply principles as you see fit. Feel free to get as creative as you want. Have participants add in their own experiences with using this tool. Also you can give homework or challenge group members to find opportunities to use this tool in their lives and journal their experiences.

# God, Grant me the Serenity
## To accept the things I can not change
## The courage to change the things I can
## The wisdom to know the difference

| | |
|---|---|
| | |

Source information for worksheet Created by Marc Pimsler

# The Starfish Story

**Group Size:** Any

**Purpose:** To increase awareness of the meaning and benefit of one's purpose in a change process.

**Props Needed:**
1. The Starfish Story—can either be copied as a handout or projected on a screen.

**Activity Preparation:**
1. Prep time needed: 5 minutes
2. The activity can be accomplished in any setting: individual or group setting.

**Time Needed:**
- ▶ Directions: Facilitator will read The Starfish Story, or have a group member read the story.
- ▶ Activity: 10–20 minutes, with discussion.
- ▶ Debrief: 10 minutes; may be more with larger group size.

**Set-Up:**
1. The activity can be accomplished in any setting: individual or group setting.
2. Participants may be seated in a classroom or gathered around in a circle.

**Activity Directions:**
- ▶ Have participants find a seat; they may be seated in classroom style or round circle group.
- ▶ If you are projecting the story onto a screen, have participants face the projected image or story.
- ▶ Explain the purpose of the activity.
- ▶ Read Facilitator's Script and The Starfish Story.

**Facilitator Script:** "Today's activity is designed to explore the meaning and benefit of one's purpose in a change process. When we think about recovery and wellness, sometimes the process may seem overwhelming. Sometimes we may feel like we are getting nowhere. One may think an easy solution is to give up when there are so many perceived obstacles in your recovery and wellness journey. Let's take time to listen closely to The Starfish Story.

## The Starfish Story (based on the story by Loren Eiseley)

A young boy was picking up objects off the beach and tossing them out into the sea. An old man approached him and saw that the objects were starfish. "Why in the world are you throwing starfish in the water?" he asked. "If the starfish are still on the beach when the tide goes out and the sun rises, they will die" the boy replied. "That is ridiculous. There are thousands of miles of beach and millions of starfish. You can't really believe that what you're doing could possibly make a difference!" The young boy reached down to carefully pick up another starfish, and remarked as he tossed it out into the waves, "It makes a difference to this one."

You see the boy knew that we can make a difference to every person we come in contact with. The choice is ours as to what type of impact we have on a person. We can do things that hurt them or we can do things to help them. Today we have the opportunity to help those we come in contact with."

---

### Debrief:

- ► What was your experience as you listened to the story?
- ► What thoughts were you aware of?
- ► What are some of the challenges one faces that may seem overwhelming?
- ► What might be getting in your way when you look at the bigger picture?
- ► How does perseverance help in accomplishing our goal(s)?
- ► What are two small steps you will focus on to strengthen your recovery and wellness?

**Recovery/Wellness Metaphor:** Participants have an opportunity to look at how they are impacting the people they come in contact with. We may have spent time hurting others but today as a result of living in recovery we can learn to help others and make a big difference in their lives.

**Role of Facilitator:** Take time to debrief the story with participants, helping them explore their perceptions that may keep them off track from their recovery. Gradually move to small steps, easily achievable, to help group participants see success in one small step at a time.

**Variations:** This can be accomplished in individual sessions or given as homework.

**Reference:** *The Starfish Story* is adapted from "The Star Thrower," authored by Loren Eiseley (1907–1977), published in *The Unexpected Universe* (1969).

https://www.goodreads.com/author/quotes/56782.Loren_Eiseley

# Stigma—A Mark of Disgrace

Activity generously provided by Christina McCleskey

**Group Size:** 5–50

**Purpose:** Create awareness of how labels and stigma affect us, facilitate discussion, increase awareness on the effect of words.

**Props Needed:**
1. Post-it notes
2. Pens

**Activity Preparation:** Prep time needed: 5 minutes
1. Familiarize yourself with the activity and concepts

**Time Needed:**
- ▶ Directions: 5 minutes
- ▶ Activity: 20 minutes
- ▶ Debrief: 25 minutes

**Set-Up:** Ask for a volunteer that would be willing to allow another group member to place labels on his or her body. Choose volunteers carefully to ensure activity will not be unsafe in any way.

**Activity Directions:**
- ▶ Pass out labels
- ▶ Instruct group to write down stigma words they associate or think others associate with addiction, addicts, alcoholics.
- ▶ Ask two volunteers to come stand in front of the room.
- ▶ One participant will read each label out loud and place it on the second participant.
- ▶ Process

**Facilitator Script:** "Have a seat everyone. Today we are going to take a look at how stigma can affect us. The word stigma is defined as a mark of disgrace associated with a particular circumstance, quality, or person. Disgrace is often associated with shame. Disgrace is defined as loss of reputation or respect, especially as the result of a dishonorable action; to bring shame or discredit on someone or something. Guilt says, 'I made a mistake' where shame says, 'I am a mistake.' Shame creates discouragement. The opposite of disgrace is honor, respect, and encouragement.

Here are some sticky notes and pens *(either pass out supplies or have them spread out prior to group)*. Take a moment to write down as many stigma words or phrases that you associate or think others associate with addiction, addicts, or alcoholics. *(Give group about 5 minutes to come up with as many sticky notes as they can.)* Write each word or phrase on a separate label.

*(When group has had enough time to brainstorm stigma labels—)* Great job everyone! Now I need my two volunteers to come up to the front. Give them a hand *(have group members cheer on their peers)*. OK, so you are going to read each label slowly and then place it on her/him.

*(Make sure that you are paying attention to the emotional tones of the volunteers as well as the group. Also make sure that the volunteer who is getting labels placed on him/her is safe. This is a very powerful experience and can bring a lot up for all. When the volunteer is done reading and placing all the labels, turn to the stigmatized volunteer and say—)*

How do you feel right now? *(Have volunteer with labels answer.)* Do you feel encouraged right now? *(Have volunteer with labels answer.)* What is your relationship with the sticky notes? *(Have volunteer with labels answer.)*

*(Ask the group—)* What do you all notice about him/her? *(pointing at volunteer)*

*(Turn to volunteer)* Do you want to keep these labels on you? *(let them answer)* OK, well you can do whatever you want to with them. *(It is empowering for the volunteer to take them off themselves or ask for help if they choose.)* You all can sit down. Give them a hand! *(Have group members cheer on their peers)*.

By increasing my awareness, I can choose to take off the labels that others may try to put on me or that I have put on myself. We can begin to choose the words that we want to carry and use for ourselves. It is our job to be conscious of the words and the effects those words have on us. Words have the power to hurt or to heal to create war or peace. Words can even shape our identity. What did you notice in this experience? *(give group ample time to debrief)*

## Debrief:

- ▶ What was it like to think of stigmatizing words that describe addiction, addicts, and alcoholics?
- ▶ What came up for you as you were writing the words down?
- ▶ What did you notice as the labels were being read and placed?
- ▶ (Ask volunteer) What was it like to place the labels on your peer?
- ▶ (Ask volunteer) What was it like to have the labels placed on you?
- ▶ How do you think wearing the labels impacts how you live your life?
- ▶ How does this relate to recovery?
- ▶ How do we begin to take off the labels that other people try to place upon us?
- ▶ How does taking off the labels empower and encourage you?

**Recovery/Wellness Metaphor:** We live in a world where addiction, addicts, and alcoholics are stigmatized. This stigmatization only serves to perpetuate addiction. Recovery allows us to renegotiate our relationship to labels and define identity for ourselves.

## Variations:

- ▶ The stigma of addiction can be substituted out for any other category of stigma.
- ▶ Instead of stigma, this group can use how trauma impacts us.

**Where to Find It/How to Make It:** Labels can be purchased anywhere. It is even more impactful to use a variety of colors for the labels as it has a greater effect.

# The Dance of Surrender

**Group Size:** 5–40

**Purpose:** Embody the lesson of surrender while exploring the concept of resistance.

**Props Needed:** None

**Activity Preparation:** None

**Time Needed:**
- ▶ Directions: 5–10 minutes
- ▶ Activity: 20 minutes
- ▶ Debrief: 15 minutes

**Set-Up:** None

**Activity Directions:**
- ▶ Have group members pair up with someone of approximate height.
- ▶ There will be 2 rounds, each with their own instructions.
- ▶ It is helpful for the facilitator to go first, demonstrating how to "resist" the push. This clues the group in to resist with their shoulders which will usually cause them to fall back.

**Safety:** Say a word about safety so participants don't hurt themselves by overly enthusiastic pushing.

**Facilitator Script:** "Gather 'round everyone. First pick a partner of similar height. *(Once pairs are in place continue with instructions—)*

## Round 1

Now that you are in your pairs determine who is partner A and who is partner B. Face each other and stand about one foot apart. Partner A is going to attempt to push partner B back using his hands and not moving his feet. Partner B is going to make an attempt at resisting partner A's push without falling backward. Watch me before trying it.

*(Facilitator demonstrates with a partner. Facilitator's partner attempts to push facilitator back; facilitator resists and tightens her shoulders and arms go forward trying to prevent the force. Consequently facilitator takes a step backward due to the force pushing her off-balance.)*

Remember the goal is not to hurt your partner; nothing is worth getting hurt over. We are simply attempting to make your partner take a step backward not push them through the wall.

Once Partner A has gone a couple of times, switch roles so that Partner B is now trying to push back Partner A.

---

## Debrief Round 1:

- ▶  What was that like?
- ▶  Did you step backward?

---

## Round 2

This time we are going to have the same task but adjust our strategy. Watch my shoulders and arms.

*(Facilitator demonstrates with a partner. This time when facilitator's partner attempts to push facilitator back, facilitator relaxes her shoulders and arms go backward absorbing the force. Consequently, facilitator's arms go backward but facilitator stays strong maintaining balance. This usually causes the other partner to lose his balance. Listen for the ooos and ahhhs.)*

What did you notice? *(Make sure participants understand the new strategy.)* Now each of you have a turn with this new strategy.

---

## Debrief Round 2:

- ▶  What was that like?
- ▶  Did you step backward?
- ▶  What was the intention the first time?
- ▶  What was the strategy? Was it effective?
- ▶  What was the intention the second time?
- ▶  How was this strategy more effective?
- ▶  How did you feel the first time?
- ▶  How did you feel the second time?

**Recovery/Wellness Metaphor:** Often when we encounter struggles, our natural instincts are to resist and push back. This usually results in us becoming unbalanced. Sometimes when we fight fire with fire we get burned. However, if we can learn to truly surrender we are actually empowered. When we know who we are we can stand strong within our core. All of a sudden, we are no longer wrestling with life we are now dancing.

**Role of Facilitator:** Support participants in thinking of their own conceptions of surrender and resistance. Process how to apply these lessons to their recovery and lives.

**Variations:** If you do not want each participant to try it you can select a partner and just demonstrate it to them.

# The Inukshuk

**Group size:** Any

**Purpose:** To increase awareness of one's response to another's struggle.

**Props Needed:**
1. The Inukshuk can either be copied as a handout or projected on a screen.
2. Variation: Let participants make their own inukshuks with rocks and a glue gun. In this instance, you would need multiple rocks and hot glue guns.

**Activity Preparation:**
1. Prep time needed: 5 minutes
2. The activity can be accomplished in any setting: individual or group setting.

**Time Needed:**
- ▶ Directions: Facilitator will read the Inukshuk story, or have a group member read the story.
- ▶ Activity: 10 minutes.
- ▶ Debrief: 10 minutes; may be longer with larger groups.

**Set-Up:**
- ▶ The activity can be accomplished in any setting: individual or group.
- ▶ Participants may be seated in a classroom style set-up or seated in a circle.

**Activity Directions:**
- ▶ Have participants find a seat.
- ▶ If you are projecting the story onto a screen, have participants face the projected image or story.
- ▶ Explain the purpose of the activity.
- ▶ Read Facilitator's Script and The Inukshuk story.

**Facilitator Script:** "Hey everyone gather 'round so we can get started with today's group. Let's take time to listen to the story of The Inukshuk.

## The Inukshuk Story

The Inukshuk (pronounced in-ook-shook), are stone monuments erected in the image of humans. They are an ancient symbol of Inuit culture traditionally used as landmarks and navigation aids in the Baffin region of Canada's Arctic. It is the Inuit word meaning "in the Image of Man." The Inukshuk are magnificent lifelike figures of stone in human form with outstretched arms and serves as a well-known symbol of northern hospitality and friendship. Built along treeless horizons, these landmarks helped travelers navigate on land and water. They endured as eternal symbols of leadership, encouraging the importance of friendship and reminding us of our dependence upon one another. The traditional meaning of an Inukshuk was to act as a compass or guide for a safe journey. The Inukshuk, like ancient trackers, helped guide people seeking their way through the wilderness. It represents safety and nourishment, trust and reassurance. The Inukshuk guided people across the frozen tundra and gave them hope in barren places to handle hardships they encountered. These primitive, stone images showed the way ahead . . . pointing you in the direction you wanted to go. These beacons of the North have now been adapted as symbols of friendship, reminding us that today as in yesteryear, we all depend on one another.

One of their purposes was to communicate direction in the harsh and desolate Arctic. As such they were a tool for survival, and symbolic of the unselfish acts of a nomadic people—the Inuit—who built them as signposts to make the way easier and safer for those who followed.

The hands of many and the efforts of an entire group were required to build these massive stone sculptures. They are the result of a consensus of purpose, of focused action by a group united in its goal and labor. The Inukshuk are the product of cooperation, teaching us that as good as our individual efforts may be, together we can do even greater things.

Each stone is a separate entity. Each supports, and is supported by, the one above and the one below it. No one piece is any more or less important than another. Its strength lies in its unity. Its significance comes from its meaning as a whole. What is true about the Inukshuk is true about people. Each individual entity alone has significance. As part of a team each of us supports, and is supported by, another. We are united by our common goals, and together we are part of a greater whole.

The stones which make up the Inukshuk are secured through balance. They are chosen for how well they fit together. Looking at the structure it can be easily seen that the removal of even one stone will destroy the integrity of the whole. So, too, with a team. Each individual in a team is necessary for the realization of the team's purpose. The removal of even one person will result in the weakening of the structure. What holds the team together is the balance—the complementary nature of the individual skills.

The Inukshuk are a symbol of the human spirit. They recognize our ability to succeed with others, where we would fail alone. They remind us of our need to belong to something greater than ourselves. They reinforce our ability to commit to common goals.

The Inukshuk celebrate our working together. They continue to remind us of our inter-dependent responsibilities to invest our efforts today, to direct a better way for all of our tomorrows.

Take a moment to think about what the Inukshuk means to them. What would symbolize being on the right path? *(Either have group process personal examples of this lesson or debrief the story.)*

## Debrief:

► What did you notice as you listened to the story?
► What were some thoughts you had as you listened to the story as to what the Inukshuk would symbolize in your life?
► Who are some of the people that help keep you on the right path?
► What are some strategies you have developed to help keep you on the right path?

**Recovery/Wellness Metaphor:** Like the Inukshuk, recovery's strength lies in unity. "We can do together what we could never do apart" is the battle cry of many groups. Personal recovery depends on the unity of the group, much like one rock does not make an Inukshuk. In recovery, we stand up as a guide for those that come behind us, leading the way, like the Inukshuk. Recovery is a symbol of the human spirit. If a man can fall, certainly that same man can rise up.

**Role of Facilitator:** Take time to debrief the story with participants, helping them explore what perceptions or actions may keep them out of balance when they detour from their wellness path. Assist participants to explore who the people are in their life that help keep them on the right path.

**Variation:** This can be accomplished in individual sessions.

**Variation:** Gather enough smooth, flat stones for participants to create their own Inukshuks. Have participants name a person for each of the rocks they use to build their structure, that have supported them in their recovery journey. Consider having participants hot-glue their rock structure together and put it in a place they will see it often, to remind them they are on the right path.

# The Other Side

**Group size:** 1–50

**Purpose:** Problem Solving, Perspective Awareness, Conflict Resolution

**Props Needed:** At least one copy of the book *The Other Side* by Istvan Banyai; two is better. The reason for two is that some of the pages are "better" than others for this activity. There are ten or so great pages for perspective in the book, so if you have a group larger than twenty people, I recommend two or more books.

**Activity Preparation:** Make sure you have laminated pages of the book *The Other Side*

**Time Needed:**

- ▶ Directions: 2 minutes
- ▶ Activity: 10 minutes
- ▶ Debrief: 15 minutes

**Set-Up:** Gather group together

**Activity Directions:**

- ▶ Invite your participants to find a partner.
- ▶ Slide one page of the book in-between each pair. Try to distribute the pages to each pair so that each person in the pair only sees one side of the page.
- ▶ Have players closely examine their side of the picture for all of the details. Let them know that they are NOT to show their picture to their partner.
- ▶ Instruct players to discuss what is happening on their side of the page and then to listen to their partner's perspective from their page.
- ▶ Have each pair try to determine what event or story is taking place.
- ▶ After several minutes of discussion, allow participants to reveal their pictures to their partner and discuss the differences in the perspective of "the other side."

---

**Facilitator Script:** "Hey everyone, gather around. Today we are going to partner up into teams of two. Go ahead and find a partner. Once you have a partner stand facing each other. I am going to come around and place a picture in-between you. Do not turn the page around. Your task is to take turns and determine what event or story is taking place. Please take about two minutes each to describe what you see. Any questions? Great, let's do this.

*(Pass out* The Other Side *pages, one per team, and give participants about two minutes each to describe what they see.)* OK, now turn it around so you can see what your partner was seeing. *(Give them a moment to see the other side.)*

*The Other Side* by Istvan Banyai is a visually dynamic and exciting book. There are few words in this book, but colorful graphic designs on each page offer intimate perspectives on the same scene. Each illustration in the book has another side. As you turn each page over, you will be surprised by the unique perspective on 'the other side.'"

---

**Debrief:** It is helpful for participants to debrief with their partner before debriefing with the large group. Ask the pairs to discuss the following questions:

- ▶ How was your perspective different from your partner's?
- ▶ Were you open to hearing the perspective of your partner's page?
- ▶ If you were in a conflict with your partner, how difficult would it be to hear his/her perspective?
- ▶ How did you communicate your page to your partner?
- ▶ What type of communication did you use to describe your perspective?
- ▶ What would happen if you openly listened in a conflict as you did in this activity?
- ▶ Why is it important to consider "the other side" and another perspective?

After participants have debriefed in small groups, invite them to sit or stand in a large circle with their partner and their page of the book. Allow them to briefly describe their page and the different perspective on "the other side" as well as any learning discovered in their small-group discussion.

**Recovery/Wellness Metaphor:** It is very helpful to increase group cohesion and to recognize there are many ways of looking at the same event. It is helpful to consider other people's perspectives. Your perspective can change, depending on which side of the story you are standing on.

### About the Author of *The Other Side*

Istvan Banyai, the acclaimed Hungarian-born creator of Zoom and Re-Zoom and illustrator of several other books for children, is also well known for his editorial illustrations, which have been published in *The New Yorker* and *Rolling Stone*, among other journals. His perspective, always unexpected (sometimes even to him), has made him one of the most original and iconoclastic illustrators today. He lives in New York and Connecticut.

**Where to Find It/How to Make It:** Purchase copies of *The Other Side* from Amazon.com.

# The Voices in My Head

**Group size:** 5–25

**Purpose:** Increase awareness, discern internal self-talk

**Props Needed:** None

**Activity Preparation:**

1. Be familiar with the different aspects of the role-play.

**Time Needed:**

- ▶ Directions: 5 minutes
- ▶ Activity: 40 minutes
- ▶ Debrief: 15 minutes

**Set-Up:** Group can sit in the round or theatre style.

**Activity Directions:**

Designate roles: Newcomer, Voice of Addiction, Voice of Recovery, Player

- ▶ Part 1: The Newcomer
  - ☐ This person is playing the role of a typical person in early recovery or simply of themselves.
- ▶ Part 2: Voice of Addiction
  - ☐ This person is playing that part of us that wants to get high again.
- ▶ Part 3: Voice of Recovery
  - ☐ This person is playing that part of us that wants us to engage recovery.
- ▶ Part 4: The Player
  - ☐ This person is playing the role of a drug-using peer.
- ▶ Introduce a role-play scenario
  - ☐ 1st role play—Newcomer has 15 days clean, Part 2 very loud, Part 3 whisper.
  - ☐ 2nd role play—Newcomer has 3 months clean, Part 2 and Part 3 speak in regular speaking voice.
  - ☐ 3rd role play—Newcomer has 18 months clean, Part 2 whisper, Part 3 speaks very loud.

**Facilitator Script:** "Have a seat everyone. OK, today we are going to do some work with the voices in our head. Some of you may have heard people in 12-step meetings talk about the committee referring to the chatter going on in here *(point to head)*. Well we are going to look at what it often sounds like. In order to do this, well, I need some help.

So I need a volunteer to come up here. *(Pick a participant to be the Newcomer. You can ask for volunteers for the remaining roles or you can ask the participant to select the players.)* OK, we are going to get a good look at what goes on inside your head. You will be called the Newcomer.

Now we need someone to be the Voice of Addiction. This is that voice in us that wants to tear us down and fool us into believing it is a good idea to get high again. *(Pick someone.)* I need for you to say anything you can to convince him to use; as if your very life depends on it.

Great, now we need someone to be the Voice of Recovery. This is that voice in us that wants to see us succeed and is basically our inner cheerleader. *(Pick someone.)* So you are going to say anything you can to keep him from getting high; as if your very life depends on it.

*(Talk to the Newcomer—)* Great, now we need someone for you to interact with. We will call this person the Player. This person is going to be offering you your drug of choice. Who would be good for that? *(Pick a participant to be the Player.)* So I need for you to be really convincing as to why he should get high with you. Like the stuff you got is really good. I mean the best he has ever had.

Great, now we have all of our people. *(Put people in their places and review their roles.)*

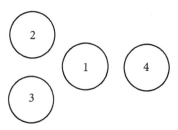

1 = The Newcomer

2 = Voice of Addiction

3 = Voice of Recovery

4 = The Player

*(Point to the Newcomer)* OK, you are the Newcomer. You have fifteen days clean. You are in outpatient treatment. With fifteen days clean you are not exactly sure if this is going to work for you.

*(Addressing the Voice of Addiction)* You are hungry and haven't been fed in fifteen days. You are used to getting your way and this is the perfect opportunity to get *(point to the Newcomer)* the Newcomer high. I want you to be very loud and strong as if there is no question as to whether or not the Newcomer is getting high today.

*(Addressing the Voice of Recovery)* You are very new on this scene, still trying to figure things out and get your footing. You are going to whisper and make simple suggestions.

*(Addressing the Newcomer)* So here is the deal, since these two *(pointing to the Voice of Addiction and Recovery)* are inside your head only you can hear and interact with them. *(Talking to the Player—)* You can only hear and interact with the Newcomer since you are the voices in his head.

*(Addressing all roles—)* Does anyone have any questions about your role or what you are doing?

Great, now here is the scenario. You *(addressing the Newcomer)* walk into a gas station and run into your old drug dealer *(point to the Player. Now talking to the Player—)* You are very happy to see the Newcomer because you just got some of the best stuff you have had in a long time and are very excited to share it with your old buddy. Convince the Newcomer to get high. And go!

*(Let it play on for about five to seven minutes.)*

Now we are going to do the same role-play but this time you *(Addressing the Newcomer)* have three months clean. *(Point to the Player; now talking to the Player—)* You are very happy to see the Newcomer because you just got some of the best stuff you have had in a long time and are very excited to share it with your old buddy. *(Addressing the Voice of Addiction and Recovery—)* You two are going to speak at your regular talking tone and volume. And go!

*(Let it play on for about five to seven minutes.)*

Now we are going to do the same role-play but this time you *(addressing the Newcomer)* have eighteen months clean. *(Point to the Player; now talking to the Player—)* You are still very happy to see the Newcomer. *(Addressing the Voice of Addiction—)* This time you are only allowed to whisper as the Newcomer now has eighteen months sober and is much stronger in his recovery. *(Addressing the Voice of Recovery—)* This time you are able to speak very loud and strongly rooted in recovery. And go!

*(Let it play on for about five to seven minutes.)*

OK, and scene . . . Great job guys, have a seat. So what did you all notice?"

**Debrief:**

► What was the experience like for each volunteer?
► How is the two parts similar to the journey of recovery?
► Do the two voices sound different for persons in early recovery versus persons in long-term recovery?
► What happened when the client listened to the Voice of Addiction rather than the Voice of Recovery? Did the body language change?
► What happened when the client listened to the Voice of Recovery rather than the Voice of Addiction? Did body language change?
► What skills are necessary to strengthen one voice over the other?
► What happens when we put our energy into the voice that gets us off-balance?
► Which voice do we respond to? Why?

**Recovery/Wellness Metaphor:** This can be a very powerful activity to showcase how the mind of a person in early recovery can be very chaotic and confusing. Many times participants exclaim that this is really what it sounds like inside their head. Process what actions make each voice louder and what quiets them down. For example, going to a meeting and calling a sponsor might make the voice of addiction quieter and make the voice of recovery louder. Listening to music you used to listen to while partying might strengthen the voice of addiction.

**Role of Facilitator:** Ensure participants are clear on their roles. Guide the role-play when stuck. Help process to drive home the imagination of The Voices in My Head Activity.

**Variations:** Additional Voices may include, the Voice of

► Higher Power
► Sponsor
► Family Member
► Roommate
► Employer
► Trauma
► Guilt
► Shame
► Drug of Choice

# These Two Things

**Group Size:** 5–25

**Purpose:** Explore change process, create group cohesion, increase awareness

**Props Needed:**
1. Natural items found outdoors

**Activity Preparation:** None needed

**Time Needed:**
- ► Directions: 5 minutes
- ► Activity: 40 minutes
- ► Debrief: 15 minutes

**Set-Up:** None needed

**Activity Directions:**
- ► Instruct participants that this is a silent activity.
- ► Each one is to go outside.
- ► They are to pick up two things. One will represent their addiction. One will represent their recovery.
- ► If a participant is not a person in recovery from a substance use disorder, ask them to think of an experience or situation in which they made a positive change, and pick up something that represents before the change experience and something that represents the after or current change.
- ► Give them ten to fifteen minutes to find their two objects.
- ► Instruct participants to gather in a circle when they have gathered up their two things.
- ► Going around one person at a time, each participant will explain to the group what their two things are and what they each represent.
- ► Participants are to then run or walk briskly around the inner circle, high-fiving every participant to receive and give props!

**Facilitator Script:** "OK, everyone we are about to get started. In a moment we are going to go outside and finish group out there. Once we leave the group room this will be a silent activity until we are all circled up. You will have ten minutes to find two objects. One object that represents your addiction and one that represents your recovery. Be as creative as you want to be. Don't just pick up a cigarette to represent your addiction. While you are looking for objects remember this is a silent activity. Don't share your objects with others until the second part of this activity. Once you have both objects bring them with you and let's meet at _____ (*pick a meeting spot where you have enough room to circle up and not be disturbed by cars*). Any questions?

OK, let's go outside and we will meet at the _____ once you have your objects.

(*Once everyone has their objects form a circle and introduce the next step in the group.*)

OK, circle up everyone. Please place your objects behind you so you have your hands free. Here is what we are going to do. You will introduce yourself with 'Hi my name is _____ and I found this (*hold hand up*) to represent my addiction. I picked this because (*and tell us why you picked it*). And I picked this (*hold other hand up*) to represent my recovery, and I picked it because' (*and tell us why*). Then everyone is going to clap like they just heard the most amazing thing (*start clapping*), everyone start clapping, and you're going to do this (*run around the circle and give everyone a high 5*). OK, any questions?"

**Debrief:**

▶ What were your feelings when explaining the two different things?
▶ Do we simply toss away the one thing identified as the before thing? Why is it important to remember both?
▶ What does it mean if we chose to avoid one over the other thing?
▶ How did it feel to run around and receive props for your new change?
▶ What did you notice about yourself when instructed to go around and get your props? If you were hesitant, what might that have been about? What was it like when you did it anyway?

**Recovery/Wellness Metaphor:** It is powerful to think about our addiction and recovery using the other half of our brain. Entering into the world of metaphor we are able to gain a different vantage point and thus arrive at a deeper inner knowing.

**Role of Facilitator:** Keep group on task and ensure we are laughing together rather than at anyone.

**Variations:** If participants cannot venture outside, feel free to bring in props or pictures that represent lots of objects one might find outside and you can disperse them around the room.

These two things can represent:

▶ One represents relapse and one recovery
▶ Career change; life change
▶ Geographic change/relocating to a new town or state

# Tree of Hope

Activity generously provided by Jared Sulc

**Group Size:** 5–10 (double the amount of supplies for every additional 10 people)

**Purpose:** To visually represent the feelings, experiences, and reality of the journey of recovery through the metaphors of the roots, trunk, and branches of a tree.

## Props Needed:

1. Enough tables and chairs for each participant to spread out.
2. Tree- and leaf-shaped templates are provided.
3. Art Supplies:
   - ☐ 10 sheets of small white poster board or multi-media paper (11 × 14)
   - ☐ 1 pack of carbon paper for tracing
   - ☐ 5 brown grocery bags
   - ☐ 15–20 magazines
   - ☐ 5–10 bottles of white glue
   - ☐ 5–10 scissors
   - ☐ 5–10 watercolor paint trays
   - ☐ A variety of decorative papers
   - ☐ 1 pack of tissue paper, assorted colors
   - ☐ 15–20 flat paint brushes, various sizes
   - ☐ 5–10 pencils for tracing
   - ☐ 10 cups for water
4. Music (optional): Ambient or instrumental music to play during the art-making to enhance the creative process.

## Activity Preparation:

1. Prep time needed: 15 minutes for set-up.
2. Prior prep time is needed for ordering/gathering art supplies, papers, and magazines.
3. Using a copier, you can increase the size of the template for legal size or larger paper dimensions. Participants can work directly on the template or cut it out and trace it onto brown paper or any other color paper of their choosing.

**Time Needed:**

- ► Directions: 10 minutes
- ► Activity: 45 minutes
- ► Debrief: 25 minutes
- ► Clean-up: 10 minutes

**Set-Up:**

- ► Option 1: (Recommended) Set up one table with all the art supplies—like a buffet of items from which the participants can choose what they need and return at times during their artistic process.
- ► Option 2: Divide out all the supplies equally among the participants.

**Activity Directions:**

1. On the poster board or multi-media paper, use the watercolor paint to make a wash of colors. This wash will be the background of the piece—the sky and the earth. It can be very loose and free. Not a lot of detail is needed.
2. Trace tree template onto a paper bag using the carbon paper.
3. Cut out the tree with scissors.
4. Glue the tree onto the poster board on top of the wash.
5. Look through the magazines and cut out images, words, symbols, shapes, and phrases to be put on the roots, trunk, and branches.
6. Look through the decorative and found papers. Choose patterns, colors, and textures that represent your tree.
7. Start gluing the images on the tree.
8. Use the leaf template to trace and cut out leaves to add to the branches. Tissue paper and decorative papers work well for making leaves.

---

**Facilitator Script:** Hey everyone have a seat. Today we are going to do an activity designed to tap into the creative aspects of our mind.

*(To explain the concepts and metaphors of the tree, read the following.)*

**The Roots:** They represent foundation, support, and motivating factors for your recovery. Choose words, images, patterns, colors, and shapes that represent what motivated you to begin recovery. These forms can represent events, people, experiences, consequences, or losses that caused suffering in your life. These images can also show how the problems in your life developed or took hold. Additionally, they can represent positive influences that encouraged you and showed you how to heal. The roots encompass all that it took to get you where you are today. For example, a cut-out of a picture of an ambulance might represent a life-threatening event. Or a lighthouse might represent a person or group who helped you out of a dangerous pattern of addiction.

**The Trunk:** It represents where you are right now. Choose images, words, patterns, and colors that represent how you are in the present. The present can be filled with struggles and victories. The ebb and flow of life in the present can be rich with beauty and at the same time touched by pain. Represent your strengths, talents, short-term goals, accomplishments, milestones, and challenges. The number 60 may symbolize 60 days of abstinence. Or a picture of a pothole in the road may represent a recent slip that needs to be processed.

**The Branches:** They represent the future, your hopes, and your dreams. Choose text, pictures, colors, and shapes that represent how you want to grow in your recovery. The future remains unseen, and your outlook may be bright and hopeful. At times, a shadow can be cast on the future. Someone might have a reservation that they cannot stay sober if this or that happens. A tombstone might symbolize a fear that the death of a loved one would trigger a relapse. On the other hand, the branches are also full of long-term goals, items on your bucket list, and spiritual aspirations. What you want more of in your life will show up in the branches of the tree. The branches call to mind the words of the poet and artist Kahlil Gibran who said, 'Trees are poems that the earth writes upon the sky.'"

The facilitator can re-read all or parts of this script once or twice while the participants are working on the collage to inspire the group and help keep them focused. Parts can also be re-read to an individual who is in a stuck place.

### Debrief:

- As much as you are comfortable, please share about your roots, trunk, and branches.
- What image or word in your collage is the most meaningful to you? Please explain.
- What image or word in your collage was difficult for you to include in your collage?
- What felt difficult about this activity?
- What did you discover about yourself by making this collage?
- What is a next step or take-away you learned from this activity? How likely are you to take that next step? Please explain.

**Recovery Metaphor:** The tree is a metaphor for a growing and changing life in recovery. Vincent Van Gogh once said, "What lives in art and is eternally living, is first of all the painter and then the painting." Allow yourself to be revealed through the art.

**Wellness Metaphor:** The image of a tree represents robust health, vitality, and the healing energy of nature.

**Role of Facilitator:** To encourage and motivate participants while they are working with the materials. Assist them with refills on glue and water so that they can focus on making the collage. Also, allow participants to move freely as they look through magazines and decorative papers to find what is needed for their collage. Help clients move through creative blocks when they ask for help. If you see a participant struggling, ask them if they would like your help. Create a safe space for talking about the artwork as you debrief. Set parameters for commenting on other people's artwork. You may want to restrict the group to only talk about their own work. If you do open it up for the group to talk about each other's work, then be sure to set boundaries around criticizing, judging, or placing value on the artwork. Remember, this exercise is not an art critique or an exhibit at an art gallery; it is a therapeutic group activity. A meaningful connection or insight gained from creating or looking at the collage is much more valuable to the group than a comment about how good or bad something looks in the collage. Encourage the group to share about how they can relate to the art or what associations they can make between themselves and the images.

**Variations:**

- Choose a specific behavior or belief that you want to change. Use the roots, trunk, and branches to show how this belief developed in the roots, how it is manifesting right now in the trunk and in the branches, how you see it shifting and transforming in the future.
- For time constraints, work directly on the template paper, but glue the template to the poster board first. The collage needs the support of the poster board or multi-media paper.

**Where to Find It/How to Make It:** See Templates.

Source information for worksheet created by Jared Sulc

Source information for worksheet created by Jared Sulc

# Vital Signs of Recovery

Activity generously provided by Eric Hrabowski & Jennifer Lockhart

**Group Size:** 5–50

**Purpose:** Create group cohesion and allow for a new way of measuring quality of recovery.

**Props Needed:**

1. Vital Signs of Recovery Handout
2. Pens

**Activity Preparation:**

1. Prep time needed: 5 minutes
2. Prior to class, print the vital signs of recovery handout and have pens for all participants.

**Time Needed:**

- ▶ Directions: 5 minutes
- ▶ Activity: 30 minutes
- ▶ Debrief: 15 minutes

**Set-Up:** Make sure participants have a hard surface to lean on so that they can fill out the form.

**Activity Directions:**

- ▶ Read activity script
- ▶ Instruct the group to fill out handout

---

**Facilitator Script:** "Hello everyone. Today we are going to look at checking in with our recovery in a slightly different way. Have you ever been to the doctor's office for a routine checkup? *(pause so participants can answer)* If you have, then you know that one of the first things a health professional checks are your vital signs. Vital signs are measurements of such things like a person's body temperature, blood pressure, pulse, and respiration. These have to be checked, because they provide us with important data used to determine if we are functioning at an optimal level, or if there are deficiencies.

In order to determine how we are functioning, our health care professional will look at certain aspects of our health like: Is our pulse regular or irregular? Is our blood pressure too high or too low? Is our respiration within normal range? If there are deficiencies in the functioning of these things, the health professional may make recommendations for lifestyle and/or dietary changes, or write a prescription, to help get our bodies back on track.

Our recovery can work in the same manner. Here are some tools to think about your recovery in a bit of a different way. These four vital signs—pulse, blood pressure, temperature, and respiration—can also be used to evaluate and monitor recovery.

## Pulse

Checking your pulse is the same as taking an inventory of where we are in the recovery process. In the context of recovery, this would also require you to ask yourself some basic self-assessment questions and answering those questions honestly. I've been told the heart doesn't lie. Therefore, being honest with yourself will provide you with a more accurate picture of where you stand and where you need or want to go from there.

So how does one measure where they might be in the recovery process? A good place to start is with the things that a person in recovery does on a regular basis, which can be compared to the consistency of a beating heart. Attending support group meetings regularly is important. Thus, one of the pulse questions could be, 'Am I making meetings a consistent part of my recovery?' Another question could be 'Do I have a sponsor?' If so, 'Am I meeting regularly with them?' Often it may be hard for us to see when we are actually making progress. Therefore, taking an inventory can be very helpful in that respect. 'Are you better off than you were compared to a previous time period?' The honesty component is critical for us to remain objective about what it is we are actually doing in our personal recovery. Not being critical enough can lead us down a path of complacency, where as being overly critical can potentially bring on feelings of frustration. It is important to keep in mind that recovery is a process, which means that it will take time.

## Blood Pressure

One of the vital signs that may help you remain invested in the process is the blood pressure. When you think of problems that may result from an abnormal blood pressure you may associate it with being too high and the presence of headaches. Although many factors can adversely affect your blood pressure, stress will be the focus of this discussion. Stressors come in a variety of forms and can be grouped into the categories of people, places, and things. Doing your part means identifying personal stressors in these categories, limiting your exposure to them when possible, and developing some ways to manage them effectively can be helpful in managing your recovery. It is good practice not to put ourselves knowingly in contact with high-risk people, places, and things. Seeking out your dealer in a place where you used to use, and picking up paraphernalia, can certainly increase your recovery blood pressure while going to meetings and talking to your sponsor is a way of keeping it low.

Other methods for managing your recovery blood pressure could include both immediate and preventative strategies. Immediate strategies are techniques that you use in the moment. A flat tire, an argument, an unexpected run-in with a former using associate or dealer are all great opportunities to implement an immediate strategy. Taking a mental or physical time-out to regroup and develop a response is one example. Counting, thought stopping, and breathing are a few more. These are important because they give us a chance to stop and think. We can use them to keep from escalating a situation to the point where we feel we no longer have a choice in our actions.

Preventative strategies are designed to maintain a low recovery blood pressure. If prior to recovery we had a high stress baseline it would be helpful to implement stress reducing skills on a daily or regular basis to lower our stress baseline.

Behaviors associated with this strategy may include listening to music, exercising, going to meetings, and talking to others regularly. We have found the best skill for reducing your stress baseline is a daily or regular meditation practice. Doing these things can help keep your recovery blood pressure at a manageable level. An assessment of your recovery blood pressure would consist of asking yourself if you are implementing these preventative and immediate strategies on a daily basis and self-correcting. The preventative ones help us to maintain a healthy balance in relieving stress and the immediate ones help us handle the unexpected. They can be a powerful combination.

### Temperature

The final aspect of the Vital Signs of Recovery is around the temperature of our recovery. The questions we ask here is are we running too hot or too cold? Checking in with our emotional life can be an important tool that can provide data about how we are responding to people, places, and things around us. If we find ourselves angry a lot of the time we might be running too hot; however, if we feel disconnected we might be too cool. Looking for the patterns might help guide where our emotional temperature has been recently.

### Respiration

Respiration is a vital sign that tells us if we are breathing properly. Doing the same things in recovery can become boring so when we think of checking our recovery respiration, let's ask this question. 'What are we doing to breathe life into our recovery?' Recovery is so much more than meetings and step work. It is a process that helps us to develop a way of living that can be fulfilling and full of excitement. If we find ourselves bored with our regular meetings we can venture out and try new ones. We can explore new activities and discover what we truly enjoy. When things get stale it is up to us to make it fresh again. 'Am I trying new things in this process?' is a great question to ask. If the answer is no, make some changes. Don't let fear and complacency steal the breath of life from your recovery.

Recovery isn't a sprint, it's a marathon. Just about anyone could write a prescription for recovery, we don't have to be doctors. The goal here is about sustainable balance. Taking the time to check the vital signs of recovery can help us write our own prescription. Answering some questions honestly and putting some strategies into play on a regular basis will go a long way in helping have healthy recovery vital signs.

Let's take a moment to fill out the Recovery Vital Signs worksheet and get a snapshot of how we are doing right now." *(Pass out worksheet and give participants about twenty to thirty minutes to fill out.)*

## Debrief:

- ▶ How can you use the vital signs of recovery to help you gauge your recovery?
- ▶ What did you notice as you listened to the vital signs of recovery?
- ▶ What did it feel like to fill out the form?
- ▶ What did you notice as others shared their form?
- ▶ What can you do with the information that the vital signs worksheet revealed for you?

**Recovery/Wellness Metaphor:** This is a great way of teaching participants to self-reflect on their recovery status periodically. This process can be done in any increments and it is helpful to keep previous checkups so that participants can compare.

**Role of Facilitator:** Help educate participants on this new way of reflecting on their own recovery.

**Variations:** Modify as needed for population.

**Where to Find It/How to Make It:** Worksheet can be found on the following page.

# VITAL SIGNS OF RECOVERY

## Pulse

What do I do daily for my recovery? What do I do weekly? Do I feel this is sufficient to sustain my recovery? What could I do more of to bring my recovery to the next level?

_____

_____

_____

_____

## Blood pressure

On a scale of 0 to 10, how stressed am I right now? _____

On a scale of 0 to 10, how stressed am I this past week? _____

On a scale of 0 to 10, how stressed am I this past month? _____

Does my current stress level allow me to function optimally? What can I do to reduce my stress level?

_____

_____

_____

_____

## Temperature

What emotions have I noticed recently? Are these new or old patterns? What can I do to work through these emotions?

_____

_____

_____

_____

Source information for worksheet Created by Marc Pimsler

**REPRODUCIBLE**

## Respiration

Am I bored with my recovery? Am I feeling stale with any part of my life? Do I feel I am living in my purpose? Do I feel excited, encouraged, and energized by my life? What can I do to breathe life into my recovery?

_____

_____

_____

_____

What did you learn about yourself and your recovery as a result of this activity?

_____

_____

_____

_____

As a result of what you learned, what are you willing to do with this new information?

_____

_____

_____

_____

Who are you willing to let help you?

_____

_____

Taking this snapshot of your recovery can help you gauge where you are currently. It could be very helpful to share this with a counselor or other helping professional to help you keep an eye on your vital signs of recovery.

# Walk the Talk

**Group Size:** 5–25

**Purpose:** Connect participants with their relationship to their addiction and recovery, create group cohesion.

**Props Needed:**
1. Assortment of old pairs of shoes
2. Assortment of art supplies (markers, paint, construction paper, glitter, glue, feathers, beads, and anything you can think of)

**Activity Preparation:** Prep Time Needed: 15 minutes
1. Make sure to have enough shoes for each participant to pick one pair.
2. Prior to group, place pairs of shoes so that each can be seen by participants.
3. Make sure that each participant has enough workspace to create and have access to ample art supplies.

**Time Needed:**
- ▶ Directions: 5 minutes
- ▶ Activity: 30 minutes
- ▶ Debrief: 30 minutes

**Set-Up:**
1. Suggestion—consider putting some butcher paper or an old plastic tablecloth to protect your tables from getting glitter glued to them.
2. Place pairs of shoes in a central location so that participants can select the one they like.
3. Have art supplies placed in a manner that participants have easy access to them. This will likely require several sets of each item.

**Activity Directions:**
- ▶ Have the participants pick a pair of shoes and have a seat.
- ▶ Instruct the group to use one shoe to create a visual representation of their addiction.
- ▶ Instruct the group to use one shoe to create a visual representation of their recovery.

**Facilitator Script:** "Come on in everybody and have a seat. There is a saying 'walk a mile in my shoes . . . see what I see, hear what I hear, feel what I feel . . . Then maybe you will understand why I do what I do.' Today's activity will be an effort to better understand each other and maybe even better understand ourselves. Today we are going to use the supplies around you to create a visual representation of both your addiction and your recovery. In a moment, I would like for you to select a pair of shoes that you would like to use for this project. You will then use one of the shoes to create a representation of your addiction and the other will represent your recovery. Feel free to get as creative as you can. Challenge yourself to get out of the box and see what you can come up with. As you are working on each shoe ask yourself what did I see, hear, and feel in addiction and then do the same thing for recovery. Let's take about twenty minutes for this part of the activity. So, think in terms of about ten to fifteen minutes per shoe. Does anyone have any questions?"

## Debrief:

▶  As much as you are comfortable, please share about each of your shoes.
▶  Which part is the most meaningful to you? Please explain.
▶  What image or aspect in your presentation was difficult for you to include in your shoe?
▶  What felt difficult about this activity?
▶  What did you enjoy about this activity?
▶  What did you discover about yourself by creating your shoes?

**Recovery/Wellness Metaphor:** Inspiration for this activity came from the saying "walk a mile in my shoes." This activity will help the group to get to know each other and their own relationship with addiction and recovery through a creative process.

**Role of Facilitator:** Be encouraging to participants as art projects can trigger all types of reactions.

**Variations:** Instead of each shoe representing addiction and recovery you can modify the activity to be Disease and Wellness or other states along the change continuum that best represent your population.

**Where to Find It/How to Make It:** We recommend buying used shoes at thrift stores or asking your network to bring you their old shoes. Churches and other large organizations might be a great place to donate throw-away shoes to you. Also, we find the dollar store to be a great resource for art supplies.

# Weather Report

**Group Size:** Any size

**Purpose:** This is a great Check-in activity for participants to identify how they are feeling, using the metaphor of the weather.

**Props Needed:** None. But if desired you could print off pictures of weather activity

**Activity Preparation:** You do not have to have anything to prepare for this activity.

**Prep Time Needed:** 5 minutes

**Time Needed:**
- ▶ Directions: 3 minutes
- ▶ Activity: 5–10 minutes
- ▶ Debrief: 5–10 minutes

**Set Up:** Check-in activity. May also be used for debriefing an activity.

**Activity Directions:**
- ▶ Gather the attention of participants. Explain that everyone is invited to check in using the metaphor of the weather.
- ▶ Give an example of weather elements (for example, sunny, foggy, clear, overcast, partly cloudy, rain, hail, sleet, etc.).
- ▶ Ask participants to think how they have been feeling (i.e., yesterday or since last session), and today.
- ▶ Using the metaphor of the weather, check in with describing your feelings or your state of mind for yesterday, today, and giving a forecast for your tomorrow.
- ▶ Facilitator can give their own weather report as an example.

**Facilitator Script:** "Let's gather around and settle in for our session. We will begin our check-in using the metaphor of a weather report. Think of a meteorologist or weatherperson you may see on the news or TV. Usually when they give a weather report, they begin with what the weather has been a few days before today, what today's weather is, and the forecast for the next days or week. So checking in now, I would like you to describe how you are feeling or how things have been for you since our last session using terms of a weather report. Describing how your weather has been for the past few days, how it is today, and what your weather forecast is looking like for the next few days."

## Debrief:

- ▶ What did you notice about yourself/others in giving your weather report?
- ▶ What made a difference between prior day/session's report and today's report?
- ▶ How do your stated weather elements represent your state of being or feelings? Represent your recovery process?
- ▶ What will need to happen to see a difference between today's session and your weather forecast?
- ▶ What is one thing you will commit to so you can realize a step in a positive direction?

**Recovery/Wellness Metaphor:** Since the weather is a common system that many can understand, it can be used in various settings and can be used as a check-in regardless of problem area or clinical domain.

**Role of Facilitator:** Introduce the check-in activity. Give an example of your own weather report so participants can follow the model. "Yesterday my weather was . . . ; today my weather system is . . . ; and my forecast for tomorrow is. . . ."

**Modifications:** Print pictures of weather activity for participants who may have trouble finding words that describes their feelings.

## Variations:

- ▶ When used as a debriefing tool for any activity, invite participants to think about their feelings or state of mind before the activity, during, and after using the weather as a metaphor.
- ▶ Traffic Report. Use same activity instructions using the metaphor of a traffic report.
- ▶ Give an example of road/traffic conditions: clear, smooth sailing, going the speed limit, excessive driving, road rage, detour, etc.

*Source:* Adapted from *The Power of One*, Page 129, Lung, Stauffer, and Alvarez.

# Who Am I?

This activity is inspired from the teachings of Ramana Marharshi as given by Ma Jaya Sati Bhagavati

**Group Size:** 5–50

**Purpose:** Explore identity and worth, increase sense of well-being, and increase group cohesion.

**Props Needed:**
1. Blank Paper
2. Pens

**Activity Preparation:**
1. Prep time needed: 5 minutes

**Time Needed:**
- ▶ Directions: 5 minutes
- ▶ Activity: 30 minutes
- ▶ Debrief: 15 minutes

**Set-Up:** None needed

**Activity Directions:**
- ▶ Ask participants to sit comfortably in chair, place their hands in their lap, relax the hands, and close their eyes if comfortable. If not, then just gently set their gaze toward something in slightly downward direction, and maintain a soft focus. They can close their eyes anytime they feel comfortable.
- ▶ Read Who Am I meditation to participants in a slow, soft tone.
- ▶ Give participants a blank sheet of paper or the Who Am I worksheet.
- ▶ Ask participants to take ten minutes to write out ten things that complete the sentence stem "I am . . . " Do not overthink it and remember first thought, best thought.
- ▶ Give examples like I am spiritual, I am hungry, I am loveable, I am frightened, I am male, I am a mother, I am in recovery, I am funny, I am frustrated I have to do this . . .
- ▶ After about five minutes let participants know they should be halfway done; if not then they are overthinking it and to keep it simple. Remind them first thought, best thought. At eight minutes give them a two-minute warning.

- ▶ Once ten minutes are up, ask for a volunteer to go first. Once you have a volunteer ask them to stand up and say I am *(then read their list)* Then go around the room until everyone has stood up and read their list aloud.
- ▶ When asked if they have to stand up I always say yes you must stand in your own truth and speak it out loud.

---

**Facilitator Script:** "Have a seat everyone so we can go ahead and get started. Take a piece of paper and a pen as you will need this in a little bit.

Today we are going to do an activity that starts off with a meditation. So find a comfortable seat that you can sustain for a short period of time. You can sit against the wall, on the floor, or in a chair. Take this opportunity to find a comfortable position to meditate in. *(Give participants some time for wiggling around and finding a seat.)*

*(Read Who Am I meditation.)*

Now grab your paper and pen and I want you to write at the top of it 'I am . . .' Then start to write the top ten things that come to mind. So for example you might say 'I am . . . smart, bored, powerful, powerless, creative, mother, addict, brother, survivor, blessed, stressed,' or whatever else comes to mind. Try not to censor yourself. First thought, best thought. Write down whatever bubbles up to the surface. Try not to judge what comes up just write it down.

Let's take about five minutes to write out our lists.

*(Give participants a time warning when they are halfway and three-quarters of the way through the allotted time.)*

OK, great who wants to start? I would like for you to stand up and read aloud your list. So it will sound like this 'I AM smart, hurt, creative, healing, in recovery, resilient' and so on." *(Encourage participants to stand up when they read their list as there is something powerful about standing in your own truth.)*

---

## Debrief:

- ▶ What was the meditation like for you?
- ▶ What was easy about coming up with your list?
- ▶ What was challenging about coming up with your list?
- ▶ What feelings did you notice as you were writing down your list?
- ▶ What did you feel when you heard you were going to read your list aloud?
- ▶ What did it feel like to stand in your own truth and read your list out loud?

**Recovery/Wellness Metaphor:** So often we hear from people in recovery that "I don't know who I am." This activity can be a powerful way to connect with aspects of who we are. Especially when combined with the meditation, intuitive thoughts will come and participants may be surprised as to what bubbles up to the surface.

**Role of Facilitator:** Practice reading the meditation in advance so that you are familiar with it. Feel free to be creative with it. Hold the space as this can be a powerful activity designed to surface all types of characteristics.

**Variations:** Feel free to do your own meditation and don't be tied to the script.

## WHO AM I MEDITATION

Find a comfortable position to start this meditation off with. If you are in a chair put your back flat against the back of the chair and your spine long and tall. Uncross your legs and rest your hands comfortably in your lap. If you are on the floor you can sit with your legs crossed or any other position you can hold for a bit.

Take a deep breath in through your nose . . . slowly exhale through your nose . . .

Check in with your feet and legs finding a comfortable place for them. Notice any sensation or feeling that you may carry in your legs. Bring your awareness to your thighs and find a comfortable place for your thighs noticing if there is any sensation in any aspect of your lower body. Finding a comfortable position for your lower body. Rising up to your pelvis and lower abdomen finding a comfortable place for your pelvis, creating a strong foundation for your spine. Checking in with your stomach and noticing any sensation that you might be carrying within your stomach. Checking in with your chest and shoulders finding a comfortable place to rest your shoulders and noticing any sensation that you might be carrying in your shoulders. Check in with your arms finding a comfortable position for your arms and hands. Noticing any sensation within your arms that might be calling out to you. Finding a comfortable position to rest your arms. Bringing your awareness to your neck and noticing any sensation that might be in your neck. Checking to see if your head is parallel with the earth. Now bringing your attention to your eyes and allowing them to rest comfortably within their sockets. Checking in with your mind and noticing any sensation within your mind and finding a comfortable place to rest your mind. Bringing your attention to your breath and seeing if you might be carrying any particular sensation within your breath . . . Breath coming in and breath going out . . .

Now begin to elongate your breath. Slow breath coming in and slow breath coming out. Begin to pause on the top of each breath hesitating before you begin the exhalation and once again at the bottom of the breath, hesitate as you begin the inhalation. Beginning to create some space between the inhalation and the exhalation.

As you inhale say to yourself I am aware I am breathing in and as your exhale say to yourself I am aware I am breathing out. Breath coming in I am aware I am breathing in and breath going out I am aware I am breathing out.

*(pause)*

Listen for your own heartbeat.

Listen for your own wisdom.

Listen

With each breath, begin to ask yourself the question "Who Am I?" As you're breathing in ask "Who Am I?" As you let go of the breath, so too, let go of the question, "Who am I?" Allow your breath to lead to you. Leading you to a space where questions have no answers and answers have no questions. Leading you into a space of simple knowing.

*(Pause)*

Breath going in and breath going out
Who Am I? Beyond Male Who am I
Beyond Female Who am I
Beyond student Who am I
Beyond addict Who am I
Beyond child Who am I
Beyond mother Who am I
Beyond hurt Who am I
Beyond love Who am I
Beyond worker Who am I
Beyond brother Who am I
Beyond sick Who am I
Beyond imperfect Who am I
Beyond perfect Who am I
Who am I
Who am I
Who am I

Slowly listen for the answer as time herself reveals the answer. Slowly listen for who is asking and who is answering. Listen.

Breath coming in and breath coming out . . .

Take a long deep breath in . . . Hold the breath in . . . and with sound let the breath out.

Take another long deep breath in . . . Hold the breath in . . . and with sound powerfully let the breath out

Take one more longest, deepest breath in . . . Hold the breath in let the moment build . . . and with sound powerfully let the breath out

Now ignore the breath and just notice what you feel

*(Give a couple minutes of silence.)*

Slowly coming back to the breath and coming back to your body begin to open the eyes about one-quarter of the way open and notice the world around you. Slowly begin to wiggle your toes and fingers coming back to the present moment. Allow eyes to continue to open. Take a deep breath in and stretch your hands way up over your head and exhale as your lower your hands.

Good job everyone.

**REPRODUCIBLE**

# Write My Eulogy

**Group Size:** 5–40

**Purpose:** To help participants identify what character traits and values one consistently identifies with over their life; or characteristics and values they want to be remembered by.

**Props Needed:**

1. Paper and writing instruments

**Activity Preparation:**

1. Prep time needed: 5 minutes
2. Have pens and paper for participants

**Time Needed:** 45 minutes

- ▶ Directions: 5 minutes
- ▶ Activity: 10–20 minutes
- ▶ Debrief: 15–20 minutes depending on size of group

**Set-Up:** This is an activity that is likely to provoke raw reactions. Considering activity sequencing, this activity should be used when increased safety and trust has been established with others and the facilitator. Also death and dying can be very unique to specific cultures. Consider any cultural context for your participants that may be relevant to them, as unique to their culture, generation, or nationality.

**Activity Directions:**

- ▶ Give participants paper and writing instruments—pen or pencil.
- ▶ Explain that today's activity involved each participant writing their own eulogy as if they were at their own funeral.

---

**Facilitator Script:** "In this activity we are going to write our own eulogy. A eulogy is what others say who stand up and speak at your funeral. Write down what you would want said about yourself when you have passed away, many years from now. Write whatever comes to mind—allow the thoughts and words to freely flow. Write words, phrase, and sentences. Don't over-think this activity. Do not edit, censor, analyze or critique your thoughts. Just write it all down. Take about fifteen minutes to complete and then we will discuss."

---

**Debrief:**

- ▶ What character traits did you consistently demonstrate over your life?
- ▶ Who did you care for? Who cared for you?
- ▶ What did you impact or change? Why?
- ▶ Who did you impact or change? Why?
- ▶ What does your eulogy really say about you?
- ▶ What were your major accomplishments in your life?
- ▶ What accomplishments did you experience at different ages (i.e., 30, 40, 50, 60, and 70 or older)?
- ▶ What were your interests? What were you passionate about?
- ▶ What is your legacy?

**Recovery/Wellness Metaphor:** The grief process is ubiquitous to all persons, and many events. Participants may write about persons, places, things, situations, events, opportunities lost or gained.

**Role of Facilitator:** This is an activity that must be carefully considered. Facilitators must be prepared to address and process grief and loss reactions, as well as possible post-traumatic stress response. The facilitator may have to offer participants an opportunity to examine their feelings about death and dying, an activity they may choose to avoid or have never thought of.

**Variations:** If this is too uncomfortable for participants, or they react adversely or with showing discomfort of writing their own eulogy, instead of writing you can facilitate a discussion. You may discuss the topic of death and dying, why people think about it or avoid it, what they think about the reality of death one day. You can also have a discussion that if one had a specific number of hours or days to live, what would they want to accomplish on their bucket list, and remembered in their eulogy.

# Photo Credits

CPSIA information can be obtained
at www.ICGtesting.com
Printed in the USA
FSHW010210230419
57489FS

9 781524 920777